Learning in Groups

A handbook for improving group work

David Jaques

THIRD EDITION

RoutledgeFalmer
Taylor & Francis Group

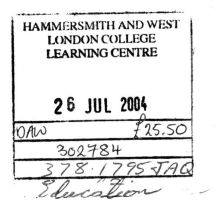
First published by Croom Helm in 1984
Second edition published by Kogan Page in 1991
Third edition 2000

Reprinted 2004
by RoutledgeFalmer
11 New Fetter Lane, London, EC4P 4EE

Simultaneously published in the USA and Canada
by RoutledgeFalmer
29 West 35th Street, New York, NY 10001

RoutledgeFalmer is an imprint of the Taylor & Francis Group

British Library Cataloguing in Publication Data

A CIP record for this book is available from the British Library.

ISBN 0 7494 3091 5

Printed and bound in Great Britain by Bell & Bain Ltd, Glasgow

Contents

Preface

Small-group discussion has a valuable part to play in the all-round education of students. It allows them to negotiate meanings, to express themselves in the language of the subject and to establish a more intimate contact with academic staff than more formal methods permit. It also develops the more instrumental skills of listening, presenting ideas, persuading and teamwork. There are greater expectations of graduates' ability to communicate and this is further underlined by the high standards set by radio and television, which make for more critical audiences. But perhaps most importantly, small-group discussion can or should give students the chance to monitor their own learning and thus gain a degree of self-direction and independence of the tutors, in their studies. All these purposes are of excellent pedigree. Yet often they are not realized to a satisfactory level and both tutors and students may end up with a sense of frustration.

Yet many tutors find the task of leading group discussion difficult to perform satisfactorily and too readily fall back in frustration on their reserve position of authority, expert and prime talker. Brown and Atkins (1988) report research to the effect that the mean proportion of time tutors spent talking in discussion groups was 64 per cent and could reach 86 per cent. Ramsden (1992) describes the 'thoroughly predictable outcomes' of group discussion as a theory of teaching that assumes the mode of telling and transmission as its basis, in which:

- the teacher gives a lecture rather than conducting a dialogue;
- the teacher talks too much;
- students cannot be encouraged to talk except with difficulty; they will not talk to each other, but will only respond to questions from the tutor;
- students do not prepare for the sessions;
- one student dominates the discussion, or blocks it;
- the students want to be given the solutions to problems rather than discussing them.

Content, process and structure

In all human interactions there are three main ingredients – content, process and structure. Content relates to the subject matter or task on which people are working. Process refers to the dynamics of what is happening between those involved. Perhaps because content is more readily definable, or at least examinable, it commonly receives more attention from all concerned. Process, on the other hand, though rarely attended to, is usually what determines whether a group works effectively or not. Group members are often half-aware of the ways in which factors like physical environment, size, cohesion, climate, norms, liaisons, organizational structure, or group goals affect discussion. These are common features with all groups and an awareness of them, as they become of consequence, should enhance a participant's worth to the group. For no one is this more true than the leader or tutor who has a crucial position in determining the 'success' or 'failure' of a discussion group. If we take the three principal aspects of group interaction: leader–members, members–content and member–member, we can see that it is probably the last of these that gains least attention and is most frequently mismanaged (Johnson and Johnson, 1987).

New lecturers are not often given suitable induction to group teaching. Even when training in small-group techniques is given, it is not easy to replicate the dynamic tension of a seminar in a training exercise. And if it were possible to do so, the traditional seminar as a model of group interaction in which anxious students present papers to a group of their equally anxious colleagues would promote a rather limited view of what small groups can contribute to learning. For this reason I would add a further ingredient, which I regard as a very enabling one, to content and process, and that is structure. Whereas attention to both content and process can lead to a wonderful intellectual exploration through open discussion, it does not always focus adequately on particular learning outcomes; and it can be difficult for shy, culturally reserved or less dominant group members to participate, especially with larger sizes of group. So, a consideration of ways to structure group activities is a further focus of this book.

Students too can benefit from training both in the group skills of discussion and project teams and in learning how to conduct the self and peer assessment of these skills.

My aim in this book is therefore not just to promote understanding of group methods but to develop group skills for tutors and students alike as well as widening the range of possible group experiences. The title *Learning in Groups* is meant to suggest that groups are not merely a valuable vehicle for learning about the skills and concepts of a subject discipline, but are also a way of learning about groups: developing abilities in cooperative work for later life.

There are several possible starting points for readers. Some may prefer to look at Chapter 6 on structures and activities first, before referring back to aims. Others may need to pick up ideas on questioning techniques and interventions before gaining awareness of theoretical bases for them. What you choose to accept and use from the book will reflect your own practice and philosophy of teaching. It might therefore be a good idea if I first state my own position on learning in groups.

I assume that students are adults and should be encouraged to learn as adults. Knowles (1979) describes this orientation as andragogy rather than pedagogy. At the same time I recognize that many students in their late teens are still maturing as they cope with identity crises (Erikson, 1971) and an uneasy relationship with authority. Nevertheless the assumption of an adult–adult relationship is one that I believe increases the likelihood of a more productive teaching and learning relationship.

Cooperation is a key word in learning groups. While competition in itself can be of great benefit in stimulating and sharpening interaction to some, it can be equally inhibiting to others. Competition in groups may sharpen the critical faculty of a few, but is more likely to dull the appetite for discussion among most. Yet competition is not inimical to cooperation: rather they are symbiotic processes. However, effective cooperation doesn't just happen, especially in a system where everyone feels they are competing with each other for approval and grades. We learn to cooperate through practice and this requires a clear and coordinated strategy for learning about working together and improving skills in cooperation. Cooperation also means each and every member of the group taking a part and sharing responsibility for its success. In sum, an effective group will have common shared aims and differentiated individual aims.

We all learn from experiences, whether happy or bitter ones, but we often fail to extend this learning beyond the immediate event. Thus when a group discussion grinds to a halt we may record that it has done so and that it is frustrating, but do little more. If we were to be a little more observant about what happened, reflect on and examine the events and our part in them, then we would be more likely to develop rules and principles to guide us in our preparation for the next, similar, experience. The 'experiential' learning cycle (Figure 0.1) is based on Kolb (1984) and contains three assumptions:

1. We learn best when we are personally involved in the learning experience.
2. Knowledge of any kind has more significance when we learn it through our own initiative, insight and discovery.
3. Learning is best when we are committed to aims that we have been involved in setting, when our participation with others is valued and when there is a supporting framework in which to learn.

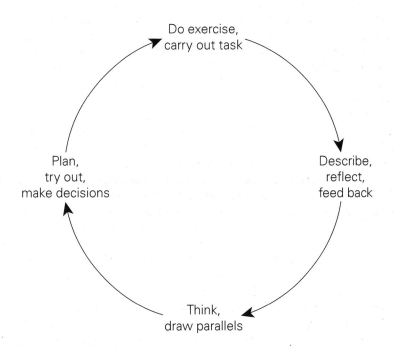

Figure 0.1 *Experiential learning cycle*

Figure 0.2 *Experiential learning cycle*

There is a further element in this cycle, which is that in every phase we are engaged in there is an interplay between thoughts, feelings and action (or behaviour), each or all of which can influence our choices in progressing round the cycle; see Figure 0.2.

Despite the pre-eminence of intellectual aims in learning groups it is often the emotional needs and undercurrents that are most powerful; yet these are most frequently neglected. The sense of identity and social belonging that a student can gain from a well-run group should not be underestimated. Nor should the inhibiting effect of tutor authority, a competitive atmosphere and the students' fear that they may make fools of themselves. Four important words seem to be missing in most academic courses: support, commitment, enjoyment and imagination. The first three may be created in a group where a climate of open communication, involving trust, honesty and mutual respect, takes place. Imagination should blossom in this climate. It might also create it.

For most tutors the first two chapters will provide a base on which to build their understanding of groups. The field of group dynamics has no unifying theme. Rather than try to present a unitary approach to the various problems and issues in groups, therefore, I have provided a rather eclectic view, drawing on various theoretical and research approaches that seem to shed light on problems, or are a source of ideas for more rewarding and imaginative approaches to group work.

There follow two short chapters on learning and communication, after which Chapter 5 examines the kind of aims that are suitable to learning groups, and relates the necessary aims of groups in general to specific ones in academic learning. Chapter 6 is a discussion of what tutors and groups might be expected to do and examines a variety of tasks and activities. Many of these are examples of more challenging and stimulating approaches than one would normally find in the traditional seminar or tutorial. Chapter 7 answers the question: what personal tasks and skills does the tutor have to learn in order to prepare for and handle group interaction? It looks particularly at the kinds of intervention a tutor could make during the progress of discussion. Chapter 8 addresses the place of learning groups in the social and educational environment of the college and several case studies of real schemes are used to illustrate it. Chapter 9 underlines the importance of group assessment, and provides some practical suggestions for evaluating both the leadership role and the group as a whole, and the book finishes with a set of training activities for improving participation in groups at all levels.

I have tried to write a book that is both readable and practical; one that permits flexibility, yet covers most of the ingredients of the wondrous mix of human behaviours apparent in any active group.

The third revised edition includes several structural changes as well as updating, though it retains a similar basic structure and content. Examples of more recent theory and practice in groups have been incorporated, and exercises based on the text added at the end of each chapter. The new layout design will also, I hope, make the book a more attractive read.

David Jaques
2000

Acknowledgements

Thank you to the late Malcolm Knowles for the inspiration and permission to use quotations from *An Introduction to Group Dynamics* in Chapter 2; to Graham Gibbs, Trevor and Sue Habeshaw for ideas and material from the *53 Interesting Things* series of books; to the Oxford Centre for Staff and Learning Development for material from various publications; Roy Gregory, Rob Pope, Gina Wisker, Peter Harris and Paul Gaffney for their contributions to the Case Studies in Chapter 7; to Sally Brown for providing the Clapping game in Chapter 10; to Zita Allen for help with the assessment processes at Alverno College; to several unnamed people whom I am unable to cite because the source is untraceable; to those who responded to my e-mail requests; and lastly, to those who otherwise helped with the time-honoured question, 'How's the book coming on?'

1 | Theories about group behaviour

No theory is good, except on condition that one uses it to go beyond.

(André Gide)

By the end of this chapter you can expect to be able to distinguish between various understandings of, and approaches to, group dynamics and to gauge their relevance to the learning groups you are involved in.

What is a group?

Many writers have attempted to establish clear definitions of groups; each one betrays assumptions about what happens in groups, both in the terminology and in what is chosen for emphasis. Rather than trying to single out or invent a unitary definition, let us look at some of the characteristics most commonly described by practitioners – a group definition if you like – in order to provide a more comprehensive picture of the range of dynamic qualities within each group. A group can be said to exist as more than a collection of people when it possesses the following qualities:

- *Collective perception*: members are collectively conscious of their existence as a group.
- *Needs*: members join a group because they believe it will satisfy some needs or give them some rewards.
- *Shared aims*: members hold common aims or ideals that to some extent bind them together. The achievement of aims is presumably one of the rewards.
- *Interdependence*: members are interdependent inasmuch as they are affected by and respond to any event that affects any of the group's members.
- *Social organization*: a group can be seen as a social unit with norms, roles, statuses, power and emotional relationships.
- *Interaction*: members influence and respond to each other in the process of communicating, whether they are face-to-face or otherwise deployed. The sense of 'group' exists even when members are not collected in the same place.

- ■ *Cohesiveness*: members want to remain in the group, to contribute to its well-being and aims, and to join in its activities.
- ■ *Membership*: two or more people interacting for longer than a few minutes constitute a group.

None of these characteristics by itself defines a group but each indicates important aspects. However, not all of them can be expected to relate to every group and some of the qualities may be seen as part of others. Interaction will not take place without some need to influence, share and be responded to – all of these give rise to attempts to communicate with others. Nevertheless, if a group is consciously to regard itself as a group, it must exist long enough for a rudimentary pattern of interaction to develop. Some group-dynamics theorists argue that a group has to comprise at least three people before significant group behaviour can occur. For the purpose of this book, however, I shall include the dyad or pair, even though it may lack some important characteristics, as a special type of group with valuable potentialities for learning.

A group may be considered as an entity, but it is illuminating to study the individual experience of members as well. Some writers (eg Allport, 1924) argue that groups have no separate reality – only individuals are real – and that all the norms, roles, relationships, etc, exist only in the minds of individuals functioning as a collection of people. Others, Freud for instance, see the dynamics of group behaviour as a sort of collective extension of individual psychopathology. The most suitable picture for our purposes is probably one in which group phenomena are held to be real to the extent that group members respond consciously or unconsciously to such phenomena as if they existed. In this book we shall consider the group from both individual and collective viewpoints, working on the assumption that a better understanding of group process will develop from consider-ing both in relation to one another.

Theory vs research

Let us now consider what contribution theory and research make to an understanding of the complex processes that take place in a group.

Opinion is divided on the most fruitful approach to studying groups. On the one hand, as Shaw (1977) explains, there are those who consider that group phenomena can be validly assessed and understood only by rigorous analysis of empirical observations. On the other hand, some maintain that research evidence will almost certainly be trivial and that theoretical analysis is the only means to a comprehensive understanding of the complex phenomena evident in groups. While it is true that, without theory, most of the research findings would merely be a collection of random and unrelated facts, it is impossible to construct a theory without some empirical understanding: empirical 'facts' serve to underline the broader statements of theoretical insights. Theory in its turn serves to illuminate and organize research data in a way that extends their meaning beyond the situations from which they were derived.

Psychodynamic theory

Freud, in his *Group Psychology and the Analysis of the Ego* (1921) claimed that people are drawn into, and remain in groups because of emotional ties between members, and that one of the principal mechanisms in the effecting of such ties is identification – the process whereby a person wants to be like his or her parent(s). To use Freud's terms, people 'introject' a preferred person (the leader), or the qualities they like in that person, into their own being, while at the same time 'projecting' some of the bad or painful qualities of themselves on to others. When each member of a group assimilates the same qualities of the leader they can identify with each other.

Introjection and projection are two processes that are common to most relationships between people and usually take place at the unconscious level (that is, the participants are not usually aware of them unless attention is drawn to them).

Transference

Another Freudian concept that has relevance to groups is that of transference, a common phenomenon in which fears, loves and longings experienced in early childhood, usually in relation to parents and siblings, are re-awakened in later life when they are displaced on to another person. It is not unusual for a student to reject, resent or conversely respect a tutor to an unrealistic extent simply because the tutor triggers the same feelings in the student (usually at an unconscious level) as did one of his or her parents. Sometimes the resentment becomes more generalized so that all people in authority and even the institution itself become the objects of hatred.

The Freudian school thus saw the basic processes in a group as outward manifestations of the inner lives of its members: the intrapersonal expressed as the interpersonal. Out of this approach has developed one of the most powerful interpretations of group interaction – that commonly known as the Tavistock model.

Bion (1961), one of its key figures, proposed that a group operates simultaneously at two levels: the work group and the basic assumption group. The work group meets to perform a specific and overt task. However, this is frequently obstructed or diverted by the powerful emotional drives of the basic assumption activity. The basic group behaves as if it shared the following tacit assumptions or motives:

- Obtaining security and protection from one individual on whom it can depend. This can be the designated leader or any member who is accepted in the role. The group unconsciously assumes that some sort of magic resides in the leader. In learning groups, students frequently direct attention to the tutor's remarks, as if he or she were the source of all wisdom, to the exclusion of their colleagues' contributions. Even if they lose respect for a particular tutor there is a sense in which the position is endowed with authority or at least that there is some external power, which determines what should be learnt, whether or not the tutor is the medium.
- Preserving itself from annihilation – either attacking something (fight) or avoiding the task (flight). Commonly the group will scapegoat some other person or group in

order to avoid a difficult problem. Flight, on the other hand, takes the form of with-drawal, passivity, dwelling in the past, or jesting. The group seems happy to distract itself from its task by focusing on some other harmless and irrelevant issue. 'In this mode, the group uses its energy to defend itself from its own internal fears and anxieties, and consequently neither develops nor achieves an effective output' (de Board, 1978).

■ Engaging in pairing. Two individuals form a bond in which warmth, closeness and affection are shown. Pairing has as its basic assumption that the purpose of the group is to bring two people together who will somehow save the group from its current predicament. Frequently this happens when the group is bored, lost or resentful in its discussion and is unable to express or otherwise cope with these feelings. In learning groups pairing may take three possible forms. In the first, two students provide mutual respect and support for each other to the exclusion of other members who are thus rendered inactive. Alternatively, the pair could engage in intellectual battle, each partner representing a different side of a conflict that has been pre-occupying the group. Again the rest of the group are mere bystanders. Finally, the tutor may pair with the group as a whole and collude with them in their wish to avoid work.

Pairing is often characterized by a sense of unreal hope: 'Everything will be OK when we get a new room', 'It'll all come right in the New Year'. The need to face up to and work through disappointments and failures is conveniently avoided by this unreal but seductive promise of things to come. Pairing can also be likened to two cells coming together in order for the group to reproduce itself – that is to say, develop another task and direction for the group distinct from the agreed one. Though this coupling may not result from an explicit sexual attraction there may well be a quasi-sexual bonding with its 'offspring' as the idea, the brainchild, that will save the group from its failings.

Dependency, flight/fight, and pairing are described as the assumptions of the basic group, whose primary task is seen as survival. It is important to recognize that the basic group that operates under these assumptions is the same one that is engaged in the work task; they are the same members operating under different models with varying degrees of intensity. Where the overt tasks of the work group and the covert tasks of the basic group meet, conflict is likely to occur.

These theoretical concepts have been developed through a wealth of experience of groups at conferences in human relations training at the Tavistock Institute and have been applied with some degree of success to industrial and organizational settings. However, they are not always easy to accept and to identify without a certain amount of training. Indeed it is sometimes said that the interpretations of group behaviour are probably 25 per cent right 25 per cent of the time. And they may be of little relevance in a well-run seminar group committed to its task of intellectual development, though it is arguable that every tutor should at least be aware of them as a latent force, because when they do surface they can be quite powerful; and the tutor might too easily be drawn into collusion on any of the basic assumptions, thus frustrating the achievement of the work task.

The Tavistock approach has brought into focus other issues of value in our under-standing of group dynamics. Banet and Hayden (1977) list these concepts as authority, responsibility, boundaries, projection, organization and large group phenomena.

Authority

Whenever decisions have to be made about process or the allocation of tasks, a group is likely to experience authority problems. Whose job is it to decide? Can the group give any one person that sanction? Where a designated 'authority person' exists, a group may either find itself dependent on them, or counter-dependent (attacking authority). Freud (1921) regarded the small group as an analogue of the family. The leader of a group is therefore likely to have childhood feelings transferred on to her or him; such feelings as infantile dependency (which arouses as many bad feelings as good) and disobedience or rebellion. Redl (1942) quoted in McLeish *et al* (1973) provided classroom pupils with different kinds of teacher personalities, and discovered that within each class there were 'conflicted individuals' who had difficulty in coping with their unconscious emotions and images in respect of a particular teacher. If and when a 'conflicted individual' acts out his or her other repressed feelings about authority with a teacher who happens to trigger them off, other students who may be incapable of expressing such feelings give tacit approval to the conflicted student as a sort of representative of their own antipathy. In this way a pattern of beliefs and behaviours, a classroom 'culture', is established for any group of students with a particular teacher.

The teacher's role when authority conflicts occur would seem to be to aid the students' growth by refusing to join battle, and to help them understand the consequences of their action. Many students who object to the authority of the teacher are not really seeking an alternative to the status quo. They are probably fighting the tutor as a way of avoiding the need to accept that learning is their own responsibility and that they have to face the consequences of the choices they make. It is important therefore for the teacher to create the conditions in which the students can make conscious choices of alternative courses of action, supportively but firmly bringing such issues out into the open.

Responsibility

There is a feeling in groups where visible authority is present that the ultimate responsibility for each person's action and its consequences resides in the figure of authority. In learning groups, students rarely take responsibility for the role they play in contributing to a successful experience. Whether they are accustomed to challenging authority overtly or to accepting it with resentment and bad grace, they may never have examined the consequences of that particular attitude. Somehow the responsibility for what happens is assumed to lie firmly on the shoulders of the tutor, who may be unable to shrug it off.

Some tutors are prone to the 'mother-hen' syndrome: they tend their 'little chicks', protecting them from the supposed deceptions practised by others. They may try to establish this sort of relationship with any person or group they encounter. It is a pattern of behaviour they have acquired through their own upbringing and which they readily transfer to any willing 'brood'. Many of us respond to a student's sense of helplessness by offering to meet it and without questioning its nature. The problem here is that teachers who are incurable helpers, in satisfying one of their basic needs, may fail to develop the student's capacity for self-growth into greater autonomy and responsibility.

Boundaries

All of us have a physical and psychological boundary in relation to others. Our own skin constitutes a physical boundary, while the distinction between our private thoughts, feelings and fantasies, and the 'known' outside world constitutes another. The same can be said of the group: both in a subjective sense and a more objective and symbolic sense boundaries distinguish one group from another. The physical space occupied by the group and the time span it covers are obvious and objective boundaries. Both of these are typically under the control of the tutor. Less tangible and more subjective are the task boundary, which determines what the group should or should not do, and the input boundary, which requires members to undergo certain social procedures before membership is acquired. Evidence of the strength of subjective boundaries can be readily perceived if a stranger – perhaps a new student – arrives unannounced in an established group, or if the tutor invites a colleague to sit in on a seminar.

Projection

Sometimes the negative feelings we have towards other people are too dangerous to permit of conscious expression and, as a mechanism to defend us against the anxiety that this produces, we attribute these feelings, motives or qualities to the person or persons towards whom our feelings are really directed. We thus experience the feelings as coming 'at us' rather than 'from us'. This is the mechanism known as projection. Some students may, for instance, see the tutor as hostile; they are in fact feeling hostility to the tutor but are unable to recognize it. They will usually hotly deny the existence of the feeling if challenged.

Just as individuals can plant their own bad feelings on others in the group, so a group can spend a lot of time and energy in projecting its own conflicts or inadequacies on to another group or the institution. This is more particularly true of staff groups and student political and union meetings than of learning groups and is what happens when a group adopts the 'fight' stance described on pages 3–4.

Organizational structure

The power relationships in the group, whether determined by outside factors (eg the curriculum, the tutor's position in the institutional hierarchy) or by internal concerns such as the qualities or skills of individuals, can have a profound effect on the work of a group. Structural relations of this kind may manifest themselves in who sits where, who takes initiatives, who defers to whom, and in the pecking order of contributions. In general, structures that are not revealed and discussed lead to feelings of mistrust. The structure of a group does not automatically exist from the beginning but develops through a process of differentiation and sorting. It can also change according to the mood of members or the special requirements of the task in hand. The recognition of this problem had led some group leaders, for instance Hill (1977), to allocate special roles and responsibilities in a group on a rotating basis.

Large groups

As the size of a group increases, so its characteristics change (see Figure 1.1). In the view of Rice (1971), six is a critical number for groups in all sorts of situations. With six or less the degree of intimacy offered by close proximity can make it difficult for group members to register their feelings about the group. Leadership tends to be fluid and inter-changeable. As the group size increases, the climate of the group changes. Individuals become less constrained by the norms of the group and become more aware of their feelings. Leadership and other roles become more established. With numbers of 12 to 25 the likelihood of full face-to-face interaction decreases and sub-groups start to emerge. When the group is over 25 in number, face-to-face interaction between everyone becomes impossible. Some people, because of the group's size, may have to sit behind others, and anyone speaking may fail to see, or be seen by, everyone in the group. When leadership occurs it takes on a clear cut, 'external' role.

Number of members	Changing characteristics
2–6	Little structure or organization required; leadership fluid.
7–12	Structure and differentiation of roles begins. Face-to-face interaction less frequent.
12–25	Structure and role differentiation vital. Sub-groups emerge. Face-to-face interaction difficult.
25–?	Positive leadership vital to success, sub-groups form; greater anonymity. Stereotyping, projections and flight/fight occur.

More cohesion (upward, left side) — *More tension* (downward, right side)

Figure 1.1 *Changing characteristics of groups with increase in membership*

Whereas in the small group it is easy to think but difficult to feel, in the large one the opposite is likely to be the case. It becomes difficult to mobilize the intellect, issues become polarized, splitting ('I all right/you all wrong') takes over as a defence against anxiety about chaos and, in order to manage this, people are likely to stereotype each other. The leader or teacher, as someone who is evidently different, is likely to be subject to these perceptions more than most and the authority/dependency problem will almost certainly be sharper and more acute.

Leaders become invested with all sorts of power and expertise. But as soon as they come up with something the group regards as 'inferior', their credibility will sag and they may be attacked for their inadequacy! Power is more sharply polarized; too sudden or big a change in the power relationship is likely to produce a flight/fight situation. If the group challenges the leader, and if in turn it is challenged back, it might retreat or withdraw. An example of this would be when a tutor, after playing a formal and omniscient role, invites the class informally to come up with some of its own ideas.

Another experience of people in large groups is that their identity becomes more fragile and their sense of reality is distorted. The mechanism of projection (see page 6) is likely to operate: unwanted parts of the self are pushed on to others, and fantasies about other people's motives, attitudes and intentions abound.

So much for the undercurrents. At the behavioural level, it becomes evident that the larger the group, the more formal and oratorical the spoken contributions become. In the educational context we can see that students have two kinds of relationship open to them: one is with small discussion or learning groups with which they already have some identity, and the other with the wider group membership, many of whom they know from social or sporting contacts, or even in another learning group. In training workshops there is a constant alternation between small groups of different sizes and the large plenary group. In some ways this mixture can provide participants with a sense of a home base (their sub-group) amid the feeling of identity loss that the large group may create. The tutor in workshops is able to circulate round the sub-groups and is thus less likely to be on the receiving end of displaced or projected bad feeling, through becoming more 'real' to participants. Yet challenges of the authority/dependency kind might still exist and they can be all the more powerful for having the support of a sub-group rather than just an individual.

The complex play of relationships in a large group and the emotional swirl that is likely to go with it are thus, at least potentially, fraught with confusion, inaction and frustration. Strong leadership is both needed and gratefully accepted. As Rice (1971) points out, 'In this condition an individual who can define some positive goal can exercise powerful leadership.' How the tutor takes that role, or dodges it, is sometimes of critical importance in large groups. It is of consequence in smaller groups too.

Group analysis

Founded by S H Foulkes, group analysis takes a more social view of group interaction, which it sees as taking place at four levels: mirroring, exchange, social integration and collective unconscious. Mirroring implies a degree of sameness between members, whereas exchange arise through difference. Zinkin (1994) observes that people in a therapy group relate to one another differently than when one-to-one:

> *they exchange experiences and pay attention to one another in a way which almost reveals a different personality . . . The group personality often seems more spontaneous and shows a much greater range of resources than when restricted to a clinical relationship of doctor and patient.*

It is perhaps interesting to compare this view with relationships in learning groups – the difference in personal behaviour between one-to-one and group tutorials – and contrast a seminar conducted by the tutor as a sequence of questions and answers between him or her and each student in turn, and one where the tutor takes a more recessive role and encourages the group to create the 'matrix' of discussion itself and, to take it one stage further, the project group. The process in tutorless groups can be likened to the kind of exchange that children have, in that they will accept from each other what they will oppose or ignore from their parents. They see themselves as being like one another, as thinking in similar ways, as inhabiting the same world: they cannot do this in the same way as their parents. Zinkin goes on to extrapolate from Foulkes' schema in which 'the free exchange (1) of information and explanations (2) between people who see one another as equals (3) goes on to build up a common pool knowledge, a specific culture and a sense of doing this together, which is of interest (4) to the participants'.

Each group will naturally, through a process of 'other than conscious' trial and error, sort out its social rules and thus acquire its distinctive culture. And each individual in the group is constantly defining him- or herself in the light of the group self-consciousness, through an awareness of its social structure. An anthropologist might approach groups in a similar way, asking questions about social rules and the system of exchange:

- What is the medium of the exchange?
- What are the rules governing the exchanges that are made?
- What is the function of the exchange and what purposes is it serving?
- In what circumstances are the exchanges fulfilling the aims for which the group was brought together?
- Are there any exchanges taking place that are detrimental to these aims?
- Are the conditions or the rules such that the exchange does not involve the exploitation of some individuals by others?
- Is everyone aware of the nature of the exchanges and of the rules governing them?

Of course the anthropologist could not reasonably expect to gain a full or even adequate answer from the group leader or any individual member simply because they do not readily think in such terms and no one person can logically hold all the answers.

Group analysis also holds notions of 'fair play' in which group members can expect to get back what they have given in transactions. On the negative side this can mean that no one in the group wants to risk 'losing out'; a positive outcome could or should be that the totality of transactions is much greater than the sum of the parts and the groups as a whole thus reaps benefits. For this to happen group members may need to recognize that they should help the group and not just themselves.

Habeas emotum

Many of the above issues may seem far-fetched to academic tutors, especially those whose central concern is not with personal feelings and group process but with the imparting of a body of knowledge. Yet, one hears of constant problems to do with lack of motivation and commitment, alienation and even 'dropout'. In a limited number of studies where some emphasis has been placed on 'process learning' and interaction in small-group work, there does appear to be a growth in student commitment. (See the case studies on pages 195–211.) Although styles of learning and shared values (Gaff and Wilson, 1971) may vary from faculty to faculty, the vast majority of students prize the sense of belonging which small groups afford them and the chance to test their understandings with their peers. Both these aims can be put in jeopardy and the student experience in groups can become most frustrating if emotional undercurrents are not recognized and coped with. This is an area where even traditional research evidence and psychodynamic theory are in agreement. The importance of emotions and feelings in learning is now being emphasized by terms such as 'emotional intelligence' and 'emotional literacy', which imply a strong linkage between the way we think and the way we feel (Goleman, 1995).

Continually throughout this book we shall be concerned with what Luft (1970) has called 'Habeas emotum' – a recognition that people's emotions are a necessary part of their existence, and that as Rubin (1967) and Jones (1972) argue, if we educate only the rational/intellectual person we do so at our (and their) peril. Behaviour is determined as much by passions, anxieties and convictions as it is by reason, the more so when we are not aware of the effects of our feelings. Negative feelings can be destructive if they are ignored, submerged or displaced into sarcasm and backbiting. Boredom, irritation or fear can interfere with the willingness of a group to engage in the learning process. Moreover, intellectual growth, as we shall see later, is closely linked to emotional development.

It is incumbent upon tutors to recognize all this and the part their own emotions may play in the process. This recognition is important, therefore, not merely for the effective functioning of the group but for the more far-reaching educational aim of developing the student as a congruent person – one who is able to hold together the different levels at which he or she experiences life and to communicate responses genuinely.

Attending to students' emotional needs should not only benefit their intellectual powers but also develop their capacity to tackle the sort of relationships that are so familiar to the industrial sector, not to speak of educational establishments. Contemporary life places a premium on the ability of people to get on with each other, to be able to handle interpersonal problems rather than to avoid them, and to do so constructively and creatively. Nowhere is it more possible to practise these qualities than in small-group work when learning is not subject to purely academic limitations. And lest we consider the emotional side of learning to be solely about what lies beneath the surface of normal human interactions, let us remember the transformational effects of fun, enjoyment and play in learning, a theme we shall return to in Chapter 6.

T-groups

This form of group training developed from the need of trainers to review their own problems in groups – the 'T' standing for training, not therapy. It is designed to help participants examine their own patterns of behaviour in a group setting and to become more sensitized to what goes on in the dynamics of a group. Typically they comprise 8 to 12 members who are strangers to each other and two trainers whose task is both to hold the boundaries of the group and to offer a commentary on what they observe happening. The group members will increasingly become able to learn from the trainers, to observe, comment and reflect on the process of the group as it develops. The task of the group is sometimes stated as: 'To study the process of the group as it evolves and our own part in it.' The focus is therefore very much on the 'here and now' experience. The group is not structured in the sense that activities are not proposed by the trainers, and whatever happens becomes data for the group's learning. Much of the learning comes in the form of personal feedback from the group and one of the trainer's responsibilities can be seen as maintaining a balance between challenge and support (Smith, 1980).

T-group courses or laboratories could well be residential, extending over several days, and usually include other forms of group experience such as large group and inter-group activity, all of them exploratory and experiential.

Unlike the model offered by the Tavistock Institute, T-groups do not operate within a strongly theoretical base of human behaviour: the trainers are more likely to be eclectic and to act as part of the group rather than making rare Olympian, and often mystifying, comments.

The value of learning from T-groups is reflected in Miller (1993) who derived the following set of rules for working with groups experientially:

- Minimize/simplify structure.
- Use inter-group as well as interpersonal communication – in order to enable people to explore structural as well as individual similarities.
- Import (selected?) bits of the real world into the laboratory environment.
- In designing laboratories, keep in mind at all times how things work in 'real life'.
- Encourage intervention/confrontation (eg, through the asking of questions as well as self-disclosure).
- Use metaphors . . . to explore interpersonal behaviour.
- Remember that past and future are experienced in the present.

The implications of these 'rules' will be evident in subsequent chapters in this book when we look at group activities, the tutor's role and groups in context.

Theme-centred interaction

As much a method as a theory, theme-centred interaction (TCI) is concerned with three constituent factors, each of equal importance: the 'I', the 'we' and the 'it' of group interaction. For productive discussion to occur, the 'I' of individual interests must be balanced with the 'we' of group relatedness and the 'it' of the theme or topic. The theme is treated as common property to which the individuals (which include the 'I' of the tutor) and the group as a whole relate and should include a gerund – for instance 'observing accurately' – in order to create a momentum and a sense of participating.

These three elements are seen to be enveloped in a 'globe' (see Figure 1.2). The globe comprises the physical, social and temporal environment in which the group takes place. It includes the shape of the room, the arrangement of the furniture and the emotional climate of the group. Each member of the group is expected to act as his or her own chairperson in charge of an inner 'committee' that comprises four members: 'What I want to do', 'What I ought to do', 'How that might affect others', and the chairperson, who has to decide which of these should have precedence.

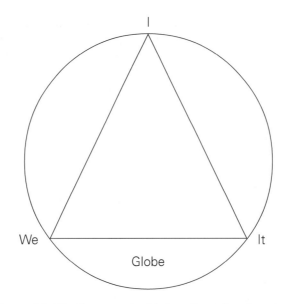

Figure 1.2 *The theme-centred interaction triangle and globe*

TCI includes two further principles: that thought and feeling should not be separated and that each person speaks for him- or herself. This latter implies that no one can speak on behalf of others (either the group as a whole or any individual) without checking with them. But more importantly it encourages group members to speak in the first person rather than the generalized 'you'. For example the statement, 'When you are in groups like this you can't think what to say' would be better as, 'When I am in a group like this I can't think what to say.' The nature and tone of the statement usually changes dramatically with the change of personal pronoun.

This basic structure is supplemented by the ground rule, 'disturbances take precedence': if a group member is unable to focus on the group task because of some distraction – being angry, bored, upset or excited, for example – he or she should say so. The emotional underlay is thus revealed in a personally responsible way. TCI has strong roots in both existentialism and psychoanalysis. It provides a framework for each individual to internalize and understand his or her own place and function in a group. It is also immensely practical and can be applied to a number of group settings to which other explanatory frameworks may not be suitable.

Shaffer and Galinsky (1974) give further details of T-groups and TCI and compare them with other group methods such as Tavistock groups.

Interaction theory

Whereas psychodynamic theory emphasizes the effect of unconscious processes in the group that exist beyond the awareness of the participant, the interaction approach is concerned with overt interpersonal behaviour between members of the group. This approach has contributed a lot to our understanding of group work, particularly by providing categories for the observation and analysis of different kinds of behaviour in small groups. These categories include qualitative and quantitative considerations, and are designed to comprise all possible types of behaviour. McLeish *et al* (1973) maintain that the interaction analysis system should include:

- the affective or emotional components of behaviour;
- the cognitive or intellectual components;
- the non-verbal or 'meta-language' components;
- content or message components;
- sociological or personal network segments of behaviour.

Although originally designed as research tools, interaction analyses have been increasingly used for training purposes to provide feedback to teachers, trainee group participants and teams. In describing apparently straightforward and overt behaviour, an interaction analysis makes it possible to provide trainees/participants with increased personal insight through objective and largely non-evaluative feedback. They may also have opportunities to practise different skills and to test them against reactions from their colleagues. In producing a comprehensive analysis of a group discussion, interaction analysis provides information on the differences between participation, and the development of different phases in a group's existence.

The basis of interaction analysis is that everything that a group says or does, including non-verbal acts, body posture, facial expressions and tone of voice, may be coded. The set of categories devised by Bales (1970) is shown in Figure 1.3. It forms a symmetrical pattern and describes different aspects of group functioning. The various categories form complementary relationships. The first three comprise the positive socio-emotional area and correspond to the last three in the negative socio-emotional area. Categories 4, 5 and 6, in the task area, comprise 'answers', while 7, 8 and 9 correspond as 'questions'. Individual categories can be paired off or 'nested'. Categories 6 and 7 focus on problems of communication, 5 and 8 on evaluation, and 4 and 9 on problems of control. Categories 3 and 10 are concerned with decision-making in the group, 2 and 11 with reducing tension and 1 and 12 with reintegration, the settling of emotional issues. These combined pairs relate to phases in the evolution of groups, too, as they move outwards from communicating the task (6 and 7) through evaluation (5 and 8) to the making of decisions in 3 and 10. It also demonstrates that in the initial stages of a task, the group should be concerned with the instrumental or task components of the interaction, and then, as it moves towards making decisions and achieving agreement, so it becomes more clearly involved in the emotional side of the process.

Theoretically, this is how a group interaction evolves. However, events rarely follow this smooth path and while the sequence may be followed in a general sense, the actual group interaction is an unstable, ever-changing process subject to all sorts of influences. The analysis assumes that members of the group are not radically affected by external factors such as previous animosities or extrinsic motives in their behaviour in the group.

Bales' position is that if one can outline behaviours in a group as objectively as possible, it will be easier for people to accept what happens and change accordingly to improve

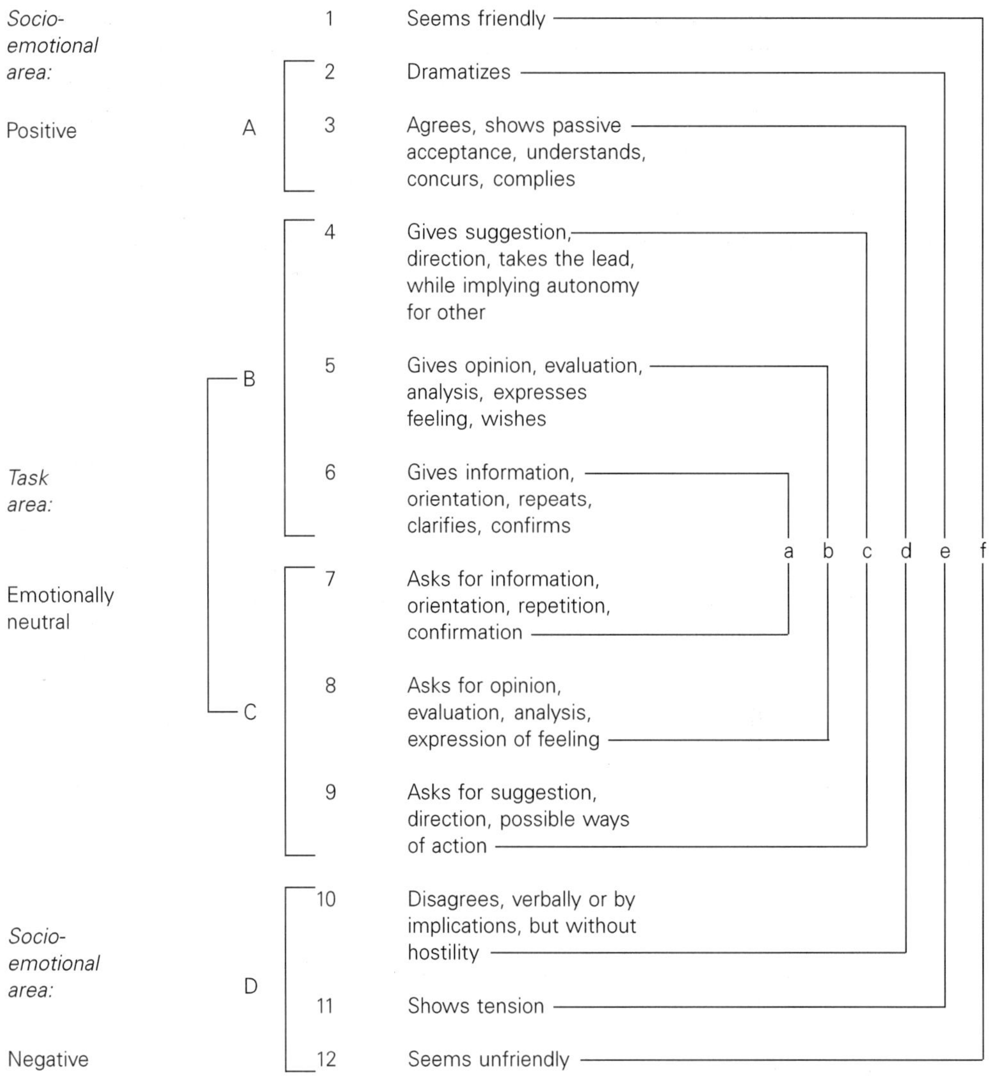

Socio-
emotional
area:

Positive   A

Task
area:

Emotionally
neutral

Socio-
emotional
area: D

Negative

1   Seems friendly

2   Dramatizes

3   Agrees, shows passive
    acceptance, understands,
    concurs, complies

4   Gives suggestion,
    direction, takes the lead,
    while implying autonomy
    for other

5   Gives opinion, evaluation,
    analysis, expresses
    feeling, wishes

6   Gives information,
    orientation, repeats,
    clarifies, confirms

7   Asks for information,
    orientation, repetition,
    confirmation

8   Asks for opinion,
    evaluation, analysis,
    expression of feeling

9   Asks for suggestion,
    direction, possible ways
    of action

10 Disagrees, verbally or by
    implications, but without
    hostility

11 Shows tension

12 Seems unfriendly

B

C

a   b   c   d   e   f

Triads
A   Positive reactions
B   Attempted answers
C   Questions
D   Negative reactions

Key to problem areas
a   Problems of communication
b   Problems of evaluation
c   Problems of control
d   Problems of decision
e   Problems of tension reduction
f   Problems of reintegration

Figure 1.3 *The verbal analysis of behaviour: Bales' system (1970)*
(All behaviour, verbal or non-verbal, is observed and classified in one or other of
12 categories.)

group process. Certainly it is my experience that group members are constantly surprised at the feedback they get from an interaction analysis in respect of both the quality and the quantity of what they contribute to discussion. However, it is not always so easy to categorize behaviours in the way indicated by Bales, more particularly in the socio-emotional area where people frequently keep their feelings to themselves or are trying somehow to compensate for various feelings they have towards other people or the whole group. The analysis makes no concession to the notion of a group culture but can be a valuable analytical tool for visible group interaction. It nevertheless fails to reveal some of the more powerful determining forces in a group.

Six-category intervention analysis

Another form of behaviour analysis is proposed by Heron (1976, 1989) and although based primarily on one-to-one interventions, can apply equally to a group setting and particularly to the tutor's role. Heron has modified and developed the categories over the past 15 years, and the analysis that follows in this book represents a selection from his two publications that seems to make best sense for learning in tertiary education. He calls it the 'six-category intervention analysis' and claims that the interventions deal with all 'desirable and worthwhile types of intervention: that is, they exclude only negative and destructive types of intervention'. The six categories are devised in a form that contributes to self-assessment and self-monitoring for group leaders of any kind; to what extent they can be extended to ordinary group members has yet to be seen.

The six categories fall into two main groups: authoritative, when the leader is in a dominant or assertive role; and facilitative, where the role of the leader is seen to be less obstructive and more discreet.

Under the authoritative mode the tutor can be:

1. Directing
   - Raising an issue for discussion, re-routing the discussion.
   - Suggesting further work to be done.
2. Informing
   - Summarizing.
   - Interrelating.
   - Giving knowledge and information.
3. Confronting
   - Challenging by direct question.
   - Disagreeing with/correcting/critically evaluating student statements.
   - Giving direct feedback.

Under the facilitative mode the tutor can be:

4. Releasing tension
   - Arousing laughter.
   - Allowing students to discharge unpleasant emotions such as embarrassment, irritation, confusion and sometimes even anger.

5. Eliciting
   - Drawing out student opinions/knowledge/problem-solving ability.
   - Facilitating student interaction.
   - Enabling students to learn and develop by self-discovery and personal insight.
6. Supporting
   - Approving/reinforcing/agreeing with/affirming the value of student contributions.

Two of these six categories – eliciting and informing – are of special importance for group work in that they form a spectrum from student-centred learning to tutor-centred learning (see Figure 1.4).

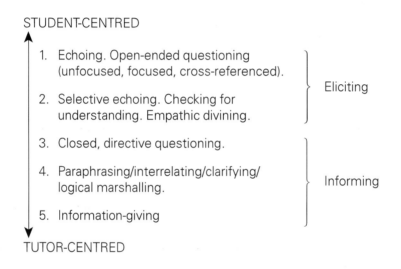

Figure 1.4 *The spectrum from student-centred to tutor-centred learning*

The details of both these categories indicate some of the particular skills the tutor should employ in performing the interventions. 'Echoing' refers to the practice of repeating, without any special emphasis, the last few words a student says before pausing. This invariably encourages the student to expand on his or her thoughts. Alternatively, the tutor may rephrase the last few words. Echoing is a way of conveying to the student, particularly when he or she has paused in the development of an argument, that the tutor is paying attention and wishes the student to continue without interruption in the flow. Various open-ended questions can serve a similar purpose. Selective echoing is the skill of picking out from a contribution a few words or phrases that seem to carry an implicit emotional charge, or that appeared to cause some sort of agitation in the student. 'Empathic divining' is a way of sensing an implicit feeling, thought or intention that is not fully expressed, and tentatively labelling it. 'Logical marshalling' involves picking up the threads of a discussion, interrelating them and sometimes indicating where they might be leading and putting this back to the group in a succinct way. Various suggestions for the use of these categories, particularly those in the facilitative mode, are given in Chapter 7.

Exercises

1. Feedback on group behaviour

Figure 1.5 shows another chart of group behaviour.

	Individuals in the group who perform these functions well
Task-based behaviour Initiating	
Giving and seeking information	
Giving and seeking opinion	
Clarifying	
Building, integrating	
Summing up	
Consensus testing	
	Individuals in the group who perform these functions well
Maintenance-based behaviour Encouraging, valuing	
Mediating	
Compromising	
Releasing tension	
Gatekeeping	

Figure 1.5 *Feedback on group behaviour*

1. Working individually, each member writes on a copy of the chart the names of group members who perform the particular functions well. They then mark, on another copy of the chart, how they see *themselves* in terms of each category.
2. When this is completed each member goes to a prepared flipchart and writes up the names in the appropriate boxes, indicating clearly the number of times that any name appears.
3. Each member in turn should then talk about how their self-assessment compared with the composite list and ask for any feedback that would help them understand any differences.
4. Finally the group can discuss what gaps there appear to be in the overall pattern and what might need to be done to remedy that.

2. Fishbowl

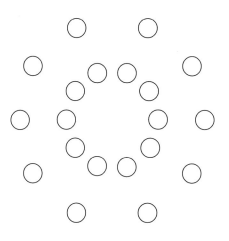

Figure 1.6 *Fishbowl*

1. Ask the leader / tutor to leave the room for the first half of this discussion. The group divides to form a fishbowl (see Figure 1.6); in this the outer members act as silent observers while a discussion takes place in the inner one.
2. Conduct a discussion on authority/dependency and organizational structure or another psychodynamic concept in relation to the group you have been working in:
    – How and when does the tutor exercise authority?
    – What feelings does it engender?
    – What do you learn for yourself from that?
    – What would happen if the group as a whole had no tutor?
3. Meanwhile the outer group can be making notes on questions like:
    – What is happening in the inner group without a tutor?
    – How is authority assumed?
    – Who takes initiatives?
    – Is there any 'pecking order' in contributions?

4. When the tutor returns (after 30 minutes), the outer group explains to the tutor what they observed, with the inner group remaining silent.
5. Finally the whole group re-assembles and the tutor joins in an open discussion based on the exercise.

Discussion points

■ To what extent do you think that a theoretical approach constrains our understanding of group dynamics and to what extent does it provide a helpful structure?
■ To what extent do you think that the problems in groups you have belonged to arose from some of the unconscious forces described in this chapter rather than an imbalance of behavioural qualities?
■ Choose a problem incident in your group. Which aspects of theory seem to shed most light on what happened?

2 | Research into group behaviour

Everything should be made as simple as possible, but not simpler.

(Albert Einstein)

The research most likely to improve teaching and learning is that conducted by teachers on questions that they themselves have formulated in response to problems or issues in their own teaching.

(Cross and Angelo, 1988)

> By the end of this chapter you can expect to be able to identify some of the essential characteristics of effective groups and a range of issues affecting the dynamics of groups.

Research into group behaviour has, over the years, largely concentrated on experimental groups performing practical tasks rather than processing academic material or experiencing personal growth. Some have focused on individual behaviour, some on the individual as a group member, some on the group as a whole and still others on intergroup behaviour. Typical criticism of the experimental approach is that the results are frequently trivial and even when put together do not add up to much (except where they can be interpreted in the light of real-life experience or a set of theoretical precepts); that they are frequently conducted with randomly selected students as subjects and are therefore unrepresentative of the population as a whole; and that they have rarely been able to touch upon the sort of complex phenomena of group interactions which appear to dominate the process in many groups.

This form of research has been described by Bronfenbrenner (1977) as 'strange people doing strange things to strangers in strange situations'. However, Argyris (1968) argues that it is more or less what happens in the shop-floor situation; in both, precise instructions are given but nobody is told why. In fact, the goals are quite frequently concealed. The same might be true of the many learning groups. There are enormous differences between patterns of behaviour in long-established groups, such as those which exist over a period of time in a course or in an industrial environment, and experimental collectivities which are drawn together solely for the purpose of a particular experiment; and patterns of behaviour change as groups develops over a period of time.

Some valuable information does of course emerge when experimental work in areas of similar interest is compared. Yet we can never be sure of cause and effect in human behaviour: which conscious or unconscious motive does it spring from? What action will a particular motive produce? The task of providing explanations for social behaviour is highly problematical and demands careful evaluation as well as scepticism from the practitioner. On the other hand, it requires an ability to see the relationship between separate bits of evidence, and between those bits of evidence and the practical situation in which decisions have to be made.

Quite apart from the so-called laboratory experiments, we can select from a range of other studies which may loosely be described as field studies. The basic characteristic of these is that the phenomenon under investigation is studied in its natural habitat. Shaw (1977) comments: 'the investigator does not create the situation or situations being studied, instead he or she examines the phenomenon as it occurs in natural on-going social events'. To this extent the evidence derived is based on local events in a special context. For the practitioner they present some problems in interpretation as there is always some uncertainty about the particular effect of the environment in which the experiment takes place – the institution, the personal qualities of the teacher and the students, the external motivating factors such as assessment and social life – all of which can profoundly affect the outcome.

An accumulation of research evidence can, over a period of time, challenge some of our assumptions about what happens in groups and change our understanding of problems. As practitioners, most teachers will need to test the relevance and value of research evidence in their own contexts, usually by incorporating some of the implied principles into their teaching procedures. Everyone must be their own translator.

What this all boils down to is that research evidence has to be interpreted in the light of practical experience with and in everyday groups. That is what Knowles and Knowles (1972) provide a ready made amalgam of research and practice in their succinct review of the common characteristics of group behaviour. The groups they refer to include families, committees and discussion groups; the properties relate to all sorts of groups and situations. All of them are relevant to the learning group and their range and variety perhaps serve to underline the limited view of group interaction we often take in our work with students. The following pages (22–30) are reproduced with the kind permission of Malcolm Knowles.

Properties of groups

Background

Each group has an historical background, or lack of it, which influences its behaviour. Members of a new group coming together for the first time may have to devote much early energy to getting acquainted with one another and with the group's task, as well as establishing ways of working together. On the other hand, a group that has often met together may be assumed to be better acquainted with what to expect from one another, what needs to be done, and how to do it. But it might also have developed habits that interfere with its efficiency, such as arguing, dividing into factions or wasting time.

Members come into a meeting with some expectations about it. They may have a clear idea of what the meeting is about, or they may be hazy and puzzled about what it going to happen. They may be looking forward to the meeting or dreading it; they may feel deeply concerned or indifferent. In some cases the boundaries around the group's freedom of action may be narrowly defined by the conditions under which it was created, or so poorly defined that the group doesn't know what its boundaries are.

These are merely illustrations of some of the elements that make up a group's background. Some questions that help to provide an understanding of a group's background include:

- How well were the members prepared for joining the group?
- What are their expectations about the group and their role in it?
- What is the composition of the group – what kind of people, what previous experience, prior friendship patterns and so on? How were they selected?
- What arrangements have been made for their meeting – physical setting, resources and the like?

Participation pattern

At any given moment every group has a particular participation pattern. For instance, it may be all one-way, with the leader talking to the members; or it may be two-way, with the leader speaking to the members and the members responding; or it may be multi-directional, with all members speaking to one another and to the group as a whole. In a given group this pattern may tend to be quite consistent, or it may vary from time to time. The studies do not indicate that any one participation pattern is always best; it depends upon the requirements of a given situation. But many studies show that on the whole, the broader the participation among members of a group the deeper the interest and involvement will be. Some questions you may ask about a group to understand its participation pattern are:

- How much of the talking is done by the leader, how much by the other members?
- To whom are questions or comments usually addressed – the group as a whole, the leader, or particular members?
- Do the members who don't talk much seem to be interested and listening alertly (non-verbal participation), or are they bored and apathetic?

It is very easy, and often useful to a group, to chart the participation pattern during periodic segments of time, thus providing objective data about this aspect of its dynamics, as in Figure 2.1.

This property has to do with how well group members are understanding one another – how clearly they are communicating their ideas, values and feelings. If some members

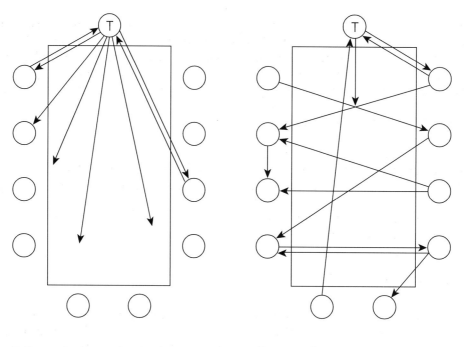

Pattern of communication in group
dominated by tutor

Pattern of communication in group
not dominated by tutor

Figure 2.1 *Participation dynamics*

are using a highly specialized vocabulary they may be talking over the heads of the rest of the group. Sometimes a group will develop a specialized vocabulary of its own, a kind of verbal shorthand, or private jokes that aren't understood by new members and outsiders.

Even non-verbal communication can often be eloquent. A person's posture, facial expression and gestures tell a great deal about what he or she is thinking and feeling. Some questions that indicate the quality of a group's communications are:

■ Are members expressing their ideas clearly?
■ Do members frequently pick up contributions previously made and build their own ideas on to them?
■ Do members feel free to ask for clarification when they don't understand a statement?
■ Are responses to statements frequently irrelevant?

Cohesion

The cohesiveness of a group is determined by the strength of the bonds that bind the individual parts together into a unified whole. This property indicates the morale, the team spirit, the strength of attraction of the group for its members, and the interest of the members in what the group is doing. In the literature it is often referred to as the 'we feeling' of a group. Symptoms of low cohesion include *sub rosa* conversations between pairs of members outside the main flow of the group's discussion, the emergence of cliques, factions and such sub-groupings as the 'old timers' versus the 'newcomers', the 'conservatives' versus the 'liberals', and so on.

Questions about the group's cohesion include:

- How well is the group working together as a unit?
- What sub-groups or 'lone wolves' are there and how do they affect the group?
- What evidence is there of interest or lack of interest on the part of members or groups of members in what the group is doing?
- Do members refer to the group as 'my group', 'our group', 'your group', 'their group', 'her group' or 'his group'?

Atmosphere

Although atmosphere is an intangible thing, it is usually fairly easy to sense. In the literature it is often referred to as the 'social climate' of the group, with such characterizations as 'warm, friendly, relaxed, informal, permissive, free' in contrast to 'cold, hostile, tense, formal, restrained'. Atmosphere affects how members feel about a group and the degree of spontaneity in their participation. Atmosphere can be probed by such questions as:

- Would you describe this group as warm or cool, friendly or hostile, relaxed or tense, informal or formal, permissive or controlled, free or inhibited?
- Can opposing views or negative feelings be expressed without fear of punishment?

Norms

Every group tends to develop a code of ethics or set of norms about what is proper and acceptable behaviour. Which subjects may be discussed, which are taboo; how openly members may express their feelings; the propriety of volunteering one's services; the length and frequency of statements considered allowable; whether or not interrupting is permitted – all of these and many more dos and don'ts are embodied in a group's norms. It may be difficult for a new member to catch on to a group's norms if they differ from those of other groups he or she has experienced, since these norms are usually implicit rather than openly stated. Indeed, a group might be confused about what its norms actually are, and this may lead to embarrassment, irritation and lost momentum. Questions about norms include:

- What evidence is there that the group has a code of ethics regarding such matters as self-discipline, sense of responsibility, courtesy, tolerance of differences, freedom of expression, and the like?

- Are there any marked deviations from these norms by one or more members? With what effect?
- Do these norms seem to be well understood by all members, or is there confusion about them?
- Which of the group's norms seem to help, and which seem to hinder the group's progress?

Sociometric pattern

In every group the participants soon tend to identify certain individuals that they like more than other members, and others that they like less. These subtle relationships of friendship and antipathy – the sociometric patterns – have an important influence on the group's activities. Some research indicates that people tend to agree with people they like and to disagree with people they dislike, even though both express the same ideas. Questions that help to reveal the sociometric pattern are:

- Which members tend to identify with and support one another?
- Which members seem repeatedly at odds?
- Do some members act as 'triggers' to others, causing them to respond immediately after the first member's comments, either pro or con?

Structure and organization

Groups have both a visible and an invisible organizational structure. The visible structure, which might be highly formal (officers, committees, appointed positions) or quite informal, makes it possible to achieve a division of labour among the members and get essential functions performed. The invisible structure consists of the behind-the-scenes arrangement of the members according to relative prestige, influence, power, seniority, ability, persuasiveness, and the like. Questions to ask about structure include:

- What kind of structure does the group create consciously – leadership positions, service positions, committees, teams?
- What is the invisible structure – who really controls, influences, volunteers, gets things done? Who defers to others, follows?
- Is the structure understood and accepted by the members?
- Is it appropriate to the group's purpose and tasks?

Procedures

All groups need to use some procedures – ways of working – to get things done. In formal business meetings we are accustomed to the use of a highly codified and explicit set of procedures. Informal groups usually use less rigid procedures. The choice of procedures has a direct effect on such other aspects of group life as atmosphere, participation pattern and cohesion. Choosing procedures that are appropriate to the situation and to the work to be done requires a degree of flexibility and inventiveness by a group. Procedures can be examined through such questions as:

- How does the group determine its tasks or agenda?
- How does it make decisions – by vote, silent assent, consensus?
- How does it discover and make use of the resources of its members?
- How does it coordinate its various members, sub-groups and activities?
- How does it evaluate its work?

Goals

All groups have goals, some very long-range – for example, 'to promote the welfare of children and youth' – and others of shorter range – 'to plan a parent education programme for the coming year'. Others are even more immediate – 'to decide on a speaker for next month's meeting'. Sometimes goals are defined clearly, specifically and publicly; at other times they are vague, general and only implicit. Members may feel really committed to them or may merely go along with them. Since goals are so important to the group's ultimate accomplishment they receive a good deal of attention in the literature. Some questions about goals include:

- How does the group arrive at its goals?
- Are all members clear about them?
- Are all members committed to them?
- Are they realistic and attainable for this group?

We shall return to each of these 10 group characteristics in the context of learning and the choices that both tutors and students have to influence group process for the better.

Social and task dimensions

It appears at first sight that there are two completely different kinds of groups. Some, such as the bridge circle, the coffee gang and the like, are highly informal, with few rules or procedures and no stated goals. People belong for the emotional satisfaction they get from belonging; they like the people, they are their friends. They tend to think of these as their social groups. Membership in these groups is completely voluntary and tends to be homogeneous. The success of the social group is measured in terms of how enjoyable it is.

In other groups, however – committees, boards, staff meetings and discussion groups – there are usually explicit goals, and more or less formal rules and procedures. People tend to think of these groups, which exist to accomplish some task, as work or volunteer service groups. The membership tends to be more heterogeneous – based on the resources required to do their work – and sometimes brought together out of compulsion or sense of duty more than free choice. The success of the task group is measured in terms of how much work it gets done.

As these dimensions have been studied more deeply, it has become apparent that they do not describe different kinds of groups – few groups are purely social or task – so much as different dimensions of all groups. Most groups need the social dimension to provide emotional involvement, morale, interest and loyalty; and the task dimension to provide stability, purpose, direction and a sense of accomplishment. Without the dimension of work, members may become dissatisfied and feel guilty because they are not accomplishing anything; without the dimension of friendship, members may feel that the group is cold, unfriendly and not pleasant to be with.

Group maintenance and group task functions

To understand the way in which various group functions are performed, it is helpful to classify these functions as: 1) group-building and maintenance roles – those that contribute to building relationships and cohesiveness among the membership (the social dimension); and 2) group task roles – those that help the group to do its work (the task dimension).

The first set of functions is required for the group to maintain itself as a group; the second set, for the locomotion of the group towards its goals. For example, some group-building functions are:

- encouraging – being friendly, warm, responsive to others, praising others and their ideas, agreeing with and accepting the contributions of others;
- mediating – harmonizing, conciliating differences in points of view, making compromises;
- gatekeeping – trying to make it possible for another member to make a contribution by saying, 'We haven't heard from Jim yet', or suggesting limited talking – time for everyone so that all will have a chance to be heard;
- standard-setting – expressing standards for the group to use in choosing its subject matter or procedures, rules of conduct, ethical values;
- following – going along with the group, somewhat passively accepting the ideas of others, serving as an audience during group discussion, being a good listener;
- relieving tension – draining off negative feeling by jesting or throwing oil on troubled waters, diverting attention away from unpleasant to pleasant matters.

The following are some task functions:

- initiating – suggesting new ideas or a changed way of looking at the group problem or goal, proposing new activities;
- information seeking – asking for relevant facts or authoritative information;
- information giving – providing relevant facts or authoritative information or relating personal experience pertinent to the group task;

- opinion giving – stating a relevant belief or opinion about something the group is considering;
- clarifying – probing for meaning and understanding, restating something the group is considering;
- elaborating – building on a previous comment, enlarging on it, giving examples;
- coordinating – showing or clarifying the relationships between various ideas, trying to pull ideas and suggestions together;
- orienting – defining the progress of the discussion in terms of the group's goals, raising questions about the direction the discussion is taking;
- testing – checking with the group to see if it is ready to make a decision or to take some action;
- summarizing – reviewing the content of past discussion.

These functions are not needed equally at all times by a group. Indeed, if a given function is performed inappropriately it may interfere with the group's operation – as when some jester relieves group tension just when the tension is about to result in some real action. But often when a group is not getting along as it should, a diagnosis of the problem will probably indicate that nobody is performing one of the functions listed above that is needed at that moment to move the group ahead. It seems to be true, also, that some people are more comfortable or proficient in performing one kind of function than another, so that they tend to play the same role in every group to which they belong. There is danger, however, in over-stereotyping an individual as a 'mediator' or 'opinion-giver' or any other particular function, for people can learn to perform various functions that are needed when they become aware of them.

In groups one can often observe behaviour that does not seem to fit any of these categories. This is likely to be self-centred behaviour, sometimes referred to in the literature as a 'non-functional role'. This is behaviour that does not contribute to the group, but only satisfies personal needs. Examples of this category are:

- blocking – interfering with the progress of the group by going off on a tangent, citing personal experiences unrelated to the group's problem, arguing too much on a point the rest of the group has resolved, rejecting ideas without consideration, preventing a vote;
- aggressing – criticizing or blaming others, showing hostility towards the group or some individual without relation to what has happened in the group, attacking the motives of others, deflating the ego or status of others;
- seeking recognition – attempting to call attention to oneself by excessive talking, extreme ideas, boasting, boisterousness;
- special pleading – introducing or supporting ideas related to one's own pet concerns or philosophies beyond reason, attempting to speak for 'the grass roots', 'the housewife', 'the common man', and so on;
- withdrawing – acting indifferent or passive, resorting to excessive formality, doodling, whispering to others;
- dominating – trying to assert authority in manipulating the group or certain members of it by 'pulling rank', giving directions authoritatively, interrupting others' contributions.

The appearance of these behaviours in groups can be irritating to other members, and they tend to react to them with blame, reproach, or counter-hostility. A group that understands group dynamics is often able to deal with them constructively, however, because it sees them as symptoms of deeper causes such as valid personal needs that are not being satisfied constructively. Often, of course, it is difficult to place a given act in one or another of these categories – what seems to be 'blocking' to one observer may appear as 'testing' to another.

Group size

The tendency for many of the above behaviours to become dominant can increase with group size for reasons explained on page 7. Even in small discussion groups participants contribute unequally and there is little doubt that the scope for participation decreases exponentially as numbers increase, as the graphs in Figure 2.2 clearly indicate.

In the first graph, which shows the percentage of contributions in a group of five, one member – the highest contributor – has made over 40 per cent of the contributions while another – the lowest contributor – has made only 7 per cent. In the second graph, in a group of eight, the difference becomes more marked. The highest contributor has maintained a similar level of contribution but the lowest six have each made only 3–8 per cent of the contributions. The implication of this is that larger groups need more structure organized for them if they are to function effectively within the usual time boundaries. Either the tutor will have to take a firmer hand and set up sub-groups with specified tasks, or some other form of leadership will emerge.

The role of leadership

In this analysis of functions necessary to the performance of groups, no distinction has been made between the functions of leaders and the functions of the members. This is because the research fails to identify any set of functions that is universally the particular responsibility of the designated leader. But the fact is that groups in our society typically have central figures with such titles as 'leader, chair, president and captain'. Ross and Hendry (1957) examine various theories that try to explain this institutionalization of the role of leader and, after assessing them as inadequate, give this view as to the current state of thinking:

> *Perhaps the best we can say at this point is that any comprehensive theory of leadership must take into account the fact that the leadership role is probably related to personality factors, to the attitudes and needs of 'followers' at a particular time, to the structure of the group, and to the situation. Leadership is probably a function of the interaction of such variables, and these undoubtedly provide for role differentiation which leads to the designation of a 'central figure' or leader, without prohibiting other members in the group from performing leadership functions in various ways, and at various times, in the life of the group.*

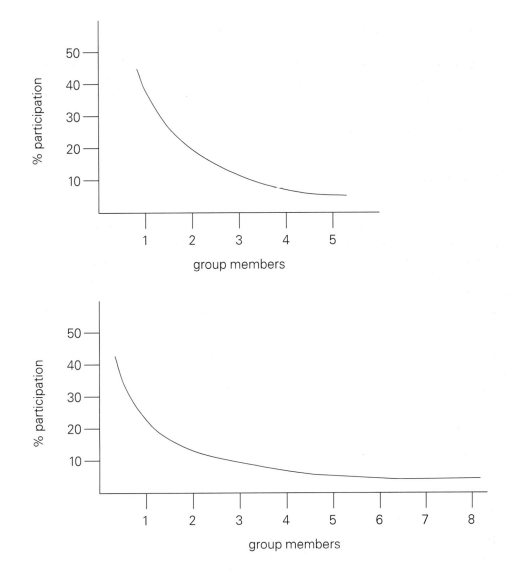

Figure 2.2 *Distribution of participation in groups of different sizes (Bligh, 2000)*

A classic series of experiments in the laboratory of Kurt Lewin often quoted in the literature of group dynamics has a bearing on leadership style. Their purpose was to measure as precisely as possible the effects of different types of leader behaviour on a number of experimentally created groups of boys. The three types of leader behaviour tested were 'authoritarian' (policy determined by the leader), 'democratic' (all policies a matter of group discussion and decision, encouraged and assisted by the leader), and 'laissez-faire' (complete freedom for the group or individual decision, with a minimum of leader participation). Their studies produced evidence for the following generalizations:

- Authoritarian-led groups produced a greater quantity of work over a short period of time, but experienced more hostility, competition and aggression – especially scapegoating, more discontent beneath the surface, more dependence and less originality.
- Democratically led groups, slower in getting into production, were more strongly motivated, became increasingly productive with time and learning, experienced more friendliness and teamwork, praised one another more frequently and expressed greater satisfaction.
- Laissez-faire groups did less and poorer work than either of the others, spent more time in horseplay, talked more about what they should be doing, experienced more aggression than the democratic group but less than the authoritarian, and expressed a preference for democratic leadership.

A mounting body of research on the leadership role since World War II supports the thesis that some situations require authoritarian and others laissez-faire leadership, but that, in the long run, in normal situations, groups thrive best when the leadership functions are democratically shared among the members of the group.

Groups in motion

Much of what we have been discussing so far has been concerned with the variables that make up a group, its properties and the membership and leadership functions. But groups are thriving and developing organisms that never stand still. Groups move both as a unit, and through the interaction of the various elements within them. A change in structure (as we shall see in Chapter 6) can affect participation which in turn may affect communication, norms, leadership and so on. Figure 2.3 from Guirdham (1990) shows a useful visual summary of the generic stages with the different emphases on individual, group and task needs indicated by the size of the circles.

Stages of group development

It might be informative to look at one approach in more detail. Of the various schema that have been proposed, the following, based on Lawrence in Bligh (1986), probably best fits the psychodynamic orientations of Chapter 1.

Forming

When a number of people come together for the first time to form a group there is an initial concern with the nature of the task: what has to be done, by what time and with what resources? Group members will equally be checking out what is appropriate

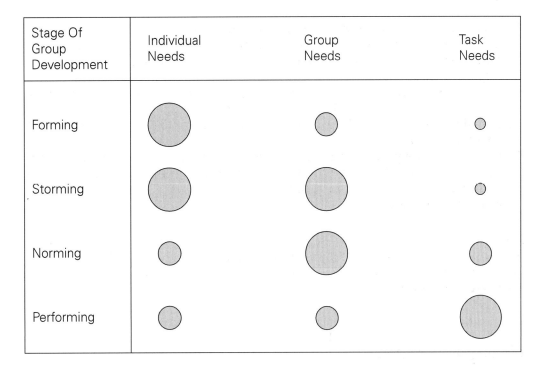

Figure 2.3 *Relative influence of individual, group and task needs on group members'
behaviour at different stages of group development*

Reproduced from Guirdham, M (1990) *Interpersonal Skills at Work*, Prentice Hall

behaviour and adjusting accordingly. There is also, at this stage, a strong dependence on
any authority in the group as a form of counterbalance to the deeper question, which is
about 'Why am I here?' or 'Do I really want to be here?'. This need to create a sense of
self in the group is labelled 'self-lodging' by Denzin (1969): 'If valued portions of self are
not lodged, recognized and reciprocated, a dissatisfaction concerning the encounter is
likely to be sensed. If self-lodging doesn't take place successfully, the person may fail to
take up a rational standpoint.' This supports the paradoxical hypothesis that a group
cannot come together until each member has established her or his own separate
individuality.

Storming

This stage typically includes conflict and an expression of interpersonal hostility within
the group. It is as if any of the uncertainties and deeper emotions from the previous

stage have become unfrozen and/or projected on to other people of the group. Bennis (1985) describes it as a stage of counter-dependence on authority. Differences are asserted and seen as all or nothing, for or against. Issues of personal freedom versus the group authority arise and leaders of opposing arguments collect followers.

Norming

Emphasis is now placed on the mutual concerns and interrelationships. The freedom/authority conflict of storming has been resolved. Behaviours now turn to listening, asking opinions, building on others, etc. Personal norms are replaced by group norms, common goals are agreed, ground rules may be established and a sense of open collaboration is created, but not without some compromise on the freedom experienced in the second stage, and some negotiation.

Performing

Now members settle into, and are reasonably satisfied with, functional roles. Schroder and Harvey (1963) called this positive interdependence with simultaneous autonomy and neutrality. The group acquires a distinct sense of itself as a culture. One role that the group will probably decide is concerned with its continuity, which naturally leads to the fifth stage.

Informing

In this the final, and sometimes ignored, phase the group starts to give voice to the outside world, communicating, for instance, with other groups, and agreeing how it will further its work.

Lawrence, in Bligh (1978) points out that the above stages depend upon certain assumptions that may or may not exist: that the group manages to survive the storming stage and does in fact move from stage to stage until they achieve their goal without falling apart; and that problems of outside hierarchy, which might distort the sense of shared purpose, are not imported into the group.

It has to be said in the context of this book that many of the classic studies of group development have involved group leaders who took a passive or non-directive role and did not directly intervene in the group process (Johnson and Johnson, 1987), and this contrasts with the typical tutor-led group in higher education. They propose the following seven-stage model for learning groups where there is a leader with clear responsibility for the effective functioning of the group:

1. *Defining and structuring procedures.* At the first meeting the group will expect the tutor/leader to explain what is required of them, what the plan and purpose of the meetings is and how the group is going to operate (whether or not this fulfilled is of course a matter of choice). Typically with a learning group, the tutor will clarify the task, explain procedures, and generally set up the group in readiness for its work together.

2. *Conforming to procedures and getting acquainted*. As members get used to the procedures and norms of the group they also become more familiar and relaxed with each other. The group are still dependent on the tutor for direction and they are happy to conform according to the process norms of the group whether explicitly or implicitly expressed. They do not yet feel a personal commitment to the group's goals or to each other.

3. *Recognizing mutuality and building trust*. The group members begin to recognize their interdependence and to build a sense of cooperation and trust. They internalize the sense that group learning is a collaborative venture and participate actively in discussions. There is a feeling of mutual support and trust.

4. *Rebelling and differentiating*. This stage represents a pulling back from the previous two as members start to resist the responsibilities they had apparently accepted and become counter-dependent, contravening many of the group-learning procedures. Sometimes this may mean returning to a more passive, minimal effort role and forgetting the previously held cooperative ethos. Despite its apparent negativity this stage is important for members in establishing interpersonal boundaries and a sense of autonomy, which can lead to a stronger, because self-owned, collaboration. Johnson and Johnson suggest that tutors should regard this rebellion and conflict as a natural and 'deal with both in an open and accepting way'. They recommend:
    –   not tightening control and trying to force conformity: reasoning and negotiating;
    –   confronting and problem-solving;
    –   mediating conflicts while helping to underpin autonomy and individuality;
    –   working towards students taking ownership of procedures and committing themselves to each other's success.

    'Coordinating a learning group is like teaching a child to ride a bicycle.' You have to run alongside to prevent the child from falling off, but still giving the child space and freedom to learn how to balance on his or her own.

5. *Committing to and taking ownership for the goals, procedures and other members*. The group becomes 'our' group, not the tutor's. The group norms of cooperation become internalized and no longer have to be externally imposed: the members are no longer dependent on the tutor as the driving force and find support and help from each other. Friendships develop.

6. *Functioning maturely and productively*. A sense of collaborative identity develops as the group matures into an effective working unit. Group members learn to operate in different ways in order to achieve group goals and can readily alternate attention between task and maintenance concerns. At this stage they can usually cope with any problems that arise in the group without the help of the tutor who in turn takes on the role of a consultant and resource to the group. Labour is divided according to expertise, members ask for and accept help from each other and leadership is shared among the members.

    Johnson and Johnson remark that many discussion groups do not reach this stage either because the tutor does not have the ability to establish cooperative inter-dependence or group members do not collectively possess the necessary skills to function in this way. Part of the tutor's job is therefore to ensure that group members are acquiring the skills they need to progress to this stage.

7. *Terminating*. Every group has to come to an end and its members have to move on. The more cohesive and mature a group has become, the more sadness will accompany its ending for both members and tutor. The last meeting must deal with this as a recognizable problem and not avoid it as they leave the group to move on to future experiences.

Most groups, if they are developing effectively, will move fairly quickly through the first five stages, devote most time and energy to the mature and productive stage, and then terminate quickly. The skill of the tutor in handing over the 'perceived ownership' of the group goals and procedures as it moves from the first two stages through the rebellion is of course critical.

Field studies

Most of the research into group work in tertiary education is naturally centred on discussion groups. It is interesting therefore to draw comparisons between this and the more general research evidence described above. Beard *et al* (1978) claim there is general agreement that some of the more important variables in discussion groups are:

- seating position;
- talkativeness;
- personality of the participants;
- a kind of leadership.

We can compare this with Deutsch (1949) who studied the effect of giving different information on the assessment of a group to members of different groups. He noted that where groups were to be assessed collectively, in cooperation, they showed more coordination of effort, diversity in amount of contribution, subdivision of activity, attentiveness to fellow members, mutual comprehension and communication, greater orientation, orderliness and productivity per unit time, as well as more favourable evaluation of the group and its products, compared with groups who were informed that each individual would be assessed independently. Davey (1969) in an experiment with 800 groups of different sizes concluded that with up to approximately seven group members the permissive style of leadership seemed most productive, but above that a controlling style seemed to work better. This leads to consideration of the value of tutorless groups. Marris (1965) found that, when staff were absent from groups, students felt far less inhibited and frequently discussed their work with each other. They felt that seeking help from staff was viewed as a confession of incompetence. Of course sub-groups within a larger group are a form of tutorless group and Beard and Harley (1989) point to the success of discussion in pairs (buzz groups) before students raise questions more formally with the teacher.

   The presence of a tutor does not of course imply his or her active participation in discussion. Abercrombie (1979), for instance, developed a technique of group work in which the tutor played the part of an onlooker who asked the occasional question or made a comment, rather in the way that a group therapist might do. In this case, the task was specific: to help students consider evidence carefully and to make valid judgements on their observations. The objects of scrutiny were radiographs or an account of an experiment. Some students were clearly unsettled by this procedure and others rejected it out of hand, though nearly all were amazed at the degree to which unconscious assumptions had appeared to influence their judgement. Upon testing at the end of the course, it was apparent that participants in this class were better able to distinguish between facts and inferences, made fewer false inferences, explicitly considered alternative hypotheses more frequently and were less often fixed in their view of the problem by dint of previous experience, than were a control group. This experience had apparently helped them become more objective in making assessments of scientific material.

It thus appears that groups are demonstrably valuable for many of the more sophisticated aims of higher education to do with critical thinking, making diagnoses or decisions, solving problems, and changing or maintaining attitudes to the subject under study. Indeed Bligh (1998), surveying the research evidence on different forms of teaching, concluded that discussion methods are more effective than didactic methods (eg, the lecture) for stimulating thought, for personal and social adjustment, and for changes of attitude and, more surprisingly perhaps, were hardly worse than the lecture for effectively transmitting information (see Figure 2.4 a–c).

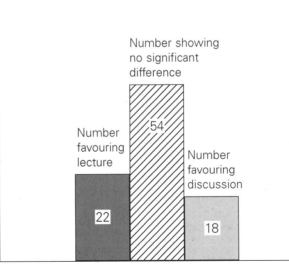

Figure 2.4(a) *Lectures compared with discussion, with transmission of knowledge as the criterion*

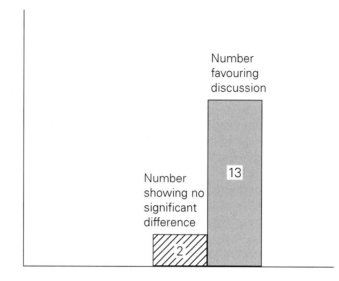

Figure 2.4(b) *Lectures compared with discussion, with promotion of thinking as the criterion*

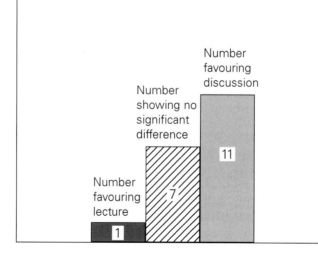

Figure 2.4(c) *Lectures compared with discussion, with attitudes as the criterion*

Preferences and problems

The disposition of tutors and students to learning in groups is of course another factor in their effectiveness. Research into this would, as Neath (1998) observes, have to take into account the whole learning environment, including the traditional culture of individualism and competition, as much as the skills and knowledge that all involved have of working and learning in groups. This is especially an issue when students are working in project teams and may suffer as a result of the inadequacies of one or more of their members or indeed the team as a whole. This commonly experienced problem is what makes books like *Learning in Teams* (Gibbs, 1995) so important as training material for both tutors and students when planning to use tutorless groups. Luker (1987) in Brown and Atkins (1988) lists a number of student and tutor likes and dislikes on the subject of small-group teaching, a selection of which is given here.

What tutors and students like about small group teaching

Tutors

- The informal atmosphere – opportunity to get to know students at a personal level and for them to get to know me.
- Feeling of informality and, when things go right, that students have learnt something and – even in statistics – enjoyed themselves.
- Seeing a student suddenly grasp an idea for the first time, which for him or her makes a number of other disjointed areas simultaneously fall into place.
- I can be stimulated by students' ideas.
- Opportunity for providing instantaneous, personal, feedback on their own thoughts and efforts.
- Being able to give praise.
- The educational goals are readily defined, almost as a contract between me and the group.

Students

- I can personally have a greater influence on what is being discussed. I can actually remember, and feel I understand what we are discussing.
- Being able to participate and to find out other people's ideas.
- I like the flexibility of a small group. We aren't bound to a rigid schedule.
- It teaches you how to converse in a literate manner.
- Helps develop your power of analysing problems and arriving at solutions.
- By being in a smaller group, one feels part of a class rather than just another face in a sea of faces. I actually feel more part of the university.

Difficulties and dislikes

Tutors

- Keeping my mouth shut.
- Getting a discussion going.
- It often requires considerable skill to direct discussion in fruitful directions.
- It requires considerably more mental alertness and flexibility than a formal lecture, and can be a bit of a strain.
- Getting students to see me as an equal, talk to me as they would to their peers, and lose their inhibitions about displaying ignorance in front of me and their peers.
- Very difficult to establish the kind of atmosphere in which students will begin to talk. They tend to be very much afraid of not saying the right thing.
- Shutting up the vociferous.
- Bringing in the meek.
- How to deal with a poor or irrelevant answer.

Students

- A small group can easily be dominated by one person.
- When members of the group will not talk.
- Long silences.
- Being asked to contribute when you don't want to.
- Being directly asked vague questions.
- A feeling of being assessed by the lecturer through your answers to questions and your attitudes.
- Sometimes you feel threatened by the closeness of the lecturers.

There is a vast amount of research evidence on group work and it is in a constant state of expansion and revision. The fact remains that it can be described as 'work done by other people in other places for other purposes' and this provides a ready excuse for teachers to reject it or at least ignore it. The notion of the teacher as researcher, therefore, has a lot to commend it.

Teacher as researcher

The concept of a teacher as one who is putting into practice ideas developed by others is not an appealing one, nor is it realistic, as Pring (1978) argues. Each teaching situation is governed by a unique set of variables which no general researcher could conceivably take into account: the personality of the teacher, the special characteristics of the students, the effects of the learning milieu in that institution and the structure of the particular curriculum being taught, to name but a few. If teachers are to research their own teaching the question arises: how can the objectivity and rigour demanded by research be obtained?

As Pring says, being objective is opening to public scrutiny the basis upon which one's judgements are made so that counter-evidence and contrary arguments might, if they exist, be levelled against what one says. I may be correct in declaring at the end of the lesson that things went well, but my judgement is subjective insofar as there is no evidence against which another might test the truth of what I say.

In order to conduct classroom research one would need to formulate hypotheses and choose an appropriate test procedure. Such hypotheses would be unlikely to embrace all the variables, yet as long as they are regarded as provisional and are stated clearly, they can be very instructive. Among test procedures one might use are:

■ an interaction analysis (for example, the one on page 14);
■ recording either with audio or video tape;
■ recording one's own comments in a diary;
■ drawing out the students' perceptions.

None of these would stand up on its own as reliable research evidence, but taken together they could be employed as a 'triangulation' technique in which each account of what happened is tested against the others. This proposal of the teacher as an activator in research, rather than as a recipient, is an exciting one in that it implies a greater sense of direction and self-autonomy for the teacher. It is firmly supported by Rowan and Reason (1981) who propose an interactive style of research in which the mutual influences of researcher and 'researched' are acknowledged.

Action research

Given the teacher's position of being researcher and partner in the researched scenario at the same time, orthodox research practices make little sense, as does the value position of watching things go wrong and doing nothing to rectify them. In a practical and very accessible book, McNiff *et al* (1996) describe action researchers, unlike orthodox researchers, as, 'intent on describing, interpreting and explaining events while seeking to change them for the better'. They also claim that action research can lead to the researchers' own personal development, better professional practice, improvements in the institution in which they work, and making a valuable contribution to the good order of society.

Action research unashamedly recognizes and values the personal part that the researcher plays as both the subject and the object of the study. The researcher therefore has to take a self-critical stance, admitting errors and taking full responsibility for mistakes. It demands the exercise of communication skills (listening in particular), management skills, quiet reflection and collaboration, all of which are agreeably congruent with the essence of good groupwork. Examples of the action research model in the review and evaluation of courses can be found in Zuber-Skerritt (1992).

Exercises

1. Places

- Ask group members to negotiate a change of place with somebody who is not sitting next to them and to describe the new experience to one of their new neighbours before speaking to the whole group about it.
- Ask each member to sit in a different place from their usual one as their arrive.
- Allocate places with numbered cards, which members are given as they arrive.
- Rearrange the furniture into an unfamiliar configuration.
- Explain the purpose and nature of the session and ask members to decide what arrangement of furniture would be most suitable.

2. Lines of communication

In a typical group, members are only half aware of how much they speak or to whom they direct most of their contribution. The group as a whole is not usually aware what the pattern of communication is over time.

In this exercise, two members of the group, or two outside observers, sit outside the group and on opposite sides, and draw a map of the group with everyone's names on it. Then over a period of time (say half an hour), as they observe the discussion, they draw lines with arrows to indicate, where possible, who has addressed or questioned whom and responded to whom. Against each person on the map they place a tick for every time they say something, so that when someone addresses the whole group the proportion of their contributions to individuals compared with the group should be visible on the map (see Figure 2.5).

Once the observers have conferred, the group is shown the maps (preferably a copy for each member) and then invited to comment in turn on the extent to which this tallied with their impression of themselves, and what they learn from that.

3. Secret leadership

Prepare as many folded slips of paper as there are members of the group and mark one of them with the letter 'L'. Tell the group that they are to take part in a discussion in which there will be a designated leader, whatever that may mean to them. Each of them is to be given a slip and whoever has the one with 'L' on it is to act as leader. Hand the slips out with the instruction that they must check their own slip privately and not reveal what is written on it to anyone.

After the allowed time for the discussion, ask the group whom they thought the designated leader was and for what reasons – what did they do, how did others relate to them that was different? Then ask the actual leader to identify him- or herself.

Discussion can then centre on how the leadership role was interpreted by the 'L' person, how comfortable he or she felt with it, and what others might have been doing in any

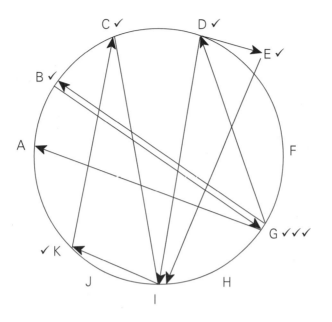

Figure 2.5 *Communication map*

form of competition for the leadership. Finally it may be useful to ask the group to generate freely a list of effective and ineffective leadership behaviours that they observed in the exercise, including any that were lacking.

Variations

- The task can be a practical or a decision-making one.
- You may choose who gets the 'L' in order to avoid any personal discomfort for any group member or for other reasons.
- Two slips could be marked with an 'L'.
- All the slips could be marked with an 'L'.

4. Norms exercise

Norms are mutual, unspoken expectations. They are mostly learnt through what is not said or through non-verbal cues. They comprise the unstated 'dos and don'ts' of the group and may be individually as well as group based.

In groups of four, discuss:

1. 'Norms in groups I belong to, lead, etc.' (10 mins)
2. 'Norms in this group.' (10mins)
3. 'Norms I/we can change in our group and how.' (10mins)

Draw up a personal list of norms for each of the three categories as you go along:

Norms in groups generally:

....

....

....

....

Norms in this group:

....

....

....

....

Norms to be broken, plus observations:

....

....

....

....

Find a partner from one of the other groups.

- Share your findings and discuss intentions for full group discussion which follows. (10 mins)
- Full group reconvenes. (20 mins)
- Open discussion (and observation of what happens in light of above insights).

Discussion points

- Take the sets of questions on pages 23–27 and answer them for, or in, your group.
- How would you describe the balance between social and task dimensions in your group? What can you do to affect this?
- How would you characterize the role of leadership in the achievement of task goals compared with social goals in your group?

3 | Learning research and theory

Learning without thought is labour lost: thought without learning is perilous.

(Confucius)

A person who 'knows everything' has a lot to learn.

(Peter Honey)

By the end of this chapter you can expect to be conversant with most of the research and theory on learning and be able to evaluate its relevance and application to groups.

Learning research has, over the past 20 years, had a marked effect in the way it has informed and influenced teaching practices in higher education. Where, previously, it was mainly focused on the activities of the teacher – the transmission model – it has increasingly recognized that what the student does is more important in determining what is learnt (Nicol, 1997). The old paradigm 'mistakes a means for an end' (Barr and Tagg, 1995). This paradigm shift , as Nicol argues, 'implies a need to change our beliefs about the teachers' role in learning' to one in which the teacher:

> *encourages participation, dialogue and interaction by students with course materials and with each other. The teacher should function as a facilitator of learning, intellectually critical, stimulating and challenging but within a learning context that emphasizes support and mutual respect.*

Equally it has changed in its conception of what learning comprises. We should be concerned not with what students take from what is available to them but their approach to learning, the personal meaning they derive, the factors that motivate and the social context and value system in which the learning occurs.

This research has begun to provide a set of helpful explanatory concepts that have become incorporated into practical ideas by trainers and developers. The effect of such research may be indirect but, when it coincides with the practical experiences of the classroom and the increasingly emphasized training in teaching and learning methods for academics, it begins to acquire meaning and relevance. We have already noted that action research on the relationships between learning and teaching can lead to outcomes that have more significance for, and effect on, those involved than 'pure' research evidence, yet the latter can serve as an excellent foundation for it as well as for forms of application deriving from inspiration rather than rigorous study.

Research evidence is thus gradually changing teachers' assumptions and the way they interpret their role. It 'sensitizes' teachers to aspects of the teaching-learning process that had previously lacked significance. It points up anomalies in the existing situation and may provide hints of alternative solutions. But it cannot indicate the single best way of tackling either lecturing or studying (Entwistle, 1977). In recent years several studies of the ways in which students learn have been conducted in Sweden, Britain and the USA. Most of them have implications for the way in which groups are organized and run, particularly because it has expanded beyond the transmission model of learning. The implication for us is that we are not trying to change students so much as change the way they experience, perceive and conceptualize things.

Learning styles

Rather different aspects of the students' approach to learning have been revealed through a series of studies by Marton and Säljö (1976) and their colleagues at Gothenburg. They identified two distinctive approaches among students in the way they read texts – surface-level and deep-level processing:

■ Surface-level processing – in which students take a passive approach and are concerned with:
  – covering the content;
  – how much they have learnt;
  – finding the 'right' answers;
  – assimilating unaltered chunks of knowledge;
  – learning verbatim.
■ Deep-level processing – in which students take an active approach and are concerned with:
  – the central point;
  – what lies behind the argument;
  – the whole picture;
  – what it boils down to;
  – what it is connected with;
  – the logic of the argument;
  – points that are not clear;
  – questioning the conclusions.

The surface-level processors divert their attention, therefore, to the sign, and the deep-level processors to that which is signified. In general those adopting 'deep' approaches are more successful in exams. Surface processors tend to pass only when they manage to overcome the tedium which that form of learning often induces.

Deep processors are more versatile: they find it easier to tackle 'surface' questions than surface processors do 'deep' questions. Strong motivation increases the likelihood that deep-level processing will occur, while anxiety induces a hurried fact-grabbing strategy. This will doubtless be familiar to the experienced tutor, who will have noticed the increasing desperation among students to memorize 'facts' and know 'what is what' as exams approach. Surface and deep approaches are therefore closely related to the level of satisfaction a student derives from the experience of learning: a surface approach can be painfully hard work while a deep approach is likely to increase motivation. Possibly the most succinct summary of the dichotomy comes from Ramsden (1992): 'Surface is, at best, about quantity without quality; deep is about quality *and* quantity' (emphasis added).

In a parallel investigation in London, Pask (1976) distinguished between two clear strategies among students for drawing up a classification system. 'Holists' adopted a broad perspective and looked for a variety of interrelationships, whereas 'serialists' were typified by their attention to details and a pattern of learning by increments. Holists ask a different order of questions, too, 'about broad relations and (they) form hypotheses about generalizations' as opposed to serialists whose questions are 'about much narrower relations and (whose) hypotheses are specific'. Lest it be thought that holists are successful in all respects it should be added that they are likely to over-generalize and to make remote and often mistaken connections. Serialists, on the other hand, are often victims of their own caution, and their inability to make connections often makes integration of knowledge a difficult task for them. Pask's continuing research into learning strategies has indicated, not surprisingly, a further category – the versatile learner who is able to adopt the holist or serialist strategy according to the task at hand. He also demonstrated that holists are not good at learning serialist material; nor are serialists good with holist material, but students whose learning style matched the material learnt it quickly and accurately.

Intellectual development

It would be sad if we reviewed student learning solely in terms of processing information and finding ways of 'working the system'. In tertiary education students are free, possibly for the first time, to learn in their preferred way, and to develop their own sense of what is worth learning.

In an interview study of students at the Liberal Arts College at Harvard, Perry (1970) found a coherent progression in the manner in which students approached learning, experienced values and construed the world during their college experience. He identified a sequence of positions through which students appear to have progressed as they moved through college. Basically the sequence comprised a development from a dualistic, authority-accepting position, through a relativistic 'anything goes' phase, to a final stage of open-minded commitment:

> **Position 1 – dualism**. There are Right and Wrong Answers to everything. Author-
> ities, whose role is to teach the answers, know what these are, and if I work hard,

and learn the Right Answers, adding more and more to my stock of knowledge, all will be well.

Position 2. Diversity of opinion and uncertainty exist but that's only because Authority is confused or ill-qualified. They set us problems only to enable us to find the Right Answer by ourselves.

Position 3. Some uncertainties and differences in opinions are real and legitimate. But this is a temporary situation for Authorities who are still searching for the Right Answer.

Position 4a. Where Authorities don't know the Right Answers, everyone has a right to their own opinion; no one is Wrong!

Position 4b. Some Authorities are not asking for the Right Answer: they are grading us like they do because they want us to think about things in a certain way, supporting opinion with data and so on.

Position 5 – relativism. All knowledge and values are relative but equally valid. Everything has to be seen in its context. Dualistic, Right/Wrong thinking is a special case in context.

Position 6. I'm going to have to make up my own mind in an uncertain world with no one to tell me whether I'm right or wrong.

Position 7. I've made my first commitment!

Position 8. Now I've made several commitments, I've got to balance them in terms of priorities. Which do I feel really committed to and responsible for?

Position 9 – evolving commitments. This is how life will be. I must be wholehearted while tentative, fight for my values yet respect others, believe my deepest values to be right yet be ready to learn. I see that I shall be retracing this whole journey over and over – but, I hope, more wisely.

According to Perry, a student moves into a new phase as the prior one becomes inadequate in coping with the uncertainties and complexities of the world and knowledge. The meanings and structurings attached to the old phase are not lost but contained within the new one to be used where appropriate, and each step is accompanied by a 'joy of realization' but also a loss of certainty and an altered sense of self. The changes and progression appear to be applicable to all ages and to varied backgrounds and situations. Though they do not necessarily develop at the same rate in all aspects of a student's life, he or she might well transfer more advanced forms of thinking to less developed areas.

One would hope that most students will enter colleges at a stage beyond position 1 and progress at least to position 5 by the end of a full-time course at tertiary level. However, fewer students appear to reach the stage of maturity implied by position 9. Even the acceptance of relativism as a perception of the world represents revolutionary change in thinking and values for many students and as such is a challenge to some of their fundamental beliefs. It is akin to the restructuring of scientific theory that takes place from time to time (Kuhn, 1973). Such a profound transformation is thus one of great significance in the intellectual development of the student, yet paradoxically it is one that is often the most quietly realized.

Perry also describes forms of 'deflection', or reversion in the process, which offer a way out at critical points. These are temporizing, where a student bides time in one position; escape, a sense of withdrawn disenchantment; and retreat, an entrenchment in the dualist, absolutist framework of positions 1 and 2.

Perry's study raises questions about structure and sequence in course design, about the presentation of knowledge and the ways in which students are grouped for teaching, about the techniques and skills that tutors bring to discussion, and about ways of assessing students. To what extent is it possible, particularly in group discussion, to assist students to growth points in their development, while allowing for the emotional dispositions to which intellectual forms are often wedded? Is Perry's scheme applicable only to the so-called liberal arts, or is it equally relevant to the learning of science and technology? Whatever the answers may be, and they will doubtless vary according to circumstances, there is little doubt that the studies of recent years stimulate thought on the nature of student learning even if they present a somewhat selective picture.

Developmental phases in the conception of learning

Säljö (1997) has demonstrated how students may change their approach to learning as they progress in their studies. Gibbs (1990) has summarized this work in a way that represents an integration of the research already discussed in this chapter. Underlying the approach students take is their understanding of what learning itself comprises. This understanding changes, influenced by the context in which they find themselves and by the learning demands these contexts make. Studies have identified five stages in the development of students' understanding, listed here with examples of the kinds of things students, who have these conceptions, say:

1. **Learning as an increase in knowledge**. The student will often see learning as something done to them by teachers rather than as something they do to or for themselves. *'To gain some knowledge is learning . . . We obviously want to learn more. I want to know as much as possible.'*
2. **Learning as memorizing**. The students have an active role in memorizing, but the information being memorized is not transformed in any way. *'Learning is about getting it into your head. You've just got to keep writing it out and eventually it will go in.'*
3. **Learning as acquiring facts or procedures that are to be used**. What you learn is seen to include skills, algorithms, formulae which you apply, etc, which you will need in order to do things at a later date, but there is still no transformation of what is learnt by the learner. *'Well, it's about learning the thing so you can do it again when you are asked to, like in an exam.'*
4. **Learning as making sense**. The student makes active attempts to abstract meaning in the process of learning. This may only involve academic tasks. *'Learning is about trying to understand things so you can see what is going on.' 'You've got to be able to explain things, not just remember them.'*

5. **Learning as understanding reality**. Learning enables you to perceive the world differently. This has also been termed 'personally meaningful learning'. *'When you have really learnt something you kind of see things you couldn't see before. Everything changes.'*

There are other developmental schemes, describing how students change in the sophistication of their perception of the learning tasks they face which embody very similar descriptions. Stages 4 and 5 are clearly qualitatively different from stages 1 to 3. Students who understand what learning is at stages 1, 2 and 3 have trouble comprehending what a deep approach consists of and are very unlikely to take a deep approach to learning tasks. Students who are at stages 4 or 5 can take either a deep or a surface approach, depending on the task and their perception of its demands. The connection between these underlying conceptions of learning and the approach students take to specific learning tasks is so strong that it is possible to predict the quality of learning outcomes directly from students' conceptions of learning. All you need to know about students is that they have a conception of learning at stage 1, 2 or 3 and you can be fairly certain that they will only derive a superficial and fragmentary understanding from, for example, reading a chapter.

For some students, then, their limited understanding of what learning comprises prevents them from approaching learning tasks in a deep way and therefore from learning effectively. Two important questions about such crude and disabling conceptions of learning are: Where do they come from? Can they be changed?

As well as being asked about what they think learning is, students have been asked what they think good teaching comprises. Some think that the teacher should do all the work and make all the decisions: the teacher should select the subject matter, present it in teacher-controlled classes, devise tests and mark students on how well they have learnt the material that has been presented. What is to be learnt and what learning outcomes should look like are completely defined by the teacher (a 'closed' conception of teaching). Others think that while the teacher has responsibility for setting the learning climate, for making learning resources available and for supporting students, all the responsibility lies with the student: responsibility for selecting learning goals, devising appropriate learning activities and for judging when learning outcomes are satisfactory (an 'open' conception of teaching). It will probably come as no surprise to learn that the former, 'closed', conception of teaching is held almost exclusively by students with conceptions of learning at stages 1, 2 or 3, while the latter, 'open' conception of teaching is held by students with conceptions of learning at stages 4 or 5. This relationship is summarized below.

Table 3.1

Conception of learning	Conception of teaching
Reproducing (Levels 1, 2 and 3)	**Closed** Teacher does all the work and makes all the decisions
Making sense (Levels 4 and 5)	**Open** Learner does most of the work and makes most of the decisions

SOLO taxonomy

As students learn, so their ways of expressing and demonstrating what they have learnt develop in structural complexity. SOLO stands for the Structure of Observed Learning Outcomes and is a developmental schema, shown in Figure 3.1, for describing the way students' learning reveals stages of increasing complexity as they master an academic subject.

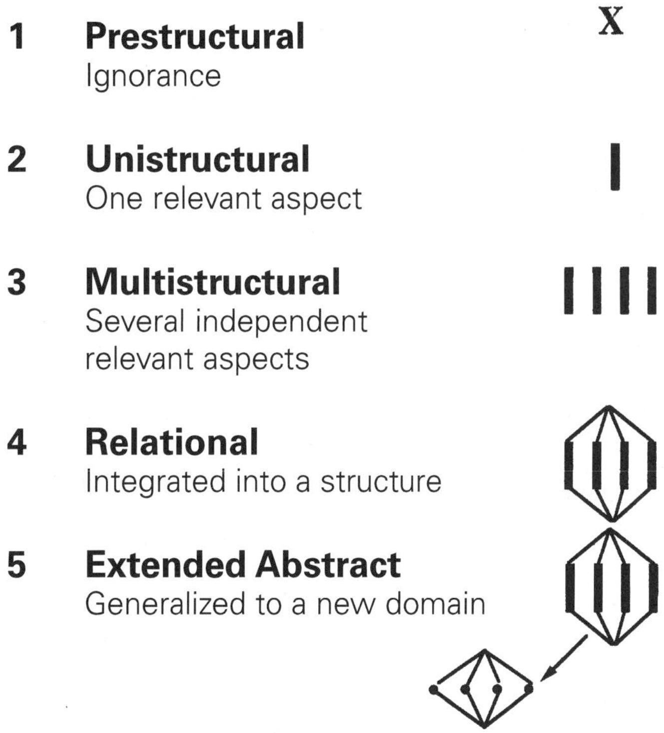

1   Prestructural
Ignorance

2   Unistructural
One relevant aspect

3   Multistructural
Several independent
relevant aspects

4   Relational
Integrated into a structure

5   Extended Abstract
Generalized to a new domain

Figure 3.1 *SOLO taxonomy*

The SOLO taxonomy, which is assumed to apply to any subject area, includes five stages:

- The first, *prestructural*, refers to that stage where students can acquire information but make no coherent interpretation of it, or meaningful response to it. While the responses may appear quite sophisticated and elaborate they do not make any overall sense. It is the quantitative accumulation of knowledge.
- *Unistructural* responses focus on one aspect adequately enough but fail to identify its significance.
- *Multistructural* responses focus on several relevant aspects but see them neither in relation to each other nor the whole: 'seeing trees is a necessary preliminary to

adequate understanding, but it should not be interpreted as comprehending the wood' (Biggs, 1999).

■ At the *relational* level the student is making sense of the various aspects of the topic or problem: 'the trees have become the wood' and points are made that pull together the whole and link to a conclusion.

■ At the *extended abstract* level, the student is able to extrapolate, to develop higher order principles and extend the topic to wider fields. Each level contains the lower level plus a bit more. As Biggs says, 'each partial construction becomes the foundation on which further learning is built'.

The SOLO taxonomy can be a very useful tool not only in prioritizing learning outcomes and objectives in the curriculum, but also in considering the development of learning in groups. As far as groups are concerned a mode of progression in discussion from the prestructural to the extended abstract has clear implications for the styles of task and intervention, which we address in later chapters. How it relates to what must be considered a related sequence – the Perry (1970) stages of intellectual and ethical development – is another issue and worthy of further research.

Metacognitive learning

There is increasing evidence (Biggs, 1999; Boud, 1995) that students who think beyond what is given, and even 'without' what is given, are able to understand more profoundly and learn more lastingly. Metacognitive learning, as the term implies, is about thinking beyond or transcending the immediate knowledge or skills, and involves thinking on at least two levels. Examples of it would include learning about learning, problem-based learning, self- and peer assessment, peer tutoring and the self- and peer monitoring of group behaviour.

Such learning is an integral part of a well-run group. Group learning gives students practice in thinking and explaining; it exposes them to multiple viewpoints, which helps them to make connections among concepts and ideas; it provides opportunities for 'scaffolding' (students supporting each other's learning); it often results in students teaching each other. Teachers can develop it by making explicit the ways in which they think and by modelling some of the processes that the students are likely to use.

Motivation

We cannot complete this section without a recognition of the powerful effect that groups can have on students' motivation to learn. Motivation derives from a dynamic interaction between students' goals and values and their experience and appraisal of situations they encounter. The rewards of commitment and hard work backed by challenge and support are themselves motivating forces for further learning. Entwistle (1998), in discussing motivation and approaches to learning, stresses the value of intrinsic motivation and achievement motivation in contributing to effective approaches to learning. Intrinsic motivation, which derives from personal goals and interest in the subject, personal engagement with the tasks chosen, feeling of competence and confidence leads to 'a deep approach and conceptual understanding and produces learning outcomes which are flexible and transferable'. Achievement motivation 'focuses on personal levels of achievement', is more competitive and self-seeking and can lead to 'a strategic, but also versatile, approach to studying' (Entwistle, 1998).

The importance of group learning in relation to these propositions is, as Nicol (1997) states:

> that when students in groups share responsibility for achievement there is a decreased risk of personal failure and increased support for individual persistence . . . Group learning involves shared goals which leads to increases in students' sense of responsibility and self-efficacy; it provides a supportive atmosphere for learning.

Implications of learning research

It is difficult to draw any hard and fast conclusions as to what learning research implies for teachers at any level of education. Although it is likely that we can equate surface processors with serialists and with those in Perry's dualistic stage (and even with Hudson's (1966) convergers), and deep processing with holists, realistic reasoning and divergers, there are no clear indications of what the teacher should do about it: the research was all investigatory rather than applied. However, we could venture a few working hypotheses based on them:

- Many courses, especially those with high student contact-hours and heavy pressure of exams, are likely to inhibit deep, holistic, relativist thinking and encourage a reproductive, fact-grabbing strategy of learning.
- Deep, holistic, relativistic students are more likely to prefer the openness of small discussion groups to the more formal, distant relationships of highly-structured lecture courses.
- The teaching style of tutors will reflect their own way of thinking about knowledge and will vary accordingly.
- A mixture of formal lectures, small-group work, individual study and project-group work may be best for the majority of students and a course sequence that focuses increasingly on the latter methods will prove acceptable on several counts.
- The most academically successful students will be able to recognize differences in teaching styles and learning tasks and adopt strategies of learning appropriate to them.

There may be implications of a need, as Entwistle (1977) suggests:

> to think more clearly about the formation of large and small group methods in relation to the particular intellectual skills, or cognitive style, they are expected to foster and whether the assignments and examination questions given to students provide sufficient encouragement for deep-level processing.

Surface processing may be the only strategy possessed by many students when they arrive at college. Whether this is a kind of personality trait or is something more superficially acquired as a means to success in school, and therefore easily shed, is something else over which to ruminate. Certainly, if we can accept what Perry says about the often traumatic nature of change, it will follow that tutors require sensitivity and skill in accommodating the variety of student styles within a climate of intellectual growth (not to speak of the tutor's own styles and predilections). Students too readily slip into disillusionment and consequent failure because the range of demands is too great. But are they always the right demands, and is their response to the demands appropriate? What we as tutors must do is to help students understand what choices there are in approaches to learning and to give them the opportunity and support in making their choices. Small groups provide the most suitable environment for this to occur.

Principles of good practice

Chickering and Gamson (1989), following a lengthy study of research into learning and teaching in the USA, produced a comprehensive set of principles of good practice for undergraduate education, all of which can be seen as supportive of, and informative about, appropriate group learning methods. The following principles are based on *Seven Principles for Good Practice in Undergraduate Education*, Johnson Foundation, 1989.

Principles of good practice for undergraduate education

Good practice encourages student–faculty contact
Frequent contact between faculty and students, in and out of classes, is the most important factor in getting students motivated and involved. A faculty that demonstrate concern help students to get through rough times and to keep on working. Students' intellectual commitment is enhanced by knowing a few faculty members well; it encourages them to think about their own values and future plans.

Good practice encourages cooperation among students
Learning is enhanced when it is more like a team effort than a solo race. Good learning, like good work, is collaborative and social, not competitive and isolated. Working with others often increases involvement in learning. Sharing one's own ideas and responding to others' reactions improves thinking and deepens understanding.

Good practice encourages active learning
Learning is not a spectator sport. Students do not learn much just sitting in classes listening to teachers, memorizing pre-packaged assignments, and reproducing the expected answers. They must talk about what they are learning, write about it, relate it to past experiences, and apply it to their daily lives. They must make what they learn part of themselves.

Good practice gives prompt feedback
Knowing what you know, and don't know, focuses learning. Students need appropriate feedback on performance to benefit from courses. In getting started, students need help in assessing their existing knowledge and competence. In classes, students need frequent opportunities to perform and receive suggestions for improvement. At various points during their studies, and at the end, students need chances to reflect on what they have learnt, what they still need to know, and how to assess themselves.

Good practice emphasizes time on task
Time plus energy equals learning. Learning to use one's time well is critical for students and professionals alike. Students need help in learning effective time management. Allocating realistic amounts of time means effective learning for students and effective teaching for faculty. How an institution defines time expectations for students, faculty, administrators and other professionals can establish the basis for high performance for all.

Good practice communicates high expectations
Expect more and you will get it. High expectations are important for everyone – for the poorly prepared, for those unwilling to exert themselves, and for the bright and well-motivated. Expecting students to perform well becomes a self-fulfilling prophecy when teachers and institutions hold high expectations for themselves and make extra efforts.

Good practice respects diverse talents and ways of learning
There are many roads to learning. People bring different talents and styles of learning to college. Brilliant students in the seminar room may be awkward in the laboratory or art studio. Students rich in practical experience may not do so well with theory. Students need the opportunity to show their talents and learn in ways that work for them. Then they can be encouraged to learn in new ways that do not come so easily.

Theories and strategies for learning

Multiple intelligences

Gardner's (1993) theory of multiple intelligences has led to a broader understanding of how people learn than is available if we take a purely academic view of learning. He defines intelligence as, 'the capacity to solve problems or to fashion products that are valued in one or more cultural settings'. His eight types (the last one added recently) referring to learners' styles, or rather learning modalities, give pointers to the need to accommodate variety in our teaching and learning strategies and methods:

1. **Linguistic intelligence** refers to a learner's capacity to absorb information best by saying, hearing and seeing words. A learner's strong ability to memorize names and places and their facility with words makes them valued in 'academic' writing.
2. **Logical/mathematical intelligence** refers to a learner's capacity to excel at categorizing and classifying. They work well with numbers and will enjoy exploring the logical patterns and relationships in what they learn.
3. **Spatial intelligence** refers to a learner's capacity to learn by visualizing and enjoying drawing and designing. They excel at puzzles, maps and charts, and minds are best stimulated by the 'gestalt' of a visual image.
4. **Kinaesthetic intelligence** refers to a learner's need to move and touch in order to learn effectively. This can apply to people or materials and may involve their recalling times when they were physically in a certain place.
5. **Musical intelligence** refers to a learner's capacity to appreciate, respond emotionally, and even create music. Certain kinds of music (mainly classical) can be used to stimulate this intelligence.
6. **Interpersonal intelligence** refers to a learner's requirement for interaction and sharing with others. They benefit from the cooperative aspects of group work and other tasks that promote interpersonal relationships both in and out of the classroom.
7. **Intrapersonal intelligence** refers to learners' capacity to enjoy working alone on projects and pursuing their own interests. They would appreciate the individualized nature, reflecting quietly on their learning through diaries or logs.
8. **Naturalistic intelligence** refers to a learner's capacity to make distinctions and relationships between natural phenomena without any necessary engagement of the other intelligences.

Gardner argues that academic work has traditionally given too much priority and emphasis to the first two intelligences – linguistic and logical/mathematical – largely relegating the others to a secondary position with a consequent exclusion of a great deal of potential talent. It also follows that, if teachers tend to design material and courses in their own dominant 'intelligence' and assess students accordingly, those whose natural propensity is towards other intelligences will not have their learning needs fully met. It also raises questions about the focus of research into learning described above, conducted by academic researchers on students already in academic institutions. On a more positive note, Gardner's theory underlines the need to provide variety in the learning experience in order to accommodate not only the diversity of preferences in any one group of students but the range of intelligence available within each student. 'We should spend less time ranking (students) and more time helping them to identify their natural competencies and gifts and cultivate these' (Gardner, 1993).

Rogers' 10 principles

Rogers (1983) bases his principles of learning not merely on his work on humanistic psychology, but on many years' experience of university teaching:

1. Human beings have a natural potential for learning.
2. Significant learning takes place when the subject matter is perceived by the student as having relevance for his or her own purposes.
3. Learning that involves a change in self-organization – in the perception of oneself – is threatening and tends to be resisted.
4. Those learnings that are threatening to the self are more easily perceived and assimilated when external threats are at a minimum.
5. When threat to the self is low, experience can be perceived in differentiated fashion and learning can proceed.
6. Much significant learning is acquired by doing.
7. Learning is facilitated when the student participates responsibly in the learning process.
8. Self-initiated learning, which involves the whole person of the learner (feelings as well as intellect), is the most lasting and pervasive.
9. Independence, creativity and self-reliance are all facilitated when self-criticism and self-evaluation are basic and evaluation by others is of secondary importance.
10. The most socially useful learning in the modern world is the learning of the process of learning, a continuous openness to experience and incorporation into oneself of the process of change.

Experiential learning

This cycle or learning sequence developed by Kolb (1984) has the underlying premise that learners learn best when they are active, take responsibility for their own learning, and can relate and apply it to their own context.

The rationale of experiential learning is as follows. We all learn from the experience of doing a task and the results of that learning can be used constructively and even assessed. But it is not sufficient simply to have an experience in order to learn. Without reflecting on this experience, possibly through discussing it with others, it may be rapidly forgotten or its learning potential lost. The feelings and thoughts emerging out of this reflection can fit into a pattern that starts to make sense such that generalizations and concepts can be generated, and relationships made with existing theories. And it is generalizations and theories that give the learner the conceptual framework with which to plan and tackle new situations effectively. The experiential learning cycle is shown in Figure 3.2.

Accelerated learning

Accelerated learning, as much a learning strategy as a theory, has become very popular in the field of language teaching. Proponents of accelerated learning claim that many students who are having difficulties with the process of learning can benefit, as can students both successful and keen, and those possibly struggling with a subject they have not chosen, such as a foreign language. It takes the view that each of us has a special way of learning that suits us best and that if we are able to learn techniques that

Figure 3.2 *Experiential learning cycle*

correspond with our preferred learning style then that learning can become faster, more enjoyable and more effective. Accelerated learning places emphasis on achieving 'mind states' that are conducive to learning. It incorporates principles from multiple intelligences, neuro-linguistic programming and experiential learning and uses music, relaxation, visualization, role play, colour and mind maps in bringing 'left brain' and 'right brain' into conjunction. Rose and Nicholl (1997) describe the 'MASTER Plan', a mnemonic that comprises Motivating your mind, Acquiring the information, Searching out the meaning, Triggering the memory, Exhibiting what you know, and Reflecting on the process. Smith (1997) cites recent research, which indicates that playing Mozart coordinates 'brain wave rhythm and acts on the unconscious, stimulating receptivity and perception'; and that Baroque music such as Bach, Handel, Pachelbel and Vivaldi induces an alpha state brain cycle, which relates to 'relaxed alertness where the receptivity to new information is high'. He goes on to list different types of music conducive to various learning tasks and phases in accelerated learning.

Conclusions

The knowledge that has blossomed over the last 20 years on the way students learn has moved the debate about quality in learning and teaching a long way forward. It is clear that deeper approaches, metacognition and active learning are consonant with qualitatively superior learning outcomes. Effective teaching implies the preparation and handling of learning events for students that support and enhance these. We shall return to this theme in Chapters 6, 7 and 8.

Exercises

1. What makes learning effective?

Think back to an occasion in your life when you learnt something really well, or which you remember vividly. It need not necessarily be when you were a student. Think of all the concomitants of the experience, what happened before and after, who was involved, the physical and social environment, your feelings, etc.

When you have done your reminiscing, find a partner with whom to talk about it. Your partner will help you explore your recollection with questions about concomitants – the context, antecedents, consequences, significant people, etc.

Jot down any notes you may need to make as an aide-memoire.

After 15 minutes join up with another pair and after describing your partner's experience, draw up a group list of completions to the sentence:

Learning is usually better when . . .

2. Surface and deep learning

Below you will see a list of factors that affect the quality of student learning. Indicate the degree to which each of them is characteristic of the modules/courses in your subject area/department, and then those on which you actually teach. 10 = high, 0 = non-existent.

Surface learning is likely to be encouraged by:	Dept	Your teaching
A heavy workload		
Relatively high class contact hours		
An excessive amount of course material		
A lack of opportunity to pursue subjects in depth		
A lack of choice over subjects and a lack of choice over the method of study		
Poor feedback on progress		
Assessment methods that emphasize recall or the use of simple, standard procedures		
A threatening and anxiety-provoking assessment system		

Deep learning approaches are likely to be encouraged by:	Dept	Your teaching
Clearly stated expectations and outcomes		
Teaches that focuses on student learning		
Opportunities to exercise choice in the content and methods of study		
A range of learning modalities is recognized and used		
Active learning is encouraged and even demanded		
Teaching and assessment methods encourage active and lifelong engagement in the learning tasks		
The learning tasks relate to the students' prior knowledge and future interests		
The teacher shows enthusiasm and commitment		

Discussion points

■   Describe (in writing) what, in general terms, you or your group learn. How?
■   In what ways can a group leader encourage deep processing, holistic thinking and intellectual development? Where are you in all this?
■   How does the balance between different approaches to learning work out in your group and how does that affect the interaction?

4 | Communication in groups

No matter how hard one may try, one cannot NOT communicate. Activity or inactivity, words or silence all have message value: they influence others and these others in turn cannot NOT respond to these communications and are thus themselves communicating.

(Paul Watzlawick, 1962)

By the end of this chapter, you should be able to observe with greater accuracy and skill the process of communication and your own part in it.

The process of communication

No amount of understanding of group behaviour is sufficient for successful participation in groups unless each person in the group has the capacity to communicate effectively. It is through communication that people achieve an understanding of one another and are thus able to influence, and be influenced by, others. Communication occurs only when a message is accurately received. Only when there is a predisposition, therefore, to observe, listen and try to understand can clear communication take place – and this implies a degree of trust and openness between participants. Without these, mutual understanding and influences are liable to distortion: cooperation is unlikely.

Communication is often regarded as little more than the process of passing and receiving information. Concern for improving communication usually centres on the skills of writing, speaking, reading and, less frequently, listening. Typically, the emphasis will be on qualities like clarity, conciseness, precision and logical sequence. Yet many, and possibly most, errors in communication occur because of psychological rather than logical factors. The feelings, attitudes, behaviours and relationships of those involved in communication are more likely to determine whether it is effective or not. The process of communication is therefore far from being the rational or mechanical exercise that many people think (see Figure 4.1).

```
         A                                                    B
Sender _____→ Receiver
```

Figure 4.1 *Model of communication 1*

Model of communication

Communication involves much more than person A saying something to person B and the latter hearing it, interpreting it and acting on it correctly. Communication is not just about words. To paraphrase Kolb *et al* (1984): A brings to the interaction with B not merely the content of the message he or she wishes to convey but much more. A brings her- or himself as a person. A has a self-image and, to varying degrees, also a set of attitudes and feelings towards B. The message to B, therefore, in addition to certain content, may well be loaded with cues as to how A feels about him- or herself as a person (eg, confident and secure versus tentative and wary), how A feels about B as a person (eg, warm and receptive versus cold and uncaring) and how A expects B to react to A's communication.

If the issue were even as simple as that we might have a reasonably easy task in communicating. The trouble is we are not always aware of what we are actually putting across. We convey things we do not intend. The message thus gets distorted so that the above picture is transformed into something like Figure 4.2.

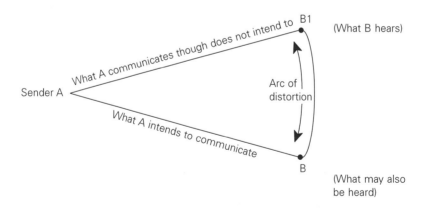

Figure 4.2 *Model of communication 2*

In addition, we often have more than one intention when we communicate something: sometimes the secondary intention becomes the stronger one, and where this is at a less than conscious level the message may well be distorted beyond recognition.

Every action, even (and sometimes especially) remaining silent, is a form of communication and is open to interpretation and response by others. Our body, face, gestures, physical proximity and eye contact all have a marked effect on what we are communicating and on how the other person feels about us and what we intend to communicate, yet are often ignored when we try to determine what goes right and wrong.

A tutor, for example, who looks stern or unresponsive when a particular student speaks, while saying, 'Yes, that's really very interesting' is communicating a message beyond words and a confusing one at that. So, too, is the tutor who, though meticulously correct in exposition, shows no enthusiasm for the subject or students, or who always sits behind a desk separate from the tutorial group. Distorting messages are conveyed by the tone of voice, facial expression, body posture, gesture or physical location. The problem is that the underlying feelings and thoughts that frequently emerge most powerfully through non-verbal cues are not usually amenable to discussion and action.

Those on the receiving end of a communication may also be party to the distortion. They have to listen and interpret appropriately and this is not at all easy when they are receiving contradictory messages simultaneously. A common problem in interpersonal communication is failure by the receiving party to attend fully to what is being said and thus missing the important points of a message. Sometimes this is because the receiver is preoccupied, or had a particular way of thinking about something (a mental set), which predetermines the interpretation. Hearing only part of a message may also serve the receiver's purpose, especially when there are contradictory signals being expressed and he or she has a legitimate choice.

The receiver's part in the hearing and interpreting of messages may be represented by a diagram complementary to Figure 4.2 (see Figure 4.3).

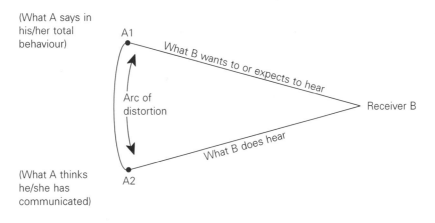

Figure 4.3 *Model of communication 3*

At times, we may consciously wish to convey more than one intention. For instance, when we express our thoughts in an interview we are usually trying to impress at the same time, to present ourselves in a favourable light. A lot of classroom behaviour is to do with impression: students trying to demonstrate their knowledge, their interest, their regard for the teacher; tutors trying to maintain an aura of objective expertise and control. There is nothing wrong with trying to impress provided it is appropriate and one is aware of it.

We are also likely to distort what we hear because of our personal needs. The need to be liked or to have everything neatly categorized, for instance, may blur our perception of what we are being told. Rather than attending to the complete message, we may block a lot of otherwise important information. Our need to be liked might cause us to be over-sensitive to negative components in a communication; our need for order and neatness or control might predispose us to miss some excellent ideas from students or colleagues who find it difficult to express themselves clearly. What we intend to do with the information when we have it can also cause us to filter and select.

An added factor that may contribute to distorted reception is threat, whether it manifests itself in a direct personal challenge from a group or an individual, or in a more general and ill-defined way. The distortion or denial that occurs as a result of threat derives from either the need to protect our self-esteem or from the anxiety that has its roots in early childhood experience. Fear of criticism, reproof, rejection or ridicule inevitably sets up defensive barriers, yet because they are at a conscious level they are at least open to scrutiny and change should we wish. Not so amenable to change are the distortions resulting from childhood conflicts, repressed because of the danger they originally posed, and reawakened at an unconscious level by particular people or events in adulthood. Both of these threats may be revived by a specific thing somebody does or says to us, or by an environment that has a high degree of evaluation, control and competitiveness.

Many of the complexities and problems of communication can be tackled through the use of metacommunication: describing the communication that appears to be taking place. For example, 'I didn't take in what you said then, could you repeat it?' or, 'This seems to have developed into a question and answer session – I suggest you talk me through what you've written on the form for a while.'

The content of communication

The words with which we choose to make our communication are important too, not just for the precision and clarity they offer but because they give colour and light to what we say. Students starting with a group are often at pains to learn how to handle the accepted vocabulary of the subject, and can easily gravitate towards the use of clichés and labels. 'Oh, that's a case of X' can cut out the possibility of open discussion when X is a concept that has been invented mainly to box in uncertainty about a phenomenon. More commonly one might hear, 'That's a mathematics problem' or whatever the subject in question is, as a way of foreclosing discussion on a topic.

Style and meaning are of relevance, too, in how people communicate. Statements that begin 'It is' or, 'They are' have a more distancing effect than those starting with personal pronouns, especially 'I think' or, 'I like'. A psychological distance is also established by the use of theoretical rather than personal understandings. Stanford and Roark (1974) divide the problem into five categories of meaning: theoretical, abstract, objective, personal cognitive and personal experiencing. Theoretical explanations are the fabric by which we write bits of experience into comprehensive explanations. Psychologically they are impersonal and distant. Theories, abstractions and objective referents can be verified by the opinions of others and are thus open to consensual agreement. But personal meanings are open to our scrutiny only; we are the sole judge.

Discussion and even lectures that focus entirely on 'what is' or 'what other people have said', may help students in jumping academic hurdles but have little personal impact on them.

To quote Stanford and Roark again, teachers often speak as if:

> subject matter has the only 'real' meaning and the students' personal meanings are irrelevant or secondary at best. The effect over a long period of time, especially for students with different experiential backgrounds from the teachers is to drive them away into a world where their meanings are never those of their environment and accepted as having worth.
>
> The effect on students is probably to encourage in their minds and culture a split between that which is acceptable for academic discussion and their more personal experience in the college as a community – a division, that is, between educational knowledge and everyday knowledge. The tendency of many students to seek solace and rewards in the social and political life of their college to the exclusion of academic work may well relate to this 'academization' of knowledge.

Improving communication

As we have already seen, the lack of trust and the existence of threat in any interaction can have a distorting effect on communication. The establishment of honest and meaningful communication can be achieved through these precepts, simple to state but not so easy to practise:

- Develop a sense of mutual trust and openness.
- Correct distortions in communication through constructive feedback.
- Engage in metacommunications; communicating about the process of communication.

The first point demands a willingness to be open to oneself (recognizing and accepting one's own feelings), to others (being able to disclose these feelings discreetly) and to the world around us. The 'Johari Window' (Luft, 1970), shown in Figure 4.4, is a helpful device for analysing and working on this problem. It is used for increasing personal and interpersonal awareness.

The Johari Window comprises four quadrants:

1. The *free and open* area refers to behaviour known to self and to others.
2. The *blind* area refers to things about us that others can see but of which we are unaware.
3. The *avoided or hidden* area indicates things we prefer to keep to ourselves (hidden agendas or personal feelings).
4. The area of *unknown activity* represents the sort of things that are accessible neither to us nor to others, but which may eventually be revealed. Such behaviours and motives could have affected our relationships, without our knowing it, all along.

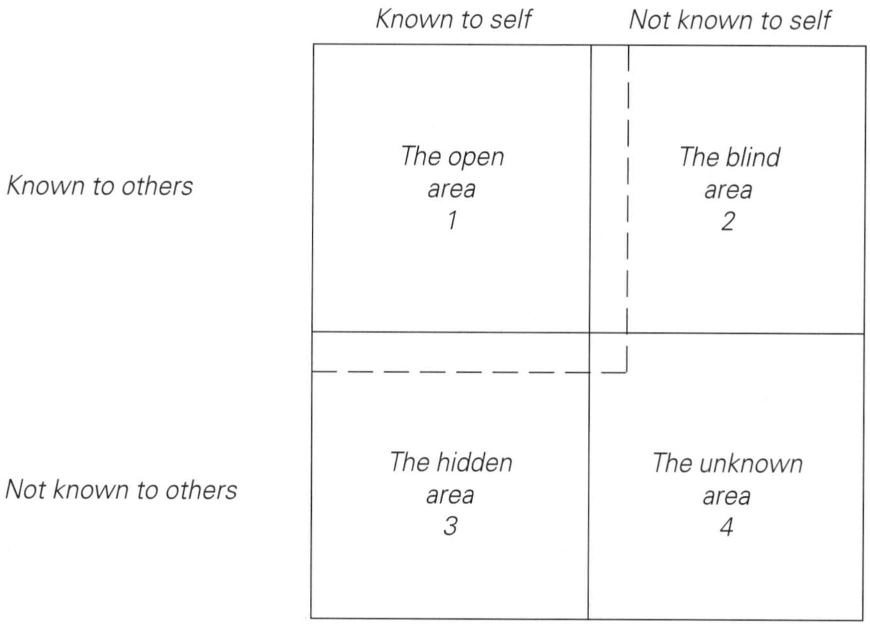

	Known to self	Not known to self
Known to others	The open area 1	The blind area 2
Not known to others	The hidden area 3	The unknown area 4

Figure 4.4 *The Johari Window*

Luft suggests that a change in any one quadrant will affect all the other quadrants. By disclosing some of our own feelings or private experiences we expand quadrant 1 into quadrant 3. This makes it more possible for other people to let us know something about ourselves that we were unaware of, for example, 'You always smile when you're angry', which in turn expands quadrant 1 into quadrant 2. This leads to the more open form of communication indicated by the broken line. Exercises using the Johari Window may be found in Pfeiffer and Jones (1974) and Kolb *et al* (1984), but it is a simple enough tool to use in any group whose members have experienced or observed each other over even a short period of time.

Giving and receiving feedback

The following simple rules about this most sensitive area of communication are likely to promote action and change. The underlying principles are existential: 'I speak of my own experience; I cannot assume yours'; and, 'I own my feelings'.

Giving feedback:

- Feedback is usually better when invited rather than imposed.
- Be descriptive rather than evaluative. Describing what we actually see or hear reduces the need of the receiver to react defensively.

- Reveal your own position or feelings vis-à-vis the other person: for example, 'I get very confused by your questions.'
- Be specific rather than general: for example, 'That's the third time you've said one thing to me privately and another thing publicly.'
- Take into account the receiver's needs as well as your own.
- Direct feedback towards behaviour the receiver can change or control.
- Timing is critical: it is usually better to give feedback as soon as possible after the particular behaviour, though one should always take into account the social situation, the receiver's vulnerability and their readiness to listen.
- Check that the receiver has understood; if you can, get them to rephrase the feedback to see if it's what you had in mind.
- When feedback is given in a group allow giver and receiver the opportunity to check with others in the group on its accuracy.

Receiving feedback:

- Listen to the person who is giving the feedback; accept what they are saying as genuine and helpful; try to understand their feelings, what they are describing and what they are suggesting you do.
- Accept feedback as a gift.
- If possible, check the feedback with a third party.
- Give the feedback serious consideration, weigh up the consequences of changing or not changing, express your thoughts and feelings about alternatives.
- Communicate your decisions to the giver.
- Tell them what they could do which might help you to change.
- Thank the giver for their concern and help.

If we accept that communication is inescapably a two-way process, then feedback is probably the best way of getting evidence on the effectiveness of our communication. It enables us to learn about how others see us and about how we affect them. It is thus a vital ingredient in the process of evaluation, which we shall examine in more detail in Chapter 9.

Transactional analysis

The 'superstructure' of the communication process is likely to be accompanied, as we have seen in Chapter 1, by a substratum of emotional forces to do with the relationships involved, whether at a conscious or unconscious level. A simple but powerful model for analysing the processes of human interaction is that devised by Berne (1968) and later amplified by Harris (1973). Taking Freud's concept as a starting point, Berne proposes that each person comprises three basic 'selves' – the parent, the adult and the child – each of which is capable of affecting the tone of communication.

These 'ego-states', as they are called, exist within each of us as a result of our early life experience. They are not – like Freud's superego, ego and id – elements of our inner world operating on each other at an unconscious level. Rather they are conscious experiences of everyday life imprinted in us as a result of internal and external events encountered during the first few years of life. Transactional analysis (TA) addresses itself to the interaction between people, rather than to their inner psyche, and is therefore more readily available for a study of relationships in teaching and learning.

The **parent** in us acts according to how we perceived our mother, father or parental figure behaving. The parent is often concerned with prescribing the limits of behaviour, issuing moral edicts, teaching 'how to', protecting, nurturing and fostering; and these functions are typically accompanied by the tones of voice and the non-verbal expressions that partnered them when we experienced them in their original form. For obvious reasons, teaching frequently puts us in the position of behaving parentally or at least of being tempted to do so. Institutions provide a broadly parental function (and in view of this it is not surprising that young people often take it out on the physical fabric of schools and colleges). This is not to say that the functions of the parent are intrinsically either good or bad. The important thing is that we be sufficiently aware of the parent in ourselves so that we can use it or not (and in any case appropriately) according to our interpretation of what is happening in any transaction.

The **adult** is that part of us that is concerned with the gathering and processing of information and with rational action in the 'real' world. It derives from the time in our childhood when we began to manipulate objects external to ourselves and to realize we could achieve something worthwhile through our own original thought. The adult in us is ruled by reason rather than emotion; it is not, however, synonymous with 'mature'. The sort of functions specific to the adult are therefore the acquiring and sorting of data (even about one's parent, adult and child states), the choosing of alternatives and the planning of decision-making processes. The adult may thus manifest itself in a variety of ways and is the side of us most concerned with analysing the very transactions it is part of.

The **child** in us is the residue of emotional responses experienced and recorded in early childhood. These responses are essentially internal reactions to external events. The re-creation of similar events in later life is likely to trigger the corresponding reactions. There are many different 'children' within us and they experience the same feelings now as they did when we were little. Where the feeling derives from parental impositions or restrictions it is likely to be that of frustration, anger, fear, rebelliousness or conformity. Where it comes from the glorious excitement of first discoveries it is likely to connect with curiosity, creative delight, desire to explore, spontaneity and trust. Other biographical traces may also include competitiveness (from sibling rivalry) and dependency.

Each of us comprises all three ego states. None of these states is better or more important than the others. 'Appropriate' behaviour is determined by the situation, the adult's analysis of it, and the adult's ability to control the parent and child according to perceived circumstances.

Needless to say, the psychopathology of individual human beings is never as simple as this model proposes, but TA is nevertheless a convenient and, at times, telling way of analysing what goes right and wrong in human communication. It can be important for the tutor to acquire the ability to pick up the verbal and non-verbal cues signifying the existence of a particular ego state. In the world of teaching one might come across cues of the kind shown in Figure 4.5.

	I'm not OK	**I'm OK**
You're OK	Get away from Pass time 'I can't do it' Frustration Do it as a matter of duty Fears failure Gives up responsibility	Get on with Use time 'I can succeed' Challenge Collaborative approach Fears are appropriate Informs and shares responsibility
You're not OK	Get nowhere with Waste time 'I give up' Ignore it Defiance Fears loss of self Takes passive stance	Get rid of Kill time 'I don't care' Promotes compliance Control Fears loss of control Puts own needs first

Figure 4.5 *The OK Corral*

Transactions

In diagrams of transactions, the ego states are commonly represented by their initial letter while communication is indicated by arrows in the appropriate direction. A transaction is complementary where the ego state of the responding person is that to which the communication was directed. It is crossed where this correspondence is not achieved and ulterior where one correspondence is intended but another conveyed. Crossed and ulterior transactions clearly lead to unsatisfied, frustrated or angry feelings. An example might illustrate these three kinds of transaction.

A student comes to see his tutor. 'I don't know, I feel like giving up the course – it's all just one big muddle.' This could be intended as a (C) -> (P) communication. For there to be a complementary transaction, ie (P) -> (C), the tutor might respond: 'I'm sorry to hear that. Here – take a seat while I make a cup of coffee' (nurturing parent) or, 'Now come on, pull yourself together, nothing's that bad' (admonishing parent).

Alternatively, the tutor might say: 'I see, well it seems to me you've got the following alternatives' or, 'OK, well what do you see as your choices?', which would be (A) -> (A) responses. This would constitute a crossed transaction, one in which the sought correspondence is denied. It is therefore likely to be inappropriate as an initial move.

If, on the other hand, the tutor responded: 'Oh, I thought you were going to go and see the counsellor', it might well sound like an adult response with overtones of critical parent or even irresponsible child. Either of these would constitute an ulterior transaction typically leading to a tangle of ill-feeling.

To quote another example from teaching; a student might say: 'I'm fed up, none of the articles is in the library like you said they would be', (C) -> (C), or (C) -> (P). The tutor could reply either: 'If you were a bit quicker off the mark there would be no problem' (P)

-> (C), or 'I've got a few copies here you can have' (A) -> (C), or 'That's not my fault' (C) -> (C).

It is typical and proper that teaching should function a great deal at the parent level. Education does after all involve the setting of standards, advising, guiding, fostering and so forth, but there is always the danger that teachers will direct such transactions indiscriminately to the student as 'child' rather than providing open choices appropriate to a given situation. A generalized parent-like posture can easily produce in students a corresponding childlike response, which in turn confirms the original parental status.

TA includes in its orbit several other useful ideas for teaching and learning. For example, Harris (1973) has expanded Berne's original scheme of transactions to include the following 'life positions':

> I'm not OK – You're OK.
> I'm not OK – You're not OK.
> I'm OK – You're not OK.
> I'm OK – You're OK.

These are likely to determine the quality of the parent–adult–child transactions. We may recognize people (including ourselves) who readily adopt the 'OK' and 'not OK' positions, though the situation can be as strong a determining factor as a predisposition. Clearly 'I'm OK, you're OK', is the most healthy and creative transaction and one we would all strive to achieve, at least for ourselves.

This scheme has been developed into a model called the 'OK Corral' (Stewart and Joines, 1987), which provides some useful insights for working with groups. Any member of a group, including the tutor, may have a general disposition to any of the positions derived from childhood, which can be triggered by a particular kind of social interaction.

If, unaware, we get drawn into one of these 'operations', we are likely to offer a predictable justification for them. But we also have the choice of adopting an 'adult' awareness of what is happening and changing the outcomes. For a tutor, possible techniques for increasing the likelihood and frequency of 'I'm OK, you're OK' transactions might be:

- warmly welcoming group members to the first session;
- smiling warmly when speaking to or being spoken to by a group member;
- making sure you know (and use) their names by using a seating/name plan, and apologizing if you forget one or get it wrong;
- having an informal chat with likely antagonists beforehand;
- thanking students;
- showing that you value their contribution – even though you might not agree with the point being made.

The important thing, as Brookfield (1990) says, is to be and present yourself as authentic and credible, even if this takes a bit of practice.

One of the strongest and boldest claims that TA brings to the world of human relationships is the belief that people, through self-awareness, are able to change themselves and develop their potential to change others. By recognizing what can cause hurt, misunderstanding and frustration in relationships, they are better able to break out of unproductive communication and bring more creativity, enjoyment and freedom into their social environment. This is a bold claim and one that needs careful examination. Nevertheless, TA certainly provides a valuable explanatory framework for human interaction, one to which it is easy to relate and to develop in everyday communication.

Barriers to communication in groups

Much of what we have discussed so far in this chapter has been based more on a one-to-one relationship than on the more complex network of group interaction. Groups involve a level of awareness of self and others' perceptions that may hardly feature in a pair. Behaviour becomes the object of scrutiny by those who are not directly engaged.

Beneath the surface of what is evident through people's behaviour in groups lie several personal needs, wishes and behaviour traits that can lead to a climate that is less than open. For instance, each individual has a personal need for survival, self-enhancement and recognition, all of which may militate against the goals of the group. Then there may be power games being played out in terms of the desire to influence and control certain members, some of the motivation for which may lie outside the actual meeting of the group. Thirdly there are often members for whom openness, trust and intimacy are felt to be risky or where the climate makes them feel at risk, and a spirit of defensiveness is created. Typical defensive strategies are:

- being concerned with self-image;
- stopping people from expressing their own ideas;
- trying to dominate the discussion;
- trying constantly to change other people's opinions;
- always responding with certainty and force;
- being judgmental;
- implying superiority;
- avoiding the expression of feelings.

Many of these can be circumvented through the promotion of ground rules and explicit codes of behaviour, which are discussed in Chapter 10.

Napier and Gershenfeld (1985) describe how we are often influenced in groups in ways that distort our perception:

> A group of people represents various degrees of acceptance and rejection, likes and dislikes, pleasant memories and distasteful ones, and it is from this complex assortment of stimuli that we conjure up a picture of our reality and build what appear to be appropriate responses – again, to maintain our own position and integrity within the group . . . Those who have limited tolerance for ambiguity create a structure for what they believe is, whether it is or not. Those who are especially sensitive to cues of others as to whether they are liked are less likely to get across the information they want to express in an efficient manner because there are paying more attention to the interpersonal information. Those who make immediate decisions about liking or not liking someone and believe that they can

size a person up and be right, set out to do just that. They make a decision on limited information and stay with it. They are 'right', and are consequently resistant to change with new information. Similarly those individuals who focus on feelings and emotions and those who prefer logical thinking and reason evaluate their participation in groups based on their own particular orientation.

But perhaps the two greatest barriers to effective communication in a group are to do with (more conscious) previous experience both of groups and of the particular group members, and of false and inappropriate assumptions about other members of the group based on this or indeed on an initial impression of them. As explained in Chapter 1, our first experience of groups (in our original family or equivalent social environment) does to a large extent determine the way we respond both to the individuals and to the group as a whole. If our experience of such groups has been painful or frustrating we may even go so far as seeing the group in a similar way when it is far from being like this. In other words it becomes a self-fulfilling prophecy. There's a further danger, too, that we are liable to stereotype people who are similar in some way to those who have affected us, perhaps adversely, in our earlier life and behave towards them as if they were such people. An extension of this is what may be called 'longitudinal stereotyping' in which there is a belief that because somebody has behaved in one way, perhaps early in the life of the group, they will behave in the same way thereafter. If, for instance, such a person has been viewed as muddled or arrogant in their contributions at one stage, the assumption can easily be made that they will continue to be muddled or arrogant in the future.

Further assumptions may include believing that we know what others mean by what they say (even though they may often not know) or that everyone experiences phenomena in the same way. But the abiding meta-assumption is too often that communication is a simple and uncomplicated process, and that one can identify anybody's intentions from their behaviour simply because we know what our intentions would be were we to behave or speak like that.

By the same token our efforts to help, to offer suggestions, to take a leadership role in the group may be misinterpreted as attempts to control or to ride roughshod over the needs of other members. As Napier and Gershenfeld say, 'these false assumptions greatly reduce our ability to communicate in a group, or even understand what seems to be happening around us'.

Exercises

1. Back-to-back. An exercise in one-way communication

In this exercise a 'sender' of information sits back-to-back with a 'receiver' and has to communicate with the latter under a set of restrictive rules. (As with many such games it may be advisable with some students to give them a little orientation beforehand.) As an introduction to this game you could, for example, chat briefly about the reality of communication by suggesting that it is a simple process and we are all superb practitioners.

Then give an example of exactly how simple it is with the situation in which the teacher says to a class: 'Does everyone understand?'

'What', you could ask students, 'do you think you would reply if you were the teacher? If you wanted to say "Yes", would you? What would be the likely consequences of so doing? If you answered "No", what would be the implications of that? So what do you do? Look at the floor? Pretend you're reading your notes? So maybe the apparently simple question has another function.' And so on.

You might also ask them about the last time they were walking down the street and a car driver stopped to ask them the way: 'As you reached the stage of your communication where you said "and take the third exit from the roundabout, if you don't count the no entry sign", you can see the glazed expression coming over the driver's face as he or she reaches for the window winder. "Is that OK?" you ask. "Fine, thanks", the driver says and drives away. As you walk round the corner you see that the car has stopped again and another pedestrian is trying to help. So what goes wrong?'

So, on to the exercise. Person A, sitting back-to-back with person B, has to tell B how to draw an apparently simple figure, such as that shown in Figure 4.6, without any checking or communication back from B to A. Subsequently the roles of A and B can be reversed using another figure (Figure 4.7).

Figure 4.6 *First figure*   **Figure 4.7** *Second figure*

The simple rule of one-directional communication can be varied to include feedback, limited questions and so forth, but the basic exercise, though it may last no more than five minutes, almost invariably produces a plethora of ideas and insights on the problems of lecturing, phone conversations, or the giving of instructions. Having asked participants to draw up a list of guidelines to improve communication these can then be compared with a prepared list like the one that follows.

To explain/instruct clearly you should:

- try to orient the other person to the task and to what is being communicated – have a clear picture of what you want the other person to understand;
- analyse your own feelings about the topic and the other person;
- assess your own and the other person's communication skills;
- try to identify yourself with the psychological state of the other person;
- make a realistic assessment of the degree of clarity obtainable in the given context;
- make the message relevant by using the other's language and terms – state ideas in the simplest possible terms;
- define before developing, and explain before amplifying;
- make it clear when you are explaining as opposed to instructing;
- develop one idea at a time;
- take one step at a time;
- use appropriate repetition;
- review when relevant;
- compare and contrast ideas;
- use analogies;
- determine which ideas need special emphasis;
- use as many channels as necessary for clarity;
- pace according to the learning capacities of the other person;
- where any two-way communication is possible, watch for and encourage corrective feedback in as many channels as possible.

The dynamics of this game, though simple, are interesting in what they reveal about opportunity and risk in personal behaviour. During the exercise proper, each pair is separate from the rest and has the reassurance of physical contact (their shoulders inevitably touch in the strain of trying to pick up words amid the background noise of all the other pairs) and the chance to avoid those embarrassing glances that go with failure and inadequacy when one is in eye-to-eye contact.

In the debriefing period the pairs themselves are asked to discuss problems privately before public discussion is invited. Anxieties and feelings can thus be shared in safety before being revealed, if so chosen, to the whole group. If anyone chooses not to, then they can silently draw comparisons between their privately shared thoughts and the public ones of others more bold or foolhardy than they.

Johari Window

The Johari Window (pages 65–66) can be used to help group members develop insight into how their communication affects others in the group:

1. Each person (the client), working alone, fills in quadrant 1 and as much of quadrant 3 as they are prepared to reveal.
2. Each client then chooses a partner and explains what they have written in quadrants 1 and 3 before inviting their partner to give them feedback for quadrant 2 for a period of five minutes (or longer if time is available). As the discussion takes place, the client may gain new insights in quadrant 4 and choose to make some notes to themselves.
3. The process is reversed with the other partner becoming the client for the same time period.
4. One of each pair moves clockwise round the group and for five minutes each way repeats the above process.
5. When members have finished receiving this feedback, a group round takes place in which each member tells the group in one minute what they have learnt, what they intend to do with that and what if anything they would like the group to do to help them in this.

Discussion points

- What barriers to communication do you notice in a) your everyday life; b) your work generally; and c) groups that you belong to or lead? How do they arise and how might you tackle them?
- What kind of transactions seem to govern your relationships in the various groups you belong to? How does this work out a) for you; and b) for the group?
- In other words, where do you feature in the OK Corral in relation to a) the group as a whole and b) to individual members, especially the leader?
- To what extent do members really listen to each other in the group? Write down on a scale from 1 to 10 the extent to which you believe you listen to others. Are there members of the group who talk more to each other than the rest? Draw a diagram of the most typical flows of communication and compare yours with those of other group members.

5 | What are learning groups for?

Education goes beyond knowing to being able to do what one knows. Educators are responsible for making learning more available to the learner by articulating outcomes and making them available to the public.

(Alverno College, undated)

By the end of this chapter you can expect to be able to identify and produce a range of aims and learning outcomes for groups that can be used by students and others to know what is expected and how well they are achieving.

Groups in the wider context (the focus of Chapter 2) form and are formed for many purposes: learning from each other, pooling resources, making decisions, mutual support, sharing ideas, creating something, to name but a few. Learning groups may include several of these options but they embody the same basic functions. In terms of group dynamics, the two major areas of aims are those concerned with task and with maintenance. In the academic context, 'task' aims will usually be the so-called intellectual ones such as the exercise of critical judgement, the ability to analyse statements and cases and to question underlying assumptions and values. They will also include those of a pastoral or remedial nature, such as recognizing when students are in difficulties, checking for misunderstandings in reading or lectures, and so on.

Group maintenance, on the other hand, will include aims like creating a sense of belonging in an otherwise anonymous institution, generating a sense of trust and openness, handling conflict in a constructive way and so forth, but also those to do with interest in, commitment to and enthusiasm for the subject and learning more about it. Maintenance aims may be said to facilitate or underpin task aims. However, 'maintenance', as in its more normal usage, implies repeated attention and adjustment to the running of the group if the task is going to be achieved. Readers may also recall, from the section on group behaviour (pages 6–7), that maintenance aims become increasingly more relevant as the size of the group increases. It is quite common, for instance, for small groups of three or four to work on a task without concern about who is doing what, or any formal leadership role being needed. Where a class is divided into small sub-groups (see pages 112–20), the maintenance problem is very much subsumed to the task. However, in a larger group, the opposite is frequently the case. If the task aims are to be achieved, either members of the group must be extremely aware of the dynamic processes within it and be skilled in handling these, or the tutor must take on a firm leadership role.

It will be seen, therefore, that in a large group, certainly one in excess of seven members, the problems of agreeing on how to set about the task, and how the distribution of responsibilities within the group should be made, will be predominant (at least in the early stages) before the group can set about its academic task. Of course it is always possible, especially in an 'experiential' group, for the task and the maintenance aims to be combined. For instance, the explicit task of the group could be to examine the processes of social differentiation or of leadership within the group (though this can become a very difficult and confusing activity to students who are not fully aware of the processes in which they are involved).

Though the 'learning' group, that is one typified by the academic seminar, may share these features to a greater or lesser extent, it has two additional and distinguishing ones. First, the group members are (generally) drawing on knowledge from outside the group in order to process it within, and subsequently use it outside. Second, and this is a particular feature of the traditional seminar, the group includes someone (the tutor) who is typically seen to be responsible for selecting the external knowledge, supervising its processing in the group and checking its use beyond the end of the group through some form of assessment. This prompts three questions to bear in mind for this chapter:

1. To what extent do learning groups have to involve a procession of knowledge from outside to inside and outside again?
2. Does it have to be the tutor who controls the input, processing and output of knowledge?
3. What can the learning group in its academic world incorporate from the aims and purposes of other kinds of group?

Before we look at these questions, however, let us consider what educational aims in particular are all about.

It seems to be a feature of educational aims that they appear more often in course documents than in discussion between tutors and students. As a public statement of values, they reflect what teachers, and those who influence them, claim to prize in what they principally do. Some of these, like key or transferable skills and intellectual rigour, may reach across many fields of study; others are more specific to a subject area and represent what is regarded as important as subject matter for the syllabus.

Several writers have described the use of aims and learning outcomes as instruments of course design (see Ramsden, 1992; Rowntree, 1981; Stenhouse, 1975; Taba, 1962; Toohey, 1999 and Wheeler, 1967, for instance) and this is not the place to get involved in the weighty arguments of curriculum theory. However, as group discussion is an important part of tertiary education, it is appropriate to examine questions about the place of aims in small-group teaching, such as:

- What are aims and learning outcomes and how do we devise them?
- Why bother to specify them, especially in group teaching?
- What are typical aims for groups?

- How can we make sense of them in terms of classroom practice?
- Is it important that they match the students' conceptions of learning? (See Chapter 4).

The nature of aims

Teaching and learning are purposeful human activities. That is to say, they may be described in terms of what we as teachers or learners believe we are doing or what we intend to achieve by what we are doing. Of course, as we carry out our day-to-day work we are not always conscious of our intentions or of what our actions achieve. Sometimes we employ, out of habit, a strategy whose origins and true functions are lost in the mists of time; or we imitate what we have seen others do without questioning its value or purpose. In some cases it seems that a teaching procedure exists purely because teachers and students expect it to be there – it has become a time-honoured ritual – and that any attempt to change it will be doomed to failure. The traditional seminar, for instance, comprising groups of 10 to 20 students discussing critical summaries presented orally by one or more of them, may fall into that category. It is used because it is familiar.

Aims, where expressed, serve to focus attention on the direction of teaching and act as a reference point in our choice of what we teach. In the words of Dewey (1944), the aim as a 'foreseen end' involves careful observation of the given conditions to see what means are available for reaching that end and to discover hindrances in the way; suggest the proper order or sequences in the use of means; and make choices of alternatives possible.

If we do not make such aims explicit and therefore negotiable, participants in a group discussion may be following their own hidden agendas and lacking any common frame of reference. The function of aims, therefore, may be not only to help establish a direction in learning but to clarify the opportunities offered by a situation. It may also lead to a better sense of collaboration among the group, and between groups, in achieving the aims.

The concept of collaborative learning is the essence of every well-run group. But it has been developed in a much more fundamental way in some institutions in the USA (Matthews, 1996). Collaborative learning in this sense involves a blurring of the lines between teacher and learner and the creation of a strong sense of interdependence between them, where aims and outcomes become a matter of mutual agreement. A typical starting activity might be students generating a list of what they are most interested in learning in the course and the background information they bring to it. Decisions about tasks and content are made collaboratively and groups who have worked on the same content through different tasks learn from each other as each contributes their learning to the whole class. Collaborative learning, rooted in the 'social construction of knowledge' claims to bridge the divide between the social and the academic sides of student life.

Aims, objectives and outcomes

A useful distinction between these three concepts is that aims indicate broad directions for teaching, are closely related to values and learning processes, and are impossible to pin down in a measurable form. Objectives can be used as descriptions of what the student should have done, experienced or completed by the end of a learning occasion. Outcomes concern what the student should have achieved or learnt and, in most cases, can demonstrate by the end. Though outcomes may give no indication of how they are to be attained, their achievement should in principle be measurable.

Learning outcomes may therefore bear a similarity to assessment questions. They are part not only of a rational and systematic approach to the teaching and learning, but of a democratic process of sharing intentions to students and colleagues alike. Teaching, so the argument for specifying learning outcomes runs, is a rational activity, and one of the conditions of rational activity is the conscious pursuit of a goal or learning outcome. To satisfy the needs of a well-designed course, one must specify a learning outcome, choose the means of achieving it and then measure this achievement so as to evaluate the effectiveness of the strategy.

Learning outcomes, in these terms, constitute a translation of aims into specific qualities – knowledge (expressed in terms of a demonstrable product or behaviour) behaviours, skills and attitudes. Aims must necessarily precede learning outcomes even if only in an implicit sense, and serve to guide them. They provide 'the ethical standards against which (learning outcomes) are judged' (Rowntree, 1981). Learning outcomes also give us some clues about tasks for so-called 'structured' groups (see pages 101–02 and Wilson, 1980). Readers will have noticed the presence of learning outcomes at the beginning of each chapter in this book and be able to make judgements about their value.

Aims of group discussion

Group discussion, as we have seen in Chapter 2, has an important place in higher education, but not an unqualified one. Used indiscriminately, without regard to what it can or cannot achieve, or its place in the curriculum, it can be wasteful of both time and resources. Brookfield (1990) suggests we should consider carefully our reasons for group discussion before we prepare for it. He proposes the following aims (slightly adapted).

Intellectual aims:

- To engage students in exploring a variety of perspectives.
- To help students in discovering new perspectives.
- To emphasize the complexity and ambiguity of issues, topics or themes.
- To help students recognize the assumptions behind many of their habitual ideas and behaviours.
- To increase intellectual agility.
- To encourage active listening.

Emotional aims:

- To increase students' emotional connection with a topic.
- To show students that their experiences, ideas and opinions are heard and valued.

Social aims:

- To help develop a sense of group identity.
- To encourage democratic habits.

These aims recognize the mutuality of the task and the socio-emotional dimensions of group behaviour underlined in Chapter 2. Group tutors are uniquely placed, according to Forster (1995), to develop higher-order intellectual functions, which are at the heart of university undergraduate education. They do so:

- by drawing on the subject expertise, setting learning tasks for students and monitoring what they make of them and responding accordingly;
- through skills of group management, encouraging students to take an active part in the group, so learning from the other students as well as a tutor;
- by exercising self-awareness as a result of which they can judge the fine line that lies between, on the one hand, contributing their subject insights to the work of the group and, on the other, so dominating the group that students are denied the space to take responsibility for their own learning.

A typical predicament for tutors is in establishing a balance between their authority as subject expert and their role as leader and facilitator of the learning group. This is highlighted when students have queries, when the natural desire to give a full and informative answer has to be set against challenging the students to think and be less dependent. The balance becomes more tricky to sustain when, as Forster comments, a tutor has engaged in excessive preparation and feels compelled to justify this by controlling and dominating the discussion.

Problems of this kind can be alleviated by the tutor making explicit what the aims or outcomes of any group session are, thus orienting the students and presenting a shared purpose to the discussion and entering into a form of mutual contract. Figure 5.1 lists some learning aims for groups and some examples of what students might do in pursuit of these.

Looking at Figure 5.1, some tutors may feel that personal growth, teamwork skills and self-direction in learning really haven't got much to do with their small-group teaching in higher education, the essential purpose of which, they say, is to make sure that students have really understood what they have been trying to get across in lectures or are able, through arguing, to develop critical judgement. Careful questioning, they argue, can bring out the major misunderstandings and difficulties and many of these can be dealt with by teachers in a way in which they can be sure that the students have really understood. Under the extreme pressures often felt by both students and staff to 'cover the ground' effectively, such a view of the main purpose of group work is very understandable. But if this purpose is pursued vigorously, it may also mean that others will not merely be ignored but will be actively discouraged. Strategies that may produce effective learning within a highly structured formal education system can leave students with little ability, or even desire, to take initiatives to promote their own learning and relearning when they leave the formal supportive structures of higher education behind them.

Aims	Related Tasks/Outcomes
1. **UNDERSTANDING** *Helping students to consolidate and enhance their understanding of a subject or discipline*	• clarifying concepts, theories and procedures • reflecting on inter-connections • testing their understanding through examples, cases, illustrations
2. **CRITICAL THINKING** *Helping students to develop their capacity for thinking critically and analytically*	• reviewing evidence in the light of theories • learning how to 'set' and solve problems or approach questions and issues • enhancing their capacity for logical reasoning and formal argument
3. **PERSONAL GROWTH** *Helping students to develop and mature as individuals*	• clarifying attitudes, articulating and reappraising values • developing in self-confidence and self-esteem • evolving a sense of responsibility and commitment
4. **COMMUNICATION SKILLS** *Helping students to learn how to communicate effectively with others*	• refining listening, questioning and explaining skills • presenting and defending a position clearly and cogently, giving and getting feedback
5. **GROUP AND TEAMWORK SKILLS** *Helping students to learn how to collaborate and work as an effective group or team*	• setting, allocating and monitoring tasks • supporting and encouraging other members of the group or team • initiating, directing and leading tasks
6. **SELF-DIRECTION IN LEARNING** *Helping students to take progressively greater responsibility for their learning*	• clarifying their own goals as learners • managing their study time and effort and setting priorities, accepting responsibility for evaluating their own work and their progress as learners
From: Forster, Hounsell and Thompson (1995)	

Figure 5.1 *Some learning aims for tutorial groups*

It could be said, therefore, that an important function of group work in higher education is to enable students to know enough about themselves and about others so that they can work independently and yet cooperatively within a team. Such teams may or may not have formal leaders, but the model of leadership is likely to be very different from that of the more traditional seminar leader who controls the activity of the class in such a way that students learn to feel little responsibility for what happens in the group beyond doing required background reading.

The group experience can, in fact, be extremely important in achieving freedom from dependency if students learn to play a variety of roles in the group and begin to develop a sense of responsibility for its success or failure. In the process of learning these roles they will need to develop more acute self-understanding, to become aware of their own inhibitions, defences and assumptions, and be able to recognize the difficulties that other students have and begin to help them to overcome them. In learning to become more sensitive to different points of view and ways of thinking, and to work cooperatively with others using the varied skills of the group, they may begin to develop a surer sense of social identity, and a feeling of belonging and commitment. This can encourage not only enthusiasm in the subject but a willingness to reveal abilities that are so often effectively hidden, even from themselves. Students' oral skills, moreover, are unlikely to develop very highly simply in response to probing questions.

Some skills can be achieved when there is a genuine sense of opportunity for self-expression, though this may be very difficult in a context where the main objective is to increase understanding and correct misconceptions and faulty reasoning.

Project aims and outcomes

There are two further circumstances in which the specification of learning outcomes may be particularly valuable for group work. One is where the students undertake a personal or peer responsibility for the conduct of their own work. In some cases this can lead to their assessing their own work. Syndicates and peer tutoring cells (see Chapter 6) may be given a direction by the tutor specifying learning outcomes for this sort of work. Knowles (1986) described a study of personal learning contracts in which students decide their own learning needs, strategies for achieving them, evidence of their accomplishment, and criteria and means of evaluating them. The development of the contract is facilitated by the tutor who encourages the students to use various combinations of teamwork in pursuit of their goals.

The other is in projects or other self-directed work where students may be encouraged to develop their own individual learning outcomes in groups and thereafter pursue them with group support. In both these cases, the specification of learning outcomes may be seen as a way of investing the authority of the absent tutor in a set of guidelines and standards.

Typical aims for projects (Jaques, 1988) may include the following:

ual skills:

- develop a personal interest and expertise in an area of the subject;
- demonstrate the ability to handle new problems;
- form independent judgements;
- collect and interpret unfamiliar information;
- show initiative;
- encounter facts, views and situations from unfamiliar perspectives;
- integrate knowledge from a range of sources.

Group skills:

- learn to work cooperatively;
- share in a decision-making process;
- exercise leadership, chair meetings;
- be flexible in adopting roles to suit the changing needs of the group.

Personal awareness:

- learn about own strengths and weaknesses in respect of the above;
- make a realistic appraisal of ability in relation to the complexities of the task;
- gain a sense of satisfaction through personal achievement;
- gain a sense of autonomy and freedom within the constraints of the task.

Communication skills:

- communicate work in a clear and effective manner in discussion and in writing;
- develop questioning and listening techniques in seeking and making sense of information;
- develop skills of logical and persuasive argument;
- write a coherent and readable account of the work done.

Though some tutors may object to the idea of promoting personal skills and values, in project work it can be extremely helpful for students to know what new team and problem-solving skills they need to develop in order to tackle the project and even to assess their development. Wellington (1998) describes a multi-disciplinary project in which students were given the following outcomes/objectives. The students were to:

- formulate, through group interactions, solutions to business problems that require the integration of design, manufacturing and marketing solutions;
- separate engineering, accounting and marketing problems into solvable elements and explore solutions mindful of the influence each discipline had on the other;
- demonstrate understanding of manufacturing design and the possible need for redesign;
- exhibit committee chairperson, secretarial and recording skills;
- negotiate responsibilities within a group to ensure effective project management;

- compile, present and defend a syndicate report on the project;
- assess personal and peer performance in achieving individual and group objectives;
- value the complexity of issues and range of people affected by the introduction of new products and technology;
- appreciate the degree of involvement necessary in the decision-making process in a typical industrial situation from disciplines including planning, marketing, finance, processing, quality, legal and human resource management.

Wellington quotes research which concludes that group motivation is optimized when students have clear goals to attain, feel efficacious about performing well, have positive outcome expectations, attribute success to ability, effort and strategy, and receive relevant and prompt feedback. Further research evidence indicates that the following factors are among those regarded as significant in group projects:

- goal activation – projects encouraging students to achieve their own goals;
- goal salience – goals being clear so that students know what is expected;
- multiple goals – lead to greater success;
- goal alignment – goals aligned with each other and not in conflict;
- optimal challenge – tasks being difficult and challenging but not excessively so.

He also cites the evidence of the importance of tasks being structured so as to highlight short-term goals that help students to feel efficacious, and for the need for assessment to be relevant to the objectives.

Devising learning outcomes

Aims and objectives (outcomes in particular) must be connected quite forcefully to the learning activities that are designed to enable the student to achieve them; they must be embodied in the actions and words of the teacher who professes them; they must be continually presented to students in order to provide a clear framework in which they can work. The most compelling reason for using (learning outcomes) is that it forces us as teachers to make our intentions for student learning explicit. (Ramsden, 1992)

As already explained, one value of learning outcomes is the way in which they enable a sharing of intentions by making them more explicit and checkable. But they also provide a useful check on the tendency to a lack of diversity in assessment methods and questions and, in describing what the student should be able to do by the end of an event, they make it possible for him or her to make choices and not be held back by uncertainty and confusion about what will be assessed.

So, a clear learning outcome should say what the students should be able to do, the conditions under which they should be able to do it, and how well they should be able to do it. It should therefore contain (if we are to follow the rubric) an active verb, an object and a qualifying clause, which specifies a context or condition. Clearly it should also identify important learning requirements, be achievable and assessable, and use language that the students can understand. So verbs like 'know' and 'be aware of' do not conform to this rubric. Let us look at a few learning outcomes and how they might be derived:

- *Content*: Legal requirements in job selection.
- *Aim*: To explain the effect of legal requirements in job selection.
- *Appropriate outcome*: Choose and apply legal requirements effectively in a range of job selection cases.

- *Content*: Rules and principles of law.
- *Aim*: To become more critical of established rules and principles in law.
- *Outcome*: Develop a commitment to looking critically at rules and principles in law, and propose reforms in the law, within an explicit value system.

- *Content*: Energy loss in hydraulic pumps.
- *Aim*: To understand the nature of energy loss and its implications.
- *Outcome*: Be able to describe the components of energy and the manner in which they are lost in a hydraulic pump and to solve simple problems from practical examples.

While it is perfectly logical to prepare and communicate learning outcomes, human activity does not always follow such a rational pattern. People tend to act on inspiration, on intuitive shifts and changes, and to respond spontaneously to the immediate situation. Nowhere are these unpredictable factors more evident than in discussion groups. The pursuit of a specific learning outcome in a group discussion could also destroy the possibility of achieving many other equally valuable aims such as those to do with creative thinking, autonomy or democratic learning. In other words, for the educational experience in a group to be valuable, the student must enjoy the freedom to question, to disagree and to make interpretations, and this may take the individual and the group in a direction other than that which was intended by the tutor or the course planner – or the examiner. In the experience of many tutors, what continually happens is that, to quote Pring (1973), 'one's conception of the enquiry or activity is altered in the very pursuit of it . . . the ends in view are constantly changing as one gets nearer them'.

Group discussion is more of a conversation than a one-way programme. What is more, there are few rational connections between means and ends except where, as previously indicated, the two are coincident. Even if it were possible to select a method to achieve a particular learning outcome, other concomitants such as the group mood, tutor / student relationships or contextual issues like the proximity of examinations could frustrate the intentions of the tutor. This is part of the problem of selecting learning outcomes as if they existed prior to and independent of the students and, more importantly, of the group upon whose very existence and energy their achievement rests.

Nevertheless the articulation of outcomes can achieve at least three important goals: to clarify not only to tutors what they are trying to achieve and hence what they might have to do; to make the same information available to colleagues working in collaboration with them; and to make clear to students what they are expected to achieve, thus establishing a form of learning contract with consequent freedom to pursue learning in alternative ways.

Some have got round the problems of prior specification of outcomes by describing them after the learning event has taken place, agreeing what these were as part of a learning process for the students. Unintended and unpredictable outcomes can thus be revealed and, dare one say, celebrated.

So, the specifying of aims and outcomes need not be restrictive: it can provide an intentional framework in which intuitive and spontaneous changes can be made, thus enabling tutors and students both separately and together to discuss their desirability (and their hidden values). All this can contribute to a sense of shared responsibility for learning, particularly because it focuses attention on what the student learns rather than what the tutor knows, but also because it releases the student from an over-reliance on the tutor's agenda. In these ways, the expressing, sharing and negotiating of aims in group teaching all help to achieve a further aim – that of creating a sense of self-direction in learning. Nowhere is this more important than in some science and technology courses where mastery of content is often stressed as an end in itself, and little is done to help the student relate to personal goals and frames of reference. If and when choice is exercised in the curriculum it is usually by the tutor. The students are deemed unqualified to select what is to be learnt – or how. It may well be, as Entwistle (1981) suggests, that students tend to specialize in subjects where the teachers suit their own personality and patterns of abilities. Yet, as we have seen on pages 47–48, there is a contradiction in students being presented with an implacable intellectual authority in subject areas (eg, science and technology) where our understanding of the world and the techniques for harnessing its forces are in a constant state of evolution and even revolution (see Kuhn, 1973), where change is the only stable factor.

Learning outcomes can be designed not only to clarify and indicate what is expected in relation to skill areas, but also at progressive levels of attainment. The following example of generic academic outcomes with indicative levels was devised for Education Studies at the University of Wolverhampton (Allan, 1994).

Generic outcomes with indicative levels

A. Make use of information:
Level 1   supplement notes with appropriate reading;
reference correctly;
Level 2   select and use relevant references and quotation to support the points you are making;
Level 3   use specialist texts and journals to substantiate your arguments;
draw together material from a variety of sources into a coherent argument;
Level 4   present an overview of an area of concern;
give a comparative and critical review of key authors, rival theories and major debates.
B. Analyse:
Level 1   identify ideas and concepts that underpin theories in your subjects;
Level 2   explain the relationship between different elements of a theory;
distinguish between evidence and argument and hypothesis;
evaluate ideas and concepts;

Level 3   recognize the difference between assertion and argument;
recognize and acknowledge inconsistencies in arguments;
Level 4   identify discrepancies and movements in positions over time;
check the consistency of hypotheses with given information and
assumptions.
C. Think critically:
Level 1   examine problems from a number of perspectives;
Level 2   question and challenge viewpoints, ideas and concepts;
make judgements about the value of evidence, concepts and ideas;
Level 3   develop and be able to justify your own opinions on significant ideas and
concepts in your own subject;
Level 4   justify and substantiate the choice of a particular approach or model.
D. Synthesize ideas and information:
Level 2   relate new ideas and concepts to previous ones;
Level 3   relate theoretical ideas to practical tasks;
integrate learning from different modules you have studied;
organize and structure ideas, concepts and theories into a coherent
whole;
Level 4   synthesize clearly theoretical perspectives and practical application
within a given professional context.

Another source of aims and learning outcomes for the group tutor can be found in educational theory. Bloom, in what became a classic educational text (1956, 1964), classified learning outcomes into two basic divisions: the cognitive (knowledge and intellectual skills); and the affective (development of attitudes and values). Clearly, in the process of learning, it is impossible to discriminate between these categories of behaviour. Skill is required to learn a piece of knowledge, to apply it or to write about it, and our attitude to both knowledge and its application in a particular environment is important in determining how well we perform these operations or, indeed, whether we do them at all.

Verbs applicable to the cognitive domain

1. Knowledge		**2. Comprehension**	
arrange	order	classify	locate
define	recognize	describe	recognize
duplicate	relate	discuss	report
label	recall	explain	restate
list	repeat	express	review
memorize	reproduce	identify	select
name	state	indicate	translate

3. Application

apply	operate
choose	practise
demonstrate	schedule
dramatize	sketch
employ	solve
illustrate	use
interpret	write

5. Synthesis

arrange	formulate
assemble	manage
collect	organize
compose	plan
construct	prepare
create	propose
design	set up
develop	write

4. Analysis

analyse	differentiate
appraise	discriminate
calculate	distinguish
categorize	examine
compare	experiment
contrast	question
criticize	test

6. Evaluation

appraise	judge
argue	predict
assess	rate
attach	score
choose	select
compare	support
defend	value
estimate	evaluate

While we may sometimes feel that the specification of desired behaviour can be an intolerable constraint on the 'democratic' processes of group discussion, a list such as this could provide tutors with a useful focus on two counts: each could form an operative verb in the instructions for a group task; a tutor could develop a repertoire of questions based on these verbs to have in mind and draw out as spontaneously as possible during the progress of a discussion. For instance the verb 'summarize' might suggest an intervention from the tutor like, 'Would anyone like to put all that together now?' (See Chapter 7 onwards for further proposals on tutor interventions.)

Realizing aims and outcomes

'No one says anything. You've prepared a lot of work and then find it's taken over by the tutor. Some just talk for two hours solid. You learn to switch off after a while.' (Student in Ruddock, 1978)

Whatever good aspirations and hopes we may have for group work of any kind, there is always the risk for all concerned of 'losing the plot' – becoming distracted by unforeseen issues and problems or being unable to deal even with predictable problems. Though group discussion clearly has the potential to provide the opportunities for students not merely to engage in intellectual discourse but also to create a social 'family' to which they can belong and become identified with, it can equally become a source of frustration despite the best intentions. Clearly, the role of the tutor in settling the atmosphere in the group will determine whether aims to do with open and cooperative styles of behaviour as opposed to closed and competitive ones is significant, as is careful preparation for students engaged in group projects.

In both discussion groups and group projects the importance of taking the risk of making mistakes and learning from them cannot be overstated. To achieve this state of affairs, the tutor has to balance a concern for academic standards with a capacity to understand and deal with the workings of group process, as well as having an attitude of generosity and praise for new solutions to old problems. The students might correspondingly applaud their tutor's resourcefulness in introducing them to new experiences in group learning.

If, finally, we return to the question posed at the start of the chapter, it will be evident that learning groups are amenable to a much wider range of aims and outcomes than is commonly supposed and that many of these bear a similarity to the aims and outcomes of groups in the wider world. Insofar as learning groups comprise a meeting of human beings with some shared goals, it seems probable that processes like pooling resources, making decisions, gaining mutual support, sharing ideas, creating something and so on would always exist in the process, at least subliminally. Yet making them more explicit, negotiating them and perhaps incorporating them into more practical, real-world tasks, might not only create more stimulation and variety of opportunity in learning for students, but also develop their awareness of group and teamwork concerns for their future careers.

The conversion of aims and outcomes into acceptable and realistic activities in the classroom is the central concern of the next chapter.

Exercises

1. Sharing aims

All members of a group are likely to have different wishes and intentions for themselves in the group, as well as for the group as a whole. In many cases the ambiguous situation of not having these clearly identified and shared can lead to a sense of cohesiveness through a greater tolerance and willingness to abandon what could not have been made clear anyway. However, there may be situations where clarity of aims is essential to progress, or at least useful in sharing values and attitudes.

This simple exercise is designed to enable group members to clarify their own aims and expectations as well as finding what these have in common with those of other members and how they differ from them.

1. Ask everyone to close their eyes and imagine what kinds of things they would visualize the group doing or achieving if it were to operate successfully. Join in this yourself as leader.
2. Ask them next to imagine themselves in the group in those conditions and to focus on what they think they would themselves be doing, or like to be doing, then.
3. Invite them to write down on cards or Post-its what they have been thinking about and express these in the form of aims, eg, to become more . . ., to take account of every . . ., to explore the way . . .

4. Ask everyone to stick their aims on a vertical surface so that they can arrange them in clusters with similar themes.
5. Ask them finally to work in threes and make pie charts that represent the three most important group aims, to give a balance of priorities and to do the same for the individual ones.

2. What are groups for?

Working with a colleague, interview each other in turn in order to draw out answers to the following questions. Try to explore those to do with the *intellectual task* and those to do with the *social and emotional climate*. Take 15 minutes each and use every opportunity to jot down your thoughts as you progress.

   Consider the groups you are involved with. What do you see as their purposes? What do you think the students see as the purposes? How do they match yours? Are there any purposes you would like to fulfil but find you cannot? Have you any ideas why that might be so? And what may you need to do to change this?

- My aims and purposes in groups.
- What I think the students' aims and purposes are.
- Discrepancies between the above and what I might do about it.
- Aims and purposes I'd like to realize but don't seem able to.
- What I might do about unrealized aims and purposes.

Discussion points

- What kinds of discrepancies appear to exist between the express aims of groups you belong to, or lead, and what actually happens? How do they arise?
- Draw up a chart like Figure 5.2 for the aims of your own group(s). To what extent do they vary within the group or between groups? What values and assumptions lie behind the aims?
- How do you think the aims of your group relate to:
  - the broader aims of your course?
  - what is actually assessed on the course?

	Task	Socio-emotional
I N T R I N S I C	Expressing selves in subject	Greater sensitivity to others
	Judging ideas in relation to others	Judging self in relation to others
	Examining assumptions	Encouraging self-confidence
	Listening attentively	Personal development
	Tolerating ambiguity	Tolerating ambiguity
	Learning about groups	Awareness of others' strengths and weaknesses
E X T R I N S I C	Follow-up to lecture	Giving support
	Understanding text	Stimulating to further work
	Improving staff/ student relations	Evaluating student feelings about course
	Gauging student progress	Giving students identifiable groups to belong to
	Giving guidance	

Figure 5.2 *Types of aims and purposes in group teaching*

6 | Structured activities

One must learn by doing the thing, for though you think
you know it – you have no certainty, until you try.

(Sophocles)

By the end of this chapter you can expect to have recognized the problems and limitations inherent in traditional seminars and tutorials and have acquired a repertoire of activities that can both address these and achieve a wider range of learning outcomes.

This chapter is about the aspect of groups most familiar to both tutors and students: the actual experience of learning in groups. In it we shall take into account not only the need to realize aims and outcomes and to take group dynamics into account, but also a respect for equal opportunities, whether to do with sex, age, race, or culture, as well as the problems arising from increased numbers in higher education resulting in larger group sizes, as indicated in Chapter 2. Each of these issues is addressed more comprehensively than we can here in Lewis and Habeshaw (1990) and Gibbs (1992b) respectively.

However, the issue of equal opportunities, whatever its ingredients, is exacerbated with large groups, as we have seen on pages 7–8. One clear way of dealing with this is to use a structured activity that breaks larger groups into smaller ones while still maintaining a sense of the whole group, as we shall see later in this chapter. Another approach, suggested by Gibbs (1992b) is to reduce the numbers in any one week by having half the group meet with the tutor one week, and the other half the next. Rather than diluting their learning by 50 per cent, during the intervening week, the tutorless group meets elsewhere with specified tasks preparing them for a return visit to the tutor the following week.

First we shall focus on seminars and tutorials as the archetypal model for group discussion and study their generic strengths and weaknesses, before going on to look at ways of organizing tasks and structures to make them a more reliable and versatile learning process. Finally we will give attention to some of the alternatives or precursors to open discussion that are concerned with creativity and the imagination.

Seminars

Most of us are familiar with the terms 'seminar' and 'tutorial' as formal titles for timetabled group sessions. The word 'seminar' is generally taken to mean a group discussion with fairly intellectual aims, led formally or informally by the tutor, and focused on issues arising from the subject matter rather than student difficulties (cf tutorials). The number of students is usually in excess of 8 and less than 20; traditionally, one of them will be asked to present a critical analysis or other preparation to introduce the discussion. However, the formal expectation of seminars is often belied by the informal experience. Treadaway (1975) describes eight types of seminar that serve to illustrate some of the common problems:

1. The monologue or 'sitting at the feet of the master' type.
2. The highly structured or 'I know what you want to say' type.
3. The duologue or 'wrestling match' type (one bright or forceful student wants to impress the tutor and a duologue ensues on areas that no one else knows about).
4. The anecdotal or 'Did I ever tell you?' type.
5. The essay-reading or Oxbridge type.
6. The article-summary or 'We've all read this anyway' type (if a student summarizes without making critical comment then his or her colleagues may not bother to read it; the tutor may not have read the article for years and the discussion can thus become sterile).
7. The examination-cramming type (the tutor seems concerned mainly with the students passing the exam, sometimes more so than the students).
8. The 'I don't believe in structured discussion' type.

The success of a seminar is dependent on the skills of the tutor and the ability of the students to overcome what are often very difficult group dynamics, not to speak of the anxiety of giving a presentation, if that is what they are expected to do. This form of discussion can of course be, when it goes well, a most exhilarating experience, but as with the lecture, the occasions on which it is so are much rarer than we like to imagine, and it becomes increasingly difficult to realize as class sizes increase. An effective seminar discussion demands a lot of skill from the tutor, adequate preparation by the students, and a suitable mix of personal qualities. It is an able tutor who can handle all the aspects of group dynamics described in Chapter 2.

The following commentary, adapted from an article by Treadaway (1975), underlines the common problems in seminars:

> My experience both as tutor and student suggests it is difficult to have a discussion in which everyone takes part fully, if the group is larger than ten. In an hour or so, even the actual time is against you – six minutes per person is not very much to develop a serious argument. But more important . . . a significant proportion of people find it difficult to speak easily and confidently to a larger group. This may be due to personal inhibition, unfamiliarity with . . . the country or the language, or a combination of these. It is very noticeable, for instance, how overseas students may be silent for a whole seminar but may be leading the discussion in a small informal group afterwards.

The size of the group (may), of course, be an administrative problem and staff/student ratios often make large groups inevitable. But, if the group is large, the answer is not, I suggest, to attempt discussion in spite of the size but to spend as much time as possible in smaller sub-groups. I have found that it is in these groups, especially when given a particular problem or project, that most learning takes place. At the same time, if the tutor feels he (or she) has particular information or ideas to put across, there is nothing wrong with spending part of the time in the larger group while the tutor gives a lecture or holds a question-and-answer session, provided it is planned as such and all concerned realize that this is different from a discussion seminar.

The second basic organizational factor is the physical one. You cannot expect a discussion if people are facing each other's backs, if they are miles apart across a huge room or table, or crowded into a tutor's small room all facing his desk, or even if the room itself is dirty or cold. All these problems cannot always be solved, of course, but at least tutors should be aware of the importance of the physical arrangement and should not be surprised if discussion fails to develop when they neglect it.

The next decision is who should lead the seminar, and how. There are no rules about this, of course, and equally successful seminars can be led by tutors or students. Most tutors seem to feel, probably rightly, that it should be led by a student, as that student may gain a great deal from having to lead it. On the other hand, few students have much experience at leading seminars and it is essential that they should be given guidance on this. This is rarely done and the result is sometimes a waste of time for the rest of the group. Whoever leads, however, the most important thing to remember is that a seminar is supposed to be a discussion. This means that the introduction should be fairly short and should deliberately raise points which will be the basis for discussion, rather than merely summarize an article or other material. The actual material for discussion should have been distributed and/or read in advance and without this a good seminar is unlikely . . . In some cases, the tutor may have the delicate task of stopping students who go on too long or summarize rather than discuss. Many tutors, quite naturally not willing to offend, fail to do this when necessary; but is it worth destroying a whole seminar by being unwilling to risk offence to one student? Advice to all beforehand should in any case make the choice unnecessary.

The most crucial factor in a seminar is, of course, the role of the tutor who has to provide sufficient guidance and structure to give the seminar a meaningful shape without dominating it and forcing it into a predetermined shape. Ultimately, there are no rules and a seminar can only be guided intuitively as it progresses. The problem is that students get the impression that some tutors are not sensitive enough to the difficulties. Good seminar leaders have to ask themselves such things as whether some time in small groups might be useful; or even whether they should withdraw altogether for a while and let the group continue on its own. There are some occasions when a seminar, divided for at least part of the time into a number of small groups with a peripatetic tutor, works much better than a single group with the tutor present all the time.

Whether they like it or not, tutors are seen as authority figures and some people will be reluctant to speak, and perhaps show lack of understanding when they are present. Sometimes a whole group can be inhibited in this way, with everyone silently thinking they are the only one who does not understand. I have often found, therefore, that the best way to get a discussion going is to leave the group, or even the room, for a while.

My ideal seminar, then, would be one prepared by a small group of people who had met in advance, discussed the topic and distributed any necessary material to the whole group. They would present the topic to a group who had already read something about it and would emphasize points for discussion rather than just summarize. Depending on the size of the group there would then be discussion by the whole group or by sub-groups with the tutor moving from group to group guiding rather than leading the discussion. There would probably be a short summary at the end by the tutor or the group leaders and encouragement for those particularly interested in the topic, or with any difficulties, to get together for further discussion later.

> *Finally, my definition of a seminar as learning through discussion should not preclude the use of other teaching methods, where appropriate (within the boundaries of the seminar).*

Treadaway's analysis of the 'seminar experience' highlights problems about group teaching in general as well as the traditional seminar. The three unconscious problems of the latter seem to be:

1. the weight of academic authority and expertise invested in the tutor;
2. the inability of tutors (and students) to recognize and try out alternative approaches rather than sticking with a respected tradition;
3. a pervading anxiety about assessment with a consequent feeling among students that they should speak only when they have something 'safe' to say.

The seminar at a research or postgraduate level, as Bligh (1981) remarks, can be very useful, particularly when new ideas and proposals for research are being discussed. In such a case, it is a discussion among equals. Bligh is singularly critical of the seminar as a general method of teaching. He describes it as 'simply inappropriate'. Its success is dependent on too many chancy factors: the 'lead' student may not do a competent job either in preparing or presenting; the essay is often not a good way to introduce a topic for discussion; there may be collusion among the students not to criticize a colleague in front of a tutor; the balance of dynamics in the group with a student leader and a tutor may be a precarious one.

In a survey conducted by the British National Union of Students, students were critical of seminars in the following respects:

- 'Tended to be dominated by one or two students.'
- 'Students tend to wait for a lead from the staff members.'
- 'Students avoid doing sufficient preparatory work.'

The students were also of the opinion that the maximum working membership of the seminar was 6 to 10 (NUS, 1969).

Students confronted with the task of the traditional seminar presentation will find some useful guidelines in 'Improving Seminar Presentations' in Gibbs (1992b).

Ideally, seminars provide an intellectual stimulus that is difficult to match. In reality, the dynamics of the group and the way tutors commonly handle the process make the traditional seminar an unsatisfactory experience for many students. The exceptional tutor may succeed in elevating it to a memorable level of intellectual ferment. Mere mortals might be better advised to try alternative means of achieving the same outcomes and, in the process, achieve some that they had not previously considered.

Benefits

- procedures accepted by general convention;
- intellectual atmosphere stimulating when well run.

Drawbacks

- task rarely clarified; leadership roles confused;
- often results in mini-lecture;
- little regard for social and emotional dimension.

Tutorials

Where the seminar is usually devoted to a critical and searching discussion of subject matter, the tutorial, at least as defined by the Hale Report (HMSO, 1964), is concerned with the development of the student's powers of thought. The tutor's task is to 'use the subject to what he considers the best advantage to promote that development'. This distinction is one of emphasis rather than of strict demarcation. The tutorial is aimed towards teaching the subject as well as the students and the seminar increases the students' intellectual powers as well as teaching them the subject. Numbers, however, do seem to be important. In a one-to-one tutorial the tutor may focus attention entirely on work prepared by the student. When the number of students increases, less and less time tends to be devoted to each individual concern and correspondingly more becomes applied to the subject matter as a way of spreading the focus. Nevertheless it is likely to develop into a series of tutor-student duologues rather than a group discussion.

Readers may recall that four to six students appears to be the critical number for effective discussion, particularly in leaderless groups. Below that sort of number, no leader is considered necessary for certain defined tasks. With more members, unless a leader is designated a group may break into disarray as leadership conflicts are fought out; this is particularly true of some (untrained) project groups. What function, then, does a tutor serve in a group whose size does not necessarily justify a leader? If the answer is none, then it follows that the tutor's presence in any tutorial is likely to be a superfluous and therefore a visible and possibly dominant one. This is not to suggest that there is anything inherently wrong with such a dynamic – it may be very necessary for certain purposes – but if as tutors we wish to avoid over-direction of student learning, with its concomitant problems, we may want to consider other techniques that allow the students more autonomy. This is never more true than in the one-to-one tutorial where, in the words of the Hale Committee, 'the inequality of intellectual power and attainment between tutor and pupil is often too great for any real discussion'. One-to-one tutorials are also extravagant in the use of tutors' time – but that is self-evident.

Tutorials appear to serve three main functions: a regular meeting ground for the checking of student progress, a means of locating misunderstandings in lectures, and an opportunity to give special scrutiny to a piece of the student's work. In two, if not three, or these respects the tutorial conforms to a teacher-based pattern of learning. However, the pastoral role of the tutor should not be under-valued; in this capacity some tutors manage to combine all the above functions quite happily. They hold a regular meeting with three or four 'tutees' where they look at a piece of written work (not necessarily for submission to them), check what difficulties the students may be experiencing in particular areas, and relate this to any reports they have of students' progress. If they are able to use the group potential skilfully – for instance by getting students to assess each other's written work – they may increasingly divest some of the responsibility for these concerns to the students, to the point where the tutorial group becomes a sort of 'learning cell' with the tutor as a resource. In this setting, learning can develop into a more mutually supportive exercise than is typically the case in tutorials.

In science and engineering the word 'tutorial' is often used to describe an exercise class of up to 30 in which students work individually on set problems while the tutor circulates. In a way the exercise class is a form of rotating one-to-one tutorial with all the virtues and drawbacks that entails. The tutor does have a chance to check how students are getting on, but many students will be wary of admitting mistakes or lack of effort to the tutor, and can quickly acquire stratagems for avoiding him or her during the all-too-short one-hour period that is conventionally allocated to the class. The alert tutor may well choose to divide the class into sub-groups, with tasks demanding collaboration between the students alternating with individual work (see horseshoe groups on page 123). A most valuable source of information on problem-solving classes can be found in Forster *et al* (1995) and Baume and Baume (1996).

Benefits

- focuses attention on individual student work and ways of thinking;
- helps tutor keep an eye on student progress;
- provides continuity in tutor/student relationship.

Drawbacks

- can be expensive of tutor time (especially with one-to-one);
- tutor in dominant role.

Tasks

If aims and outcomes are to represent more than good intentions, they must, as we have already discussed, be related to corresponding tasks and activities. Each of these demands of the tutor particular skills and the playing of a special role. Tasks specify the activities in which the students individually or collectively are engaged, whether it is to do with a process like 'Observe the behaviour of a white rat' or an end product like 'List 10 issues that strike you as important and rank them'. Activities are the ensemble of tasks, rules and procedures that comprise a coherent educational experience. In order to establish and maintain a task or activity, a tutor needs imagination and skill in prescribing the structure, monitoring what is happening, gently enforcing rules or adjusting them to advantage, and avoiding the risk of being drawn into the sort of relationship with the group that could subvert the purpose of the exercise. Here is an example of the way aims, tasks, activities and roles might fit together:

Outcome: Students will be able to identify and competently use three different strategies for solving problems.

A suitable set of group tasks might be:

- to try and solve a given problem;
- to monitor the strategies involved;
- to share the findings and compare them with research evidence;
- to draw up a classification of the findings.

An activity which could match this might be to organize sub-groups with observers in a 'fishbowl' layout (see page 115). The tutor's job would be to prepare any materials, explain and check agreement on the tasks, monitor their development and control time boundaries.

Setting tasks

As already explained, students are often unsure about what to do in groups and might well take up the pursuit of separate individual goals while ostensibly engaged in collaborative discussion. In the traditional seminar the very vagueness of the task often means that students fail to get their teeth into anything substantial and end up with a feeling of dissatisfaction. They are unsure about whether they have achieved anything or even what it was they were supposed to achieve. After several meetings the task might become clear to them, but even then it may well be diffuse and perceived differently by each student. What is more, the rules or conventions of behaviour may not be explicit and may possibly be unrelated to the task. There seems to be tacit confusion about all sorts of things and this creates uncertainty and stress.

Stenhouse (1972) suggests that students evolve a secondary task of their own, which is to study the tutor's behaviour in order to understand the situation in which they find themselves. If this muddled situation is to be avoided, it is important for the tutor to make the task, and his or her role in relation to it, explicit. For a large class working in sub-groups or where students have to do work outside the classroom it is essential, if confusion is to be avoided, that the task be carefully worded and written out. On other occasions it may be better to negotiate a task with the group, especially where this is the first time it has been tried.

By placing the emphasis on task, the tutor can partly sidestep the ever-present problem of authority and dependency in the group. In setting a task for a group the tutor assumes authority in order to delegate it to the group. The tutor may organize any structuring of sub-groups, set time limits, confine his or her authority to a position that is set by agreed rules and procedures, monitor what is happening and make consequent adjustments.

Having set the task the tutor may monitor the work of the sub-groups to check that it is making sense to them and be ready to change or adjust the task to one that is more relevant to the immediate concerns of the group. Sometimes ideas for such changes occur spontaneously with remarkable results. Abercrombie (1979) reports the experience of Baker (1974) who converted the uninspiring experience of a group studying French prose into a 'small new awakening' by giving responsibility to the students for the assessment of each other's work as a group task.

Boredom in a group can often be relieved by a change of task, with remarkable results. The boredom may be due to a lack of 'grounding' in the discussion: that is, it is not rooted in the personal experience of the students. The sort of real-life process encountered in case study, role play, or marking each other's essays can reactivate the dormant energy of the group. On the other hand, the boredom may comprise no more than subdued anger, which can arise from the group being trapped in an authority/dependency tangle (see pages 4 and 5), and a tutor may be wise to spend time getting the group to look at its assumptions about the teaching/learning relationship.

The problem of how to relate group discussion to personal experience or real-life processes is discussed by Parker and Rubin (1966) who argue strongly for the introduction of real-world experiences (as opposed to academic artefacts) in the classroom. One model they suggest for this purpose comprises four stages:

1.   Creating and acquiring knowledge: students observe phenomena, read expository material, collect evidence and listen to presentations.
2.   Interpreting knowledge: students derive meaning from what they have learnt; they relate new knowledge to old. The necessary skills include analysing, reorganizing and experimenting with information and relating it together.
3.   Attaching significance and communicating knowledge: students infer generalizations, relate information to new situations and learn or reorganize the information in new ways. These activities precede communication.
4.   Applying knowledge: students use information to recognize, clarify and solve problems.

Several of these processes could be converted into group tasks and elaborated as the discussion progresses. Parker and Rubin's approach reminds us that we can learn a lot about ways of education by considering 'natural' activities in the outside world. Many of the tasks and activities listed on the following pages are derived in this way.

Tutors will also need to consider some practicalities in preparing group tasks. Forster *et al* (1995) suggest some thought be given to the following:

- an estimate of how long the activity will take;
- whether the available room arrangement is suitable;
- the availability of resource materials;
- whether it requires the tutor's involvement, if so, when and in what roles (see Chapter 7);
- whether the method it involves will assist continued building of a supportive learning climate – for example, activities that provide opportunities for individual work followed by sharing in pairs or threes are useful for this purpose;
- what briefing students will require and whether this needs to be put on paper beforehand.

It is worth mentioning here that, while any task or activity may embody a unique complex of aims and objectives, any one aim could be achieved by a number of tasks or activities. Tutors who can build a repertoire of tasks and activities should thus find themselves more versatile in the pursuit of all sorts of aims.

Types of task

The possibilities and permutations of tasks are endless and they will vary according to whether they are for the whole group, sub-groups or individuals. Here are some broad categories and specific examples.

Tasks for groups as a whole, or sub-groups:

- argue with tutor / students – disputation, debate;
- discuss a presentation;
- discuss misunderstandings;
- draw up a list of similarities and differences;
- list items from experience;
- list ideas, difficulties, preferences from reading;
- list items from observation in the group;
- list items from reading;
- establish principles embodied in a text;
- mark own or each other's essays;
- set criteria for essay marking;
- generate ideas;
- pool information – for example from different readings, interpretations, data;
- put items in rank order, rate them;
- make categories;
- make a list of relevant experiences;
- clarify problem / solve it / evaluate it;
- enact;
- agree a question or a statement worth making about a text;
- discuss critically;
- diagnose;
- mark each other's work;
- try to fill gaps in a solution or a text (eg, a poem with a missing line);
- report back on previous session;
- argue relative merits;
- share anxieties;
- evaluate a case study with various possible answers and compare the results between groups;
- solve a problem and compare results between groups;
- compare and contrast items;
- identify the origins or purpose of something;
- share essay plans;
- share study methods;
- watch a video (with prepared focal questions or tasks);
- read and evaluate text.

Tasks for individuals followed by discussion in groups:

- mark off checklist;
- rank or rate and compare values;
- make decisions/proposals about case;
- construct model, etc;
- observe group process;
- make choices;
- analyse text;
- allocate individual tasks – project work;
- suggest thesis and argue it;
- solve problem.

Tasks for peer tutoring (see pages 143–44):

- teach;
- question to check learning;
- prepare questions;
- prepare tasks;
- counsel.

Any tutor wishing to devise a new task might find it useful to apply some of the principles underlying these tasks:

- consider the ways in which knowledge in the subject is created, interpreted, communicated and applied;
- create situations in which social comparison and cognitive dissonance can take place;
- incorporate and vary the use of different roles and functions described in Chapter 2.

Structuring tasks

As we have already seen, large groups (10 or more) find some difficulty in working cohesively on a task and will tend to split into sub-groups unless held together by strong leadership. When it is important to mobilize a sense of commitment and immediate purpose among a largish group of students, therefore, it may be sensible to capitalize on the group's desire to divide into smaller units by 'doing what comes naturally'. As tutors, we might for example invite the students first to work individually to make a list for five minutes, share their ideas in pairs for 10 minutes and finally, in groups of four to six, to write up categories on a large sheet of paper, followed by 25 minutes of open discussion between groups. We could explain our role as that of wandering round to check that everyone understands and accepts the task and is doing it in an appropriate way, and to help students in formulating categories. The nature of the students' encounter with each other would thus vary over a period of time, and with each change would come a different kind of learning experience.

The skills required of the tutor in setting up these 'task-oriented' groups differ somewhat from those required in tutor-led groups. They are more to do with a considered negotiation of a mutual contract than a sensitive response to the unfolding group process. These skills are discussed in more detail in Chapter 7.

Group tasks alone do not lead to integrated learning. They have to be coordinated into a schema that not only pinpoints roles and relationships within the group, but also puts them in a valid and coherent learning sequence. Though the following task from Nisbet (1966), quoted in Rudduck (1978), is elaborate, it is a nice example of such integration. The amount of detail thought necessary may be an indication of the number of pitfalls inherent in the traditional seminar, which must consciously be avoided if new structures are to take shape. The course is in Theory of Education.

> *Each student chooses a field of study and has two-and-a-bit meetings in which to complete the task. At the introduction meeting, the tutor explains the procedure. Within each field the student responsible must first produce six statements worth making. What this involves has to be clearly understood: a 'statement worth making' (worth making, that is, in the context of this seminar) is one that is clear, succinct and important; that is controversial enough to require careful decisions before it is accepted or rejected; and that represents the personal belief, based on study, experience and reflection, of its author. To put it negatively, statements not worth making are high-sounding platitudes, trivialities, vague abstractions whose acceptance or rejection would make no observable difference in practice, disingenuous 'OK' phrases, inadequately grounded opinions, or assertions that no one is likely to dispute. Each statement must consist of only a single sentence, but the author will in due course be given every opportunity to provide supplementary details and explain why he or she chose to formulate each statement in its present form. No attempt must be made to 'cover' the whole field. The six chosen are to be regarded as a selection from the hundreds he or she could presumably produce in the given area of study if called upon to do so. When the list is made up, the student is expected to provide enough copies (with recommended references to relevant literature appended) to go round the group.*

The second meeting begins with the distribution of the copies of Student A's statements and a short talk by that student to introduce them. The remainder of the meeting is devoted to free and informal discussion. 'Spontaneity and freedom are the characteristics of this meeting.'

At the third meeting the statements are quickly reintroduced; in an atmosphere of discipline and urgency (in contrast to the previous meeting), Student A tries

> *to obtain unanimous agreement for each statement in turn. Whenever this is not immediately forthcoming, the student and the other group members, including the tutor, suggest amendments, which might a) satisfy the critics and yet b) retain the support of those who approve the statement as it is and c) still leave 'a statement worth making'. If, after a long discussion, a compromise proves impossible, the dissident member(s) will be left to compose a 'minority view' on the statement in question. Each member of the group, including the tutor, knows that when the first is promulgated in its final form his or her name will appear as one of the supporters. At the end of the meeting Student A takes home the group minute book to write up the official account of the two meetings for which they were responsible.*

These minutes are checked with the group at the beginning of the next meeting. What seems particularly interesting here is that the task is similar to the traditional seminar in which a student presents views on prior reading, yet it places a very explicit and more comprehensive set of demands on the students. Above all, decisions have to be made and this almost invariably draws out values and beliefs into open conflict – they cannot in this case be avoided by mere verbal felicity. The alternating of free and disciplined styles of discussion is a structure worth looking at also. Too often a group vacillates between the two styles, so that the benefits of neither are convincingly achieved.

In these seminars, then, the broad ground rules for discussion are clear and explicit (we shall return to this matter later on page 168). The role of the tutor is also made clear.

> *The method makes it easy for tutors to sustain their rightful role* ad primus inter pares – *'primus', in that he or she is chairman, and is responsible for the conduct of the meetings, occasionally supplying factual information, tactfully bringing in the less vocal members, keeping an eye on the clock, and exercising self-restraint by remaining silent where necessary, even when he or she would like to say a lot; 'inter pares' because he or she participates in the discussion on the basis of equality, criticizing and being criticized, asking and answering, revealing his or her own personal values as well exploring those of the students.*

These tasks, rules and roles are of vocational benefit to the students, the writers claim. For their postgraduate students (average age 27) the practice of shaping a consensus view and reconciling opposing positions has direct relevance to their professional work on committees and the like. They are also of great value to the tutor who cannot fail to be stimulated by the flux of new and unexpected ideas and confrontations (see also Wilson, 1980). The above tasks emphasize processes of discussion and decision-making. Another fruitful task field is evaluation and assessment.

Students may be asked to do one of the evaluation exercises described on pages 245–47 or to assess what they have learnt (in perhaps a general sense) and what they have contributed to, and got from, the course. This latter task can be given a keener edge by asking students to rate themselves on a numerical scale according to agreed criteria on work or performance. These criteria can be worked out by the class as part of the exercise. Following this, the students might rate each other and compare their self-ratings with the mean of the peer ratings. If these are then put alongside the assessment of the tutor, a fascinating discussion can ensue, as a result of which students begin to internalize some of the criteria and standards of academic learning. This task is yet another that could equip students for more autonomous learning and self-appraisal in their subsequent careers. It also introduces the idea of triangulated assessment (self–peer–tutor) in which a degree of objectivity is obtained by having three separate judgements on the value of the student's achievement.

Clarifying tasks and roles can be enormously helpful to group project students too. Projects (in this context) consist of several successive and overlapping tasks. Choosing a problem or topic, choosing partners, researching solutions, analysing results, writing a report, making a presentation and so on, all occur with varying degrees of overlap and weight. Pervading all of these is the task of group maintenance – how to get the best out of a collection of students with disparate experience, skills, knowledge and personal qualities. One task for the tutor in this regard is therefore to alert students to leadership issues and decision-making processes as the project progresses. Kuiper (1977) suggests an 'internal' contract for project groups that comprises aims and values on which members can agree, and an 'external' one that describes the practical purpose to which the project is to be put. The external contract involves a third party, possibly outside the institution, whose aims and needs may differ from the educational ones required inside. We shall return to the subject of projects later in this chapter.

Game tasks

Games are essentially tasks with added rules. Making rules and procedures clear is important enough in group teaching, but sometimes it is useful to introduce some imaginary scenario into the task, as in a role play or simulation. An engineering laboratory can be enlivened without any loss of standards by encouraging students to adopt a professional role in problem solving, as the following three examples demonstrate.

A. Dear Sirs,

I am designing a series of submerged pipelines to cross rivers in different parts of the UK (details given). I am in urgent need of a reliable check on the forces I might expect them to withstand and would be most grateful if you could test various models in a wind tunnel in order to give me some working data. Please send me your report within three weeks from this date.

Yours, etc.

B. The first year students are currently interested in the differences between static and dynamic forces. Could you please conduct the following experiement to check on the nature and magnitude of these differences and, having undertaken suitable rewording, write out a set of explanatory notes for the first-year students?

C. The valley of Erehwon (map and relevant data enclosed) is being considered as the site of a huge new dam and reservoir. You are to divide into three professional groups: engineers, technicians and journalists. The engineers must conduct a feasibility study on:

- dam structure;
- water supply;
- hydroelectric power.

The technicians must determine measuring techniques for [a list of purposes given] and the journalists must compile a public relations brochure on the study. Your written reports should be submitted two days before the meeting of the study commission where they will be formally introduced and discussed.

In these three cases, and especially the last one, the rules and procedures, though not very explicit, are no longer embedded in the teacher/student relationship but in an understanding of everyday life outside the educational system, to do with the consultant/ client relationship, students in a teaching role and feasibility studies repectively. Approaches like this are admirably suited to group-teaching in professional subject areas or those that have low intrinsic interest and need some imaginative boost to get them going. Games and simulations are indeed most valuable in this regard. Many examples of their use in Language Teaching are given in *Take Five* (Carrier, 1981).

Roles do not have to be imagined ones, however, they can be practical and purposeful in the context of a course. As students begin to engage with experimental work and have to learn all the new techniques and skills that they need, it may make sense to introduce them gradually, in stages, to the various aspects of their experimental work. This can be done by, for example, limiting the variables at the start so as to focus on factors like observation, errors and cross-referencing, before moving into more open-ended experiments.

In one chemistry practical (Moore & Exley, 1993), a clearly-structured sequence had each group of eight students in four pairs doing four experiments:

	Expt 1	Expt 2	Expt 3	Expt 4
Week 1	Pair 1	Pair 2	Pair 3	Pair 4
Week 2	Pair 4	Pair 1	Pair 2	Pair 3
Week 3	Pair 3	Pair 4	Pair 1	Pair 2
Week 4	Pair 2	Pair 3	Pair 4	Pair 1

The experiment allocated to each group in Week 1 became their experiment and they had responsibility thereafter for the progress of that experiment throughout the four weeks. They were responsible for:

- learning the aims, theoretical principles, calculations and techniques associated with that experiment;
- carrying out the first week's work on the experiment;
- instructing and directing the work of the other pairs in subsequent weeks;
- collecting and collating the results from the other pairs in the subsequent weeks;
- writing the final report of their experiment including the calculations and results of the other pairs;
- presenting an oral report of the investigation to all the students.

The output of each week's work was assessed by the students leading the experiment, and the final report was assessed by the teacher and the oral presentation by both class and teacher. This method involved an initial briefing of all the students on the operation of the scheme and with each group on their own experiment, weekly meetings between the student groups to brief and debrief, and a training session on presentation skills with the whole class. An advantage of this scheme is that the students' learning is sharpened by their having to instruct other students with great care because the results contributed to the final presentation. Other advantages are that each pair of students has to write up only one report each and the staff have less repetitive marking.

Another approach to the sequencing of laboratory work set out to desegregate theory and practice. Rather than keeping lectures, reading, practicals and writing all separate, the different activities can be mixed (which is what usually happens in practice). For example, you could:

- design the experimental work during lectures;
- introduce a bit of theory or send students off to the library in the middle of the practical;
- allocate the first half hour of a laboratory to the completion, and handing in, of the previous week's report;
- hold a seminar on the ethics of a particular practice or experiment during the laboratory session.

The case studies in Chapter 8 include further examples of group tasks in the context of the curriculum.

Group structures and activities

Thus far we have looked at aims and tasks and the educational and psychological principles that support them. When these are integrated into an established pattern of rules, roles and procedures, we have an ensemble of means – what I shall call an 'activity'. In this section we will look at some of these activities and the principal aims they are designed to serve. Subsequent chapters describe the skills required of the tutor in preparing and operating the activities, and how they may be organized into the curriculum. The activities are roughly grouped into the following pattern:

- those that involve a structure either in terms of an explicit pattern of interaction, a change in the use of space or time sequence;
- those that are designed to stimulate creative thinking;
- those that stimulate the imagination by importing an external scenario;
- those that students can operate on their own.

The way the various activities are used will vary enormously from group to group. Some, like synectics, a creative problem-solving technique, are fairly specific in their format; others, like the seminar, are infinitely variable. Some are incorporated with others. Whichever category system one uses, there are always too many exceptions.

A further classification indicates those activities especially, but not exclusively, suited a) in observing or promoting equal opportunities, and b) for larger groups. The former will be indicated by *E* and the latter by *L*.

The intention of this chapter is to encourage tutors to break out of the mould of traditional seminars and tutorials and to recognize the range of variations and alternative activities or methods they can use; techniques that are less frustrating, more enjoyable, and which challenge and stimulate the minds of students and give credit to that under-used faculty – the imagination. Many of these less-than-familiar activities may be included within the bounds of what is, for timetabling purposes, called a 'seminar'. Others may need to be pursued in their own right.

Structured approaches

The first three methods involve the group as a whole remaining as one unit, the first two being of particular relevance for larger groups where the communication of knowledge is clearly directed through the tutor.

Controlled discussion (L)

This method is commonly used as a means of checking for knowledge and understanding of presented material. Discussion is controlled by the tutor; either students ask questions or make comments, or the tutor fires questions at students in the manner of a Socratic dialogue.

Benefits

- convenient to organize at the end of (or as a follow-up to) a lecture;
- quick feedback;
- large and 'economical' number of students.

Drawbacks

- inhibiting to open communication;
- reticent students not heard;
- little peer discussion.

Step-by-step discussion (L)

Though similar to controlled discussion in its communication pattern, this method is based on a prepared text, audio or video tape that provides a sequence of subject matter. In leading the students through the sequence, the tutor draws out and guides the students' developing knowledge in discussion and, by using open-ended questioning skills (see page 176), allows students some freedom to explore the realism of their own knowledge. The input for step-by-step discussion may be a sheet of notes, or a text shared by tutor and students alike, or even a video/audio tape where a 'stop-start' procedure can be employed. This technique brings together several of the qualities of the lecture and the seminar.

Benefits

- economical use of large groups;
- 'authority' can be invested in shared text or tape – students not dependent on tutor for content;
- combines information-giving, processing and feedback aims.

Drawbacks

- as for controlled discussion, but to a lesser extent;
- sequence and structure of discussion pre-ordained – may not correspond with students' needs.

Free or associative discussion (L)

The benefits of giving people freedom in a controlled environment to talk about whatever comes to mind have long been understood in psychoanalysis and group therapy (see Chapter 1). The therapist is trained to listen and generally refrain from comment while the patient 'freely associates', thus revealing underlying patterns of thought and feeling. Free discussion operates on a similar principle. The tutor says very little but encourages spontaneity of speech among the students. What the tutor does say is by way of directing students' attention to anomalies and inconsistencies in what they have said, pointing out patterns and relevances in what might otherwise seem a vague and rambling discussion, and helping them 'to see themselves as capable of change' (Abercrombie, 1979).

Although free discussion may comprise a great number of apparently random exchanges, its permissiveness allows the student to become increasingly aware of some of the habitual attitudes and assumptions which to a large extent determine his or her ways of thinking about the subject. McLeish (1973) states that:

Students discover, in the course of discussion, that they have highly specific, even idiosyncratic reactions to problems, to situations, to individuals; that they always slow down their ability to solve problems. An understanding of the nature of knowledge and self-insight is given them in a manner no other teaching method can provide. It is first-hand, personal experience of the shifting character of experience, the ambiguity of evidence, the tenuous nature of our most profound convictions.

In these senses free discussion is a means to intellectual growth – the sort of personal development that Perry (1970) describes as students move from the dualistic to the relativistic phases, and even onward to commitment.

The tutor's job is not to correct mistakes (other participants quickly pick up this task) but, with a good sense of timing, to inject comment on the nature of the argument; otherwise to listen attentively. By clearly specifying the aims and by intermittently restating them in the context of what is being said, the tutor sets a direction. By occasionally expressing feelings – 'I don't know what I've done to shut you all up' – the tutor encourages a recognition of the important part that emotions play in our thinking. By referring to his or her own habits when students are talking about theirs, and encouraging 'oscillation of attention between different contexts', eg from the present group to the whole class or profession, the tutor promotes the transfer of learning and a reflexive understanding of problems. The tutor's role is therefore to clarify the field of discourse and set its boundaries as well as to draw associations within the general aim. For this reason Abercrombie expresses preference for the word 'associative' rather than 'free' to describe the group discussion.

In her earlier book, *The Anatomy of Judgement* – a classic text that merits study by all teachers and students – Abercrombie (1969) describes tasks set to groups of medical students. The tasks were designed to elucidate for the participants 'some of the factors that had affected their judgement on scientific matters'. Each of the tasks was undertaken in the climate of free/associative discussion:

Task 1. Students were shown two similar but different radiographs and asked to 'list the differences you can see between the two hands'.
Task 2. Students were given a short extract from a book in which the words 'normal' and 'average' occurred. They were asked to 'Write what you think the author means by these terms and give all the definitions of "normal" you can think of'.
Task 3. Students wrote a short essay on classification and discussed in the group.
Task 4. Students first read a scientific paper reporting an experiment and its conclusions. They were then asked to answer the following:

- Quote a statement that summarizes what the author claims she has discovered.
- Compare this with observation actually made.
- How could you set out to test the hypothesis that [author's hypothesis stated]?

The students were thus being asked to reveal how they interpreted, ordered, commented on and judged scientific information, and to improve in and through the process. Several students claimed this caused them to think seriously and to continue doing so well beyond the group session. In some cases it appeared that the time effect was delayed by months.

One student claimed that it was two years after he had finished the course before he understood it. It was remarked that the course helped students express themselves clearly, to understand what others were saying and to listen. The last, as Abercrombie remarks, is a much-neglected skill.

A variation of the free/associative group model was used in a basic biology course at the University of Sydney. The tutor was originally placed outside the group and the students were told she was present only as a resource and would not enter discussion unless the whole group agreed it was necessary. Later, a five-minute limit for 'non-intervention' by the tutor was introduced. Tasks ranged from the arrangement of specimens, diagrams or cards to intriguing questions such as 'Was Jack's Beanstalk possible?'. Two of the themes that come through strongly in all the literature on these groups are the somewhat painful moves from a state of dependency into one of responsibility, and the need for some sort of training for tutors in what is a very unnatural role for most. The authority/dependency conflict is deeply rooted in the culture of teaching and learning. It takes a lot of courage, care and personal insight to handle it successfully.

Benefits

- promotes intellectual growth, greater student responsibility for learning;
- encourages flexibility;
- has long-term value.

Drawbacks

- apparently rambling kind of discussion;
- time needed for adjustment to process;
- learning difficult to assess by traditional means as often very internal;
- difficult role for many tutors.

The next set of group activities specifically involve direction by the tutor for the students to follow a sequence or a spatial pattern which can enable not only greater freedom to express ideas but also a focus on specific skills at different stages and from various positions.

Rounds (E)

Each person has a brief time – 20 seconds or one minute, for example – to say something in turn round the group (see Figure 6.1). This can go clockwise or anticlockwise: the direction can be decided by the first contributor; or members can speak in a random order as the spirit takes them. More interest and energy is usually generated if the person starting the 'round' chooses who should go second, the second person, who should go third and so on.

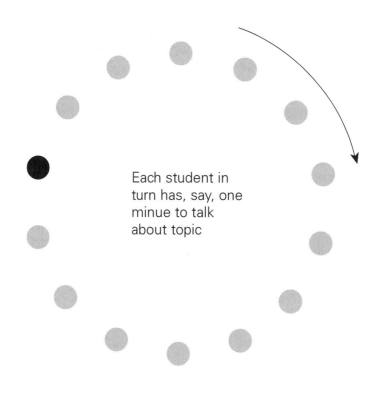

Each student in turn has, say, one minue to talk about topic

Figure 6.1 *Group 'rounds'*

Rounds are particularly useful at the beginning of any group meeting in order to bring everyone in from the start and, depending on what the group is asked to address in the round, as a way of checking on learning issues.

Benefits

- everyone contributes and can therefore feel included in the group;
- the tutor gets a sense of everyone;
- can be used as a gentle check on work done in preparation.

Drawbacks

- as with all 'rule-bound' activities, natural spontaneity is curbed;
- if done in a circular sequence the last few can become quite anxious.

Buzz groups (E) (L)

Frequently, where the group is large, there is a need for a break in the more formal proceedings in order to provide a stimulating change in the locus of attention, for the tutor to gain some idea of what the students know, and for the students to check their own understanding. If, therefore, during the course of a lecture or other one-directional communication, students are asked to turn to their neighbours to discuss for just a few minutes any difficulties in understanding, to answer a prepared question, or to speculate on what they think will happen next in the proceedings, a sense of participation and some lively feedback can be quickly achieved. (See Figure 6.2.)

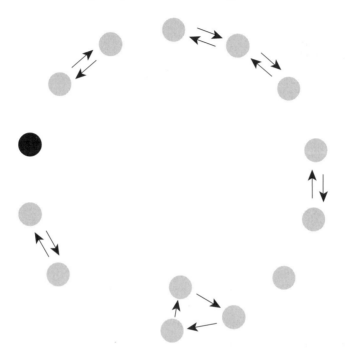

Figure 6.2 *Buzz groups in a seminar*

Buzz groups enable students to express difficulties they would have been unwilling to reveal to the whole class without the initial push of being obliged to say something to their neighbours. Taken by itself, the buzz group technique has little meaning. Yet in the context of a lecture or other large group event it can rekindle all sorts of dying embers. Its incorporation into a pattern of teaching events is described on pages 190–92.

Benefits

- can be used in any teaching situation for as short or as long as desirable;
- helps students and teacher check on misunderstandings;
- creates a stimulating break.

Drawbacks

- can destroy intellectual and emotional cohesion if timed wrongly.

Three minutes each way (E) (L)

A variation of the buzz group, this allows each partner in turn to take a listening role for three minutes (or five) and to give unconditional attention to what the other is saying. The tutor has to be quite firm in making sure that the students know that this is not a conversation or discussion but a disciplined and focused opportunity for each person to explore their experience without interruption. The only intervention the listener may make is if the speaker drifts too far from the topic, to bring them back.

One particularly useful application of this method is with 'learning partners' where at particular times pairs form to explain in turn what they have learnt, how well and what they will do to maintain or improve that learning. It can also be very useful at the end of a workshop in presenting action plans.

Benefits

- simple and easily repeated once understood;
- develops reflective mode of learning.

Drawbacks

- none if timed right.

Snowball groups (Pyramids) (E) (L)

Buzz groups can easily be extended into a progressive doubling in which pairs join up to form fours, then fours to eights, which finally report back to plenary session. This developing pattern of group interaction is known as a 'snowball'. It is amazingly effective in ensuring comprehensive participation, especially when it starts with individuals writing their ideas in the first stage before sharing them. Lest students become bored with repeated discussion of the same points, a sequence of increasingly sophisticated tasks is often desirable (see Figure 6.3.)

Benefits

- good for encouraging the creation of well-integrated ideas;
- allows students to think for themselves before discussing;
- generates full and lively participation in plenary discussion.

Drawbacks

- breaks up cohesive feeling in some groups; takes time to unfold.

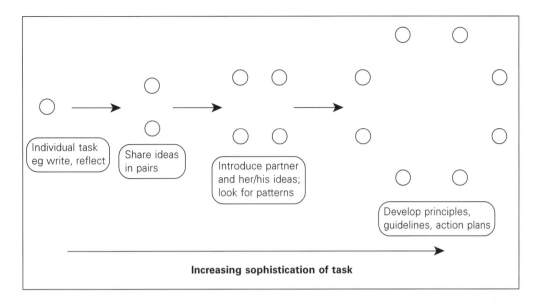

Figure 6.3 *Snowball or pyramid groups*

Fishbowls (L)

Though a very simple format, fishbowls can incorporate many of the best processes and structures of group practice. The concept of a fishbowl group springs from an obvious metaphor: one group of sentient beings observing another group of sentient beings who are swimming around in a less rarefied medium, and are aware of being studied while behaving in their usual manner. The observer feels at once detached and envious; superior and yet wanting to be part of the action.

Fishbowls differ from other inter-group methods in that there is a mutual process and a differentiation of task: the inner group in a cognitive and the outer group in a metacognitive activity (generally).

The normal fishbowl configuration has the inner group discussing an issue or topic while the outer one looks for themes, patterns, soundness of argument, etc, or uses a group behaviour checklist to give feedback to the group on its functioning; and the roles are then or at a later date reversed (see Figure 6.4). They can of course be reversed without any feedback discussion. But as we shall see in the following three pages, the tasks and the structure of fishbowls can be varied in many creative ways.

Inter-group meeting
The outer group could be another seminar group who are there either to observe how a parallel group discusses a topic and give them a commentary, or to conduct a peer group assessment.

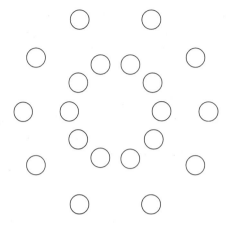

Figure 6.4 *Fishbowl*

Empty chair
The inner group includes an 'empty chair', which enables anyone in the outer group to move to the inner group and ask a question or to make a brief statement before returning to the outer position.

Alter ego
Here, any outer person has permission to tap an inner person on the shoulder, either to take their place or, standing behind them, to put their point in a different way. This can be combined with the empty chair method. Alter ego can be used to advantage in evaluating a group where two people start with a prompt like a sentence completion, and talk about the group/workshop/course. Anyone can take the place of either person in the middle, even the tutor, and two useful ground rules are that everyone must have contributed by the end and that anyone in the middle who wants to come out can invite a replacement.

Role plays
Provided confident-enough students are selected, role play can be done like 'theatre in the round'. Or parallel role plays (say A interviews B) can be done in a number of small groups and then all the As come together to discuss the experience with the Bs observing, and vice versa.

Five-minute theatre
This is a special and very effective version of the above. Groups of three to six select a problem that concerns them and that they are prepared to present to their fellow-students as a five-minute drama. They have 20 minutes to prepare and are advised to do a 'dry run' privately before the performance. The enactment is usually given without any

'prologue' to the others 'in the round'. The task of the outer group is to report what they observed and particularly any insights and interpretations that may not have been transparent to the 'actors' or could have been revealed only through the drama.

Paired feedback

Less commonly, pairs are matched between the inner and outer group, members of the former briefing the latter who acts as 'consultant' to their partner. The consultant then observes the inner group discussion and after a period of time gives confidential feedback to his or her 'client'. The inner group then resumes discussion, integrating the comments from 'outer' colleagues into a new round of discussion. (See Figure 6.5.)

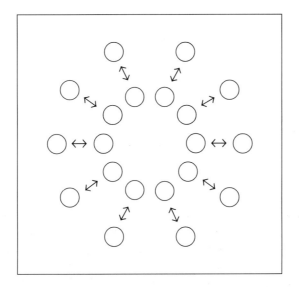

Figure 6.5 *Fishbowl with paired feedback*

Representatives observed

When a number of sub-groups are first asked to make a decision like putting a list of items in rank order, all the groups could then elect leaders/spokespersons who sit in an inner circle to make a final, agreed, decision, observed by the others. After reaching the decision they could then 'face the music' back in the first groups.

Mix-up

After a round of normal fishbowl activity (discussion and observations), you could sub-divide each group: half the inner with half the outer to form two new groups who either work independently of each other or form a fishbowl relationship.

Hot seat

This was a method devised by some students for me after an experiential course I had run. They put a rotating chair in the middle asked me to sit in it and proceeded to ask me questions about the course as I rotated.

Outward facing

A fairly bizarre but interesting way to organize a fishbowl is to have the members of either group facing outwards. If the inner group face outwards, they may have problems in picking up non-verbal cues but they may find themselves listening more carefully and able to pick up cues from the outer group, especially if they are paired for the purpose. Alternatively the outer group can face outwards in order to fine-tune their listening skills.

Benefits

- useful for generating and examining divergent views, and for cross-cultural or inter-group understanding;
- can add a new dimension to problem solving;
- a reasonably safe way to learn and get feedback on group behaviour;
- can be used to set agendas and objectives, for assessment and evaluation and to energize a group.

Drawbacks

- the ground rules for the outer group may be difficult to maintain if their task is not clearly explained and understood;
- the outer group may become bored;
- the inner group may find the presence of observers inhibiting.

Crossover groups (E) (L)

One continual problem with the division of a class into sub-groups is how to avoid a tiresome plenary session when each group reports publicly to the others. In the crossover technique, students are divided into groups of roughly equal sizes. There are then two (and possibly more) ways of proceeding, each requiring group members to meet at least one from each of the other groups. If we take a group of 36 students organized as in Figure 6.6 into sub-groups and hand each a colour (blue, red, pink, green, yellow, white) the two distinct procedures are as shown in the figure.

After a given time, all 'reds' leave their original groups to form a 'red group', and the same for all the other colours (see Figure 6.6 B).

The task of each student as he or she moves into a new group can be to report what has been said in the previous group before discussion in the new group proceeds. This

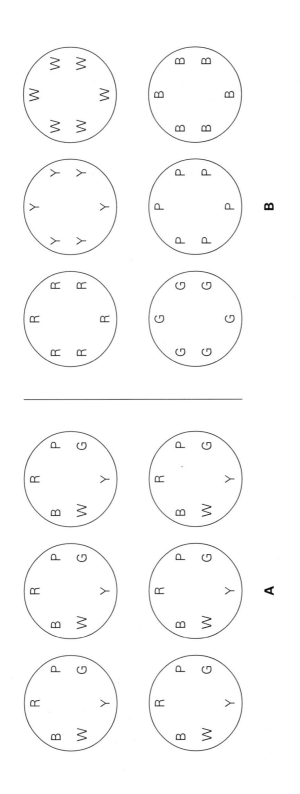

Figure 6.6 *Crossover groups*

technique is helpful in mixing a new group of students on part-time courses where the circulation of ideas is never very rapid (Bligh, 1981), and with cross-cultural groups where there may be equal opportunities problems to do with language or culture, or both.

A variation on the crossover model, described by Brookfield and Preskill (1999) and based on Slavin (1990) is the Jigsaw method. In this, the students are asked to study topics in preparation for a discussion in which they feature as 'experts', first by themselves and then in conjunction with other 'experts'. The topics, chosen by the students for their own interest within the course outcomes, are distributed on a 'square root' basis – 16 students in a group means four topics, four for each student. The students individually undertake the necessary study to become experts and, on return, meet in groups with the experts concerned with the same topic to share and upgrade their expertise. That done, they split into crossover groups, each group containing an expert from each topic who has to lead the discussion. This phase ends when all the groups have expressed reasonable satisfaction that the expertise has been shared and understood. Finally, the whole group may reassemble for an open discussion.

Benefits

- excellent for mixing people and information;
- simple to organize; students enjoy it;
- avoids plenary discussion;
- everyone has to contribute and present a view, not necessarily their own.

Drawbacks

- can lead to confusion about learning outcomes;
- can break up absorbing discussions.

Circular questioning (E) (L)

One method of engaging the whole group from the start is to conduct a 'round' in which each member of the group in turn asks a question (see Figure 6.7). In its simplest version, one group member formulates a question relevant to the theme or problem and puts it to the person opposite, who has a specified time (one or two minutes) in which to answer it. Follow-up questions can be put if time permits. The questioning and answering continues clockwise round the group until everyone has contributed, at which point a review of questions and answers can take place; this could of course include answers that others would like to have given.

Questions thought up spontaneously can sometimes be a little facile and shallow. If we want to encourage deeper levels of learning, it may be wise for students to prepare their questions on cards for prior inspection by the tutor. Whether these are then returned to the originator or placed face down in a pile for students to pick at random (obviously ensuring ownership cannot be identified) is a matter of choice and depends on whether

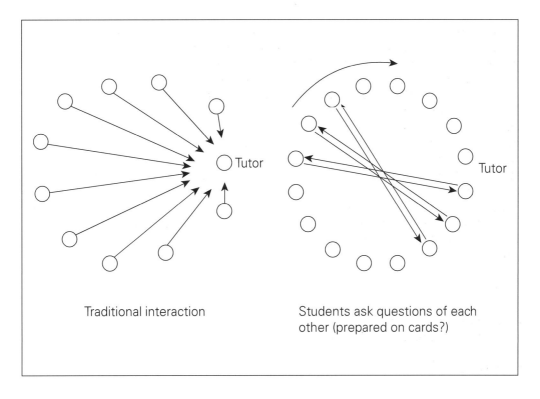

Figure 6.7 *Circular questioning*

the main objective is merely to get discussion started or to present something more like a test to the group.

As an alternative the tutor could prepare the cards, or mix the best of the students' with some of his or her own.

Circular questioning can also be used to advantage in problem-solving and decision-making groups.

Benefits

- a simple and quickly understood process;
- it ensures everyone is engaged in and has contributed to the topic in the first 10 or 20 minutes.

Drawbacks

- the questions can be facile;
- it can be frustrating for those wanting to contribute when it is not their turn;
- it can stifle a natural wish for open discussion.

Line-ups (E) (L)

In line-ups the students are asked to adopt a position in a line, which represents their view on an issue. Line-ups serve two valuable purposes: to get members of a group to tease out opinions, values or attitudes that might otherwise remain obscure; and as a means of organizing sub-groups.

The line in which the students are asked to stand denotes a range from one predefined polarity to another and they are asked to negotiate their position in it with others, in order to establish they are in the correct place (see Figure 6.8 for an example).

Figure 6.8 *Line-up 1*

It is useful to place two chairs to represent the extremes. If, as is quite common, nobody feels strongly enough to stand at one end, you can stretch the scale by asking the person who feels nearest to that value to take the physically extreme position.

When used in this way a line-up can form a sort of opinion poll, which enables both tutor and students to see what the balance of opinion is and make whatever relevant decisions are necessary (see Figures 6.9 and 6.10).

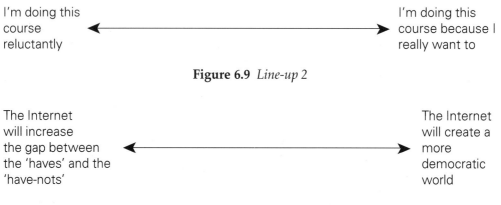

Figure 6.9 *Line-up 2*

Figure 6.10 *Line-up 3*

It can also help when there is a sense of simmering hostility or resistance in a group in that, by having it brought out into the open, its 'owners' can lose a lot of their negative energy.

If the intention is to form sub-groups, then by organizing a mix of value positions in the sub-groups drawn from the line-up you are less likely to get cliques and splits in the group or workshop. The simplest way to effect this is to ask them to number off, according to the number of sub-groups you want, from one end to the other and ask all the 1s to form one group, the 2s another, the 3s another, and so on. You will thus achieve a membership in each group that is heterogeneous in opinion. The criteria can be more arbitrary, for example according to height, shade of hair, length of little fingers or any other visible criterion.

Benefits

- they are a quick way of getting a survey or 'straw poll' of opinion in a group;
- they provide a visible and fair way of dividing into heterogeneous sub-groups;
- they create physical movement and informal negotiation.

Drawbacks

- they can bring out opinion differences too early in the proceedings;
- sometimes students are afraid to admit to any extremes and so cluster in the middle.

Horseshoe groups (L)

This describes a way of organizing a class so that it can alternate with ease between the lecture and discussion group formats. Rather than the students facing the front in serried ranks, they are arranged around tables in a horseshoe formation with the open end facing the front, as in Figure 6.11. A tutor can thus talk formally from the board for a time before switching to give the groups a task such as a problem or an interpretation; the task should of course be one demanding collaboration among the students. The horseshoe format can be of great benefit in science and engineering exercise classes if students are given problems at the start and then the tutor circulates round the groups, listening and asking or answering questions. Should any general problem emerge, an explanation can be offered by the tutor or indeed by any student to the whole class.

Whether the groups are given identical, similar, or entirely separate problems, there is always the opportunity to open up discussion on a sticky point or to ask groups to explain their solutions or decisions to each other. If a sense of inter-group competition can be infused into the situation, not only can the level of interest and work be heightened but also the cohesion in each group. To give each group a different role in relation to the task can also add energy and interest.

The plenary session can be run in several ways apart from the traditional one of a reporter presenting from each group. Written reports could be circulated for comment, groups can interview each other (A to B on C, etc) or one member of each group could circulate. Groups could produce and display posters, everyone can be given a number and the tutor picks a group and number at random (A3, D5, etc). The tutor could pick up the necessary information from each group and present a unified report him- or herself

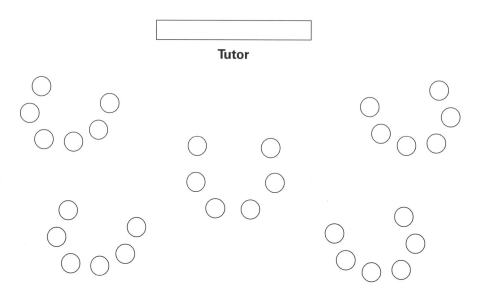

Figure 6.11 *Horseshoe groups*

(Bligh, 2000) or simply change the room layout to form one large group and let discussion emerge naturally without any structure. This is also an occasion where two other methods can be used to great effect. Reporters can form the inner group of a fishbowl or everyone can be involved in reporting using the crossover method. The horseshoe group format may also be used for syndicate meetings (see page 142).

Benefits

- students can clear up misunderstandings;
- students share uncertainties and teach each other;
- tutor has flexibility of talking or listening; students help each other.

Drawbacks

- some students do little or nothing;
- tutor cannot easily identify students in difficulty (unless a 'remedial' exercise is set up);
- many 'problem' tasks not suited to group work.

Delphi and nominal group techniques (L)

Two group methods that do not involve discussion in the normal sense are the Delphi technique and the nominal group technique. In each of these the interchange takes place through the processing of written statements or ideas and they are therefore useful tools when a group cannot meet face-to-face or there is a risk of a quiet minority being submerged by a more vocal majority.

Delphi technique

This is essentially a method for reaching consensus on issues, a purpose that can be very relevant in collecting opinions on a course. Information is separately collected from all those contributing and then analysed and summarized, before being fed back to everyone. Each person then has the chance to reconsider his or her view in the light of the summary before sending in a further, more developed, contribution. This cycle can be repeated as many times as is practicable and effective.

Variations may include feeding back opinions that differ from the majority and asking those who submitted them to justify their viewpoint and then to note and inform the 'group' of any changes of opinion.

A form of the Delphi technique can be used in a face-to-face situation, too, where group members are asked to write their comments or problem solutions on Post-its and to place them on the wall before agreeing how the responses should be clustered and reorganizing them into theme areas. The collation and sorting of ideas can be done by one or two members of the group, thus delegating more responsibility for learning.

Benefits

■ each person can put forward his or her view anonymously without evident influence from the others;
■ when the group cannot easily meet in the same place it makes consensus achievable;
■ contributors do not have to spend travel time getting to a meeting place;
■ they are likely to give more considered thought to the issues;
■ there is a clear and safe framework in which to express opinions;
■ it lends itself to e-mail as the medium of communication.

Drawbacks

■ it can be time-consuming to organize;
■ it can take much longer than face-to-face discussion;
■ participants do not get the stimulus of face-to face contact;
■ as it is not a public discussion, the integrity of the collators is critical.

Nominal group technique (NGT)

This differs from the Delphi method in that ideas are collected in a face-to-face situation and pooled publicly. Typically a problem or theme is proposed and individuals are given a sheet of paper on which silently to respond with short written phrases. They are then invited, in turn going round the group, to read out one idea and this is recorded as presented on a board or flipchart. If anyone is stimulated with a new idea by that of someone else they can add that to their sheet. The tutor/facilitator continues to elicit one idea per person for a second or third round until all ideas have been gathered.

In the next stage the ideas are labelled, usually with a letter of the alphabet, in order to make reference to them easier and the subsequent ranking of solutions (if it is a problem-solving session) to be achieved. Time is then allocated to clarification of the ideas in open discussion: members are invited to ask for the meaning of words and phrases and the thoughts behind them.

The final phase is a process for deciding the relative importance of the ideas. Each member has a set number of cards (not more than five) on which to write the items recorded on the flipchart that have the highest priority for them and to write a number on the card against each item to indicate its rank order. The cards are collected and the numbers processed on a master sheet.

Benefits

■   ideas can be expressed freely without pressure to conform;
■   a wider range of ideas is usually produced within a shorter space of time than in traditional discussion and debate;
■   everybody's ideas are given due and balanced consideration;
■   NGT can be used to determine and promote interest in topics for a course.

Drawbacks

■   the restriction on free and open discussion can cause irritation among those who enjoy (but sometimes dominate) free discussion;
■   the tutor/facilitator has to take a dominant role in maintaining the proper process and pooling the results – though the latter could be delegated.

Creative thinking

We shall now look at two approaches to creative thinking that are popular in the world of business for producing imaginative solutions to problems. Both of them introduce ground rules and special roles for the leader which, by limiting the scope of communication, can paradoxically release a great deal of creative energy.

Brainstorming (L)

This is the best-known and most frequently employed procedure to stimulate creative thinking. It was devised by Osborn (1963) as long ago as 1938 in reaction to much of the cramped thinking he saw being applied to the solution of problems at business meetings. In fact, it is only one part of a creative problem-solving procedure designed to generate ideas. The full procedure includes the stages of fact finding, idea finding and solution finding.

Fact finding involves the definition and preparation of problems; definition in the picking out and refining of the problem; preparation in the gathering and analysis of relevant data. Idea finding deals with the production and development of ideas through brainstorming. Solution finding relates to the evaluation of tentative solutions and the choosing and implementation of the agreed one.

The two main principles of brainstorming are the 'deferment of judgement' – evaluation and criticism inhibit the freedom of creative thinking – and 'quantity breeds quality', based on the premise that we have to work through conventional ideas before we can get to original ones.

During brainstorming sessions four rules operate:

1. *Criticism is ruled out* – any attempt at evaluation must quickly be declared out of order. This includes discussion as it usually raises doubts and qualifications.
2. *Free-wheeling 'is welcomed* – the wilder the idea the better. 'It is easier to tame down than to think up (ideas)' (Osborn, 1963).
3. *Quantity is wanted* – the more ideas suggested, the greater the likelihood of an original one coming up.
4. *Combination and improvement are sought* – participants are encouraged to build on and improve each other's ideas and combine them to form new ideas.

The participants in a brainstorming session should ideally have knowledge of the problem areas though not be too close to the problem, and be of such a mix as to provide a variety of experience and personal style. Osborn (1963) regards the ideal size of group as 'about a dozen' and this is the experience of most practitioners. The leader must be both alert and pushing yet be able to maintain a friendly and informal atmosphere. A typical session might proceed as follows:

1. The leader makes sure that the problem has been properly defined and background information prepared.
2. Having arranged everyone so that open communication can take place, the leader runs a warm-up session (especially for newcomers). For this purpose, the leader may place an object, eg a plastic beaker, brick, paper clip in the middle of the floor and invite a quick generation of ideas on possible uses of the object. In order to free members from the usual inhibitions the leader might throw in some less conventional ideas: very often those of a lavatorial, aggressive or sexual nature have an astounding effect! (This arises from the taboos that commonly operate in these areas.)
3. The leader reminds everyone of the rules and principles and prepares to write up on a board or large sheet a title for each of the contributions; constantly pushes for more, proposing own ideas where necessary; stimulates further lines of thought by asking how the 'thing' could be changed in terms of colour, shape, motion, etc.

    In a brainstorming session on the problem of 'How to remove oil slicks from the surface of the sea' the dialogue might go as follows:
    –   Burn it (write 'burn it').
    –   Let it get washed ashore and scrape it off the beaches (write 'scrape beaches').
    –   Sink it with sand (write 'sink with sand').
    –   Blow it out to sea (write 'blow out to sea').

- That won't get rid of it (reprimand for evaluating).
- Soak it up with seagulls (write 'soak with seagulls').
- Harness it to seagulls (write 'harness to seagulls').
- Train seagulls to dive down and suck it up into straws and drop these into a waiting tanker (what shall we write down for that? Sucking gulls!) and so on.

4. The ideas may then be evaluated by the same group, a completely different one, or a mixture of the two. As a first step it is often fruitful to ask ,'What is the wildest idea on the list?' and try to translate this into a practical proposal. The above list might, for example, throw up 'sucking gulls' as the idea to develop, and this could lead to the more practical proposal of helicopters holding the suction end of a pipe on to the slick with the delivery end held in an adjacent tanker.
5. Finally, discussion focuses on the implementation of the chosen solution(s).

Brainstorming has been well-tried and successfully proved in the production of creative solutions to all manner of real-life problems. In an education system that generally pays much lip service to creativity but does little actively to promote it, the very simplicity and quickness of this technique makes it well worth a try, especially in design, project work or other areas where open-ended problems are of consequence.

Benefits

- simple, easy to learn;
- good fun;
- can easily be generalized to include many aspects of life.

Drawbacks

- can be facile and unproductive;
- some people unable to function in it.

Synectics (L)

A more structured and thorough scheme for creative problem solving was developed by Gordon (1961) and Prince (1970). Synectics is built around many of the psychological states known to be helpful in overcoming blocks to creative thinking. It uses analogues and metaphors, encourages a wide range of ideas, and pays particular attention to the role of the leader in this. The psychological states are: involvement and detachment – an oscillation between close personal resonance with the problem and detachment from it; deferment – avoiding the danger of the quick and superficial solution; speculation – the freedom to let ideas flow easily; hedonistic response – a recognition that the feeling aroused, as a solution is approached, is an indication of where the discussion should go. These psychological states are induced through a series of 'operational mechanisms' that serve to 'make the familiar strange' – people are distanced from the problem in order to free them from their prior concepts of it – or 'making the strange familiar' in order to bring them closer to it. The operational mechanisms are as follows.

Personal analogy

Each person is invited to imagine themselves to be the object under consideration, to merge themselves with its physical existence. In the case of a concrete object such as a spring, or an oil slick (the problem being considered) the individual would attempt to feel the tension, the glutinousness, or whatever. With personal and social problems, role play may do the same thing. In personal analogy, group members are asked first to describe the facts about their identified-with object, its everyday experience and how it feels about its existence.

Direct analogy

Now the group thinks of instances where comparable modes of operation, function or movement exist. The oft-cited case is that of Brunel getting his idea for the design of caissons from seeing shipworms tunnelling into wood.

Symbolic analogy

Here the emphasis is on finding a visual or metaphorical image that helps to free the mind from the constraints of literal thinking. One group used the Indian rope trick as a symbolic analogy for the design of a jacking device to fit into a box 4 inches square.

Fantasy analogy

The value of fantasy is in the way it can act as a releasing mechanism for the unconscious motives and wishes we all have. Fantasy analogy is based on Freud's notion that creative work is the result of 'wish fulfilment'. It is an effective way of making the familiar strange. The group is asked to abolish their rational understanding of the object or problem and indulge in daydreaming. For instance, members might be asked, in tackling the problem of inventing a vapour-proof closure for space-suits, 'How in your wildest fantasies do you want the closure to operate?'. Alternatively, the group may be led into a story fantasy based on how the initiator of the concern senses the problem. The 'hedonistic' responses are picked out to see what they reveal.

In a synectics session on how to design a training workshop for administrators, a fantasy story conducted as a group 'round' led into the notion of poodle dogs floating down from the sky by parachute. This was quickly 'forced' into the somewhat more practical proposal that random individual tasks be 'showered' upon participants at the beginning of each day.

Unusual techniques abound in synectics. Because creative thinking is essentially a free-flowing and undisciplined process, structure has been built in to help clarify and emphasize what is happening. The interested reader should refer to Stein (1975) for a review of all the procedures of synectics as well as the original work of Gordon and Prince.

Apart from its use for stimulating creative thinking, synectics has potential for more general learning purposes. For instance, in metaphorical thinking for 'unsticking' discussion (see Pirsig, 1974), students are encouraged to suggest what something is like – perhaps the influence of Socrates on the Athenians could be likened to a river cutting into a bank of clay – and to play with that for a while. This approach seems to have been particularly successful with underachieving students. It has even been used with success in the teaching of philosophy.

The role of the synectics leader in facilitating the creative process is illuminating to a host of group-dynamic problems. Prince is concerned, as is Osborn (1963), about the effect of prematurely evaluating ideas in a problem-solving group and in avoiding comment on their negative aspects. He offers the following advice to the leader:

- 'Never go into competition with your team' – everyone else's ideas have precedence over the leader's.
- 'Be a 200 per cent listener to your team members' – in order to understand someone's view the leader might paraphrase or build on it.
- 'Do not permit anyone to be put on the defensive' – there is value in what everyone offers and the leader's job is to find it; those seeking negative aspects should be asked what it is they like or would prefer.
- 'Keep the energy level high' – the leader should be alert, interested, involved, and demonstrate this with body movements; he or she should use humour, challenge and surprise.
- 'Use every member of your team' – verbose members should be thanked rather quickly after a contribution, their eyes avoided when inviting a response and if all else fails, talked to frankly; quiet members should be brought in.
- 'Do not manipulate your team' – whatever ideas of his or her own the leader may want to have adopted, he or she should work towards the group over solutions being reached; the leader's job is to keep them informed on their stage in the synectics process.
- 'Keep your eye on the client' – the person presenting the problem should be constantly referred to.
- 'Keep in mind that you are not permanent' – the leader is the servant of the group, and must keep lines of communication open and emphasize imagination and flexibility; assuming that traditional leaders accrue power and that everyone wants the role, the leadership should be rotated.

Synectics is both a problem-solving technique and a means of training people to be more creative. In utilizing so many of the conscious, preconscious and even unconscious psychological mechanisms of human ability it appears to stimulate hard work, spontaneity and a happy connection between the rational and the emotional. For these reasons some of its procedures carry lessons for us in the more strait-laced context of tertiary education.

Benefits

- taps subconscious mental processes, stimulates creative thinking, people work hard and intensively;
- provides clear procedures.

Drawbacks

- demands considerable skill and time;
- is unfamiliar to most – not usually germane to academic learning.

Groups with imported scenarios – games, simulations, role plays and case studies

There is a growing interest at all stages of education in methods that allow students to act out the problems and issues under discussion and make decisions about them based on a more personal understanding of their nature and implications. If we were to take a cynical view, this interest might be viewed as a response to the sense of alienation among students towards the learning of knowledge as if it existed independently of them and for purposes (eg, examinations) extrinsic to the knowledge itself. From a more positive standpoint the interest in games could result from a recognition that enactment of issues can serve to integrate even pedestrian knowledge into the framework of values, beliefs and personal behaviour of students. The medium for this 'gestalt' is the imagination, that faculty of mind so often written off because of its association with fun and the supposedly childish connotations that holds. The assumptions that underpin this argument were exposed early last century by Dewey (1916):

> *The difference between play and what is regarded as serious employment should not be a difference between the presence and absence of imagination, but a difference in the material with which the imagination is occupied. The result (of overlooking this) is an unwholesome exaggeration of the fantastic and 'unreal' phases of childish play and a deadly reduction of serious occupation to a routine efficiency prized simply for its external tangible results.*

It appears that among those students who get most out of games and simulations are those who are able to maintain a delicate balance between play and reality. They can commit themselves wholeheartedly to what they are continuously aware is an exploratory device, and the energy seems to be released through the creative interplay between fantasy and reality. The experience of games and simulations therefore brings a further meta-dimension to the experiential cycle, that of play, a factor that in a successful game with suitable players is likely to suffuse all parts of the cycle. It allows people to imitate and experiment safely with new behaviour in the context of a prepared situation and to gain instructive feedback on it in the knowledge that the boundaries between the imagined world and the real one are safe.

Games and simulations and their concomitant debriefing provide an excellent example of the experiential learning cycle in action. Before we discuss the games and simulations as techniques, a few definitions are called for.

The term *games* is usually taken to describe a group exercise in which players cooperate or compete towards a given end within a regime of explicit rules. Players behave as themselves (even if they do display exceptional behaviour at times). Cricket, chess and charades are obvious examples of popular games; educational games include 'The Colour Game' (six people with hidden agendas have to agree on a colour), 'Back to Back' (where a drawing is described so that a back-to-back partner can draw a copy) and 'Starpower' (players trade tokens to acquire power). Games are generally given no real-life context and people act as themselves.

Simulations are working representations of reality; they may be an abstracted, simplified or accelerated model of the process. They allow students to explore social or physical systems where the real things are too expensive, complex, dangerous, fast or slow for teaching purposes. A game may be transformed into a simulation by the addition of a specific context or scenario, which could vary from the highly complex ('virtual reality') to the outline that allows players space to invent their own details.

Role play involves people imagining that they are either themselves or someone else in a particular situation. They are asked to behave as they feel that person would, and to try behaviours that may not normally be part of their repertoire in order to broaden their sensitivity to, and understanding of, interpersonal problems. The role may be prescribed: 'You are the leader of a pressure group opposed to the siting of a new youth club on land adjacent to an old people's home', or self-defined where individuals are invited to enact a situation as themselves. Sometimes roles are written in the form of aims, eg, 'Your aim is, without revealing it, to become chair of this committee.'

Exercises are games, simulations and role plays stripped of their roles and scenarios. Participants work either in groups or individually on a task, eg devising a set of guidelines on how to write essays based on the pooled experience of the students. The source of information could be the participants themselves or resource material. In design-and-build exercises the participants typically have the task of constructing something with a given set of materials, such as a number of index cards or Lego pieces. In-tray exercises have participants working independently through a sequence of papers, each requiring a decision, and then comparing the results with what others have done.

Case studies are descriptions of a real-life event presented to illustrate special and/or general characteristics of a problem. They allow students to study quite complex problems that include elements that could not be contrived in a classroom simulation. Case studies have the advantage of depth and complexity, but involve a more distanced, second-hand style of learning. They can, however, incorporate role play where the problem is one that requires exploration of the dynamics of human interaction rather than armchair speculation.

Games and simulations

A game becomes a simulation when a scenario is provided – it thus constitutes a simplified representation of life. The scenario might be a public meeting, a classroom or a radio station. If play is not prescribed by rules then it is usually shaped by roles, as described above. What is called role play is often therefore an exercise in which interpersonal encounters can be explored with some degree of freedom. Whereas in games the interplay occurs within a pattern of clear and often artificial rules, in role play what happens is governed by the implicit rules of everyday life in a defined situation.

All of these definitions are a matter of degree and balance – combinations abound. It is possible, for instance, to have a simulation in which communication between groups is governed by rules, where the activity in the groups is determined by roles and where each group has a singular objective to fulfil in competition with the others. Most simulations are depicted in the diagrammatic model shown in Figure 6.12.

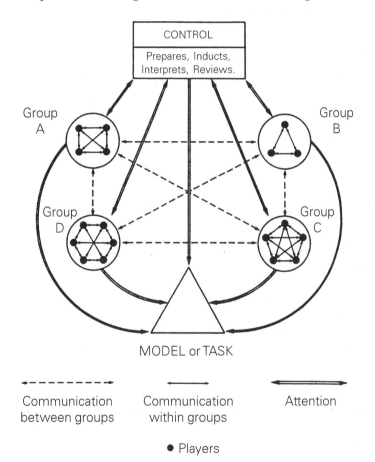

Figure 6.12 *Diagrammatic model of games and simulations*

The model in Figure 6.12 may be contracted or expanded to suit. As depicted here it comprises a number of groups – A, B, C and D – each with a goal and possibly a shared role (eg, a pressure group). The inter-group communication may replicate what happens in real life (eg, if there is a hierarchical relationship there might be more communication channels available 'downwards' than 'upwards'). The relations between each group may be ordained by roles. Each group's attention is focused on a model that may be a concrete object (eg, a 'Lego' town), or map, or an imagined problem scenario. The task of the tutor in a simulation/game is usually that of referee (though this may be delegated) who plays a benign 'god', and who supervises the setting up, smooth running and debriefing of the exercise. All of these operations require qualities often ascribed to a deity – prediction, an element of mystery, apparent control of the elements, the creation of ad hoc roles and rules, and a tendency to ignore requests.

Debriefing, the review of a game or simulation, is the most important part of the task educationally and should last for at least half the duration of the exercise itself in most cases. Abstract games often require double or triple this amount. This reflective discussion helps students to generalize from their particular experience and to think beyond the immediate experience. The following pattern for debriefing is one that seems to put the students' learning into perspective:

- How are you feeling right now? (Often this needs to be asked in order to tap some of the emotional charge of the exercise.)
- What was going on in the simulation? Who achieved what? What different perceptions were there of what happened? (These are particularly important questions to put when, by accident or design, a lot of intense feelings have been aroused.)
- What did you learn about yourself, each other, social groups, social systems, limitations of science and so forth?
- What did the simulation tell you about the 'real world'?
- How did it parallel the 'real world'?
- How could the simulation be improved?
- How is everyone feeling now?
- What might you do differently as a result of your experience in the simulation?

The debriefing discussion, though typically conducted as a plenary, can often be enlivened by dividing the class into sub-groups, especially ones whose membership cuts across the grouping in the simulation. Following the debriefing, the often loose and variable learning can be better tied up and consolidated with students in syndicates or task-oriented groups with activities like:

- Discuss and report back on generalized insights.
- Make links with learning from more traditional sources: lectures, reading, for instance.
- Or, if it can be video-recorded: use a video-playback to look at the whys and wherefores of interaction in the simulation (a step-by-step discussion works well here).

Games and simulations are considered to be particularly valuable in promoting social and professional skills such as communicating, role-taking, problem-solving, leading, decision-making and so on, not to speak of their less academic but more affecting function in opening the eyes of participants to what it feels like to be in someone else's position. Games and simulations are also claimed, with good justification, to increase the level of motivation and interest in the subject matter, develop a greater sense of self-awareness and personal power, and create a freer and more democratic climate. As for cognitive learning, apart from the impact of all the above in energizing the learning process, games and simulations can facilitate the understanding of relationships between separate areas of subject matter, particularly those where personal action is demanded. Nevertheless, without the consolidating effect of debriefing and further tasks, a lot of this learning may remain only half-realized.

The number of possible permutations of the game and simulation format is vast: as varied, one might suppose, as life itself. Ready-made and tested exercises with full instructions for the tutor/organizer are available from a variety of sources. Reference to these may be found in books such as Christopher and Smith (1991), Davison and Gordon (1978), Jones (1991), Krupar (1973), Pfeiffer and Jones (1972 through 1990) and Taylor and Walford (1972). The Society for the Advancement of Games and Simulations in Education and Training (SAGSET) includes many examples in its journal, *Simulations/Games for Learning*, and produces resource lists for different subject areas. Should readers want to design their own exercises, some helpful advice may be found in Davison and Gordon (1978), Chesler and Fox (1966), Jones (1988) and Stadsklev (1974). Such an exercise could come under any of the following categories, or combinations of them:

- public meeting;
- assessor's panel;
- communication network;
- competitive or cooperative interaction in group;
- committee role play;
- critical interactions role play;
- board game;
- in-tray exercise;
- card game (usually with Rummy rules).

Role play

Role play is usually taken to mean the enactment of an encounter or relationship, often within an agreed scenario, in order to get inside the human experience of a case or problem, and to practise some of the interpersonal skills required for its solution. It can illuminate and clarify at both the level of the original problem and what the particular 'players' bring of themselves into it; in other words to provide personal feedback. For role play is not just about acting: it reveals much about the real feelings and skills of those involved, and it is possibly this that makes it so threatening to some. But, run effectively, it is capable of realizing a set of rather special aims:

- developing sensitivity and awareness from first-hand experience;
- understanding and empathizing with other's perspectives;
- trying out new skills and behaviours;
- providing 'live' material for study by observers;
- integrating thought and feeling;
- testing out a model.

But who really plays roles in real life? Of course, we all do most of the time. To quote Shakespeare in *As You Like It*:

All the world's a stage,
And all the men and women merely players:
They have their exits and their entrances;
And one man in his time plays many parts.

Whether as teacher, student, parent, domestic partner, committee chair, or fund negotiator, we readily adopt a particular set of behaviours and attitudes, in so far as we have them in our repertoire, to meet the needs and expectations of the situation and the others involved. Where our repertoire is less than adequate, we may need practice, rehearsal, coaching and feedback in order to improve.

Many of the supposed problems can be overcome through the expertise and sensitivity of the trainer, and some of these are difficult to pinpoint with written guidelines and the like. In this section we will touch on a range of role play options, look at the role (sic) of the trainer in setting them up, supervising and debriefing them, and finally at a simple rubric for handling problems:

- don't start from here;
- use structures;
- choose interventions.

Role plays in context
It may be useful to view role plays as a part of a spectrum of simulated reality, bound less by rules than games, and with more freedom to explore personal feelings and behaviour. Games are played when one or more players compete or cooperate for payoffs, according to an agreed set of rules. Players behave as themselves (no roles) though they may well display exceptional behaviour. Games are designed so that success is achieved by the use of the materials to be learnt. Many games are abstract in that the materials are shapes, colours or numbers that have to be manipulated in some way. As a result the players can ascribe all sorts of meanings to the activity, so the games are capable of a rich variety of application.

Devising a role play
Ready-made role play exercises do exist. However, there will be occasions when you simply have to create your own exercise to suit particular purposes and consequently take the risk of improvising with groups of trainees. In so doing you may find the following points useful. Role play can take many forms and several of them can be, time permitting, combined in order to focus more clearly on particular areas. Some involve more risk and skill in handling than others.

Positional role play
The aim here is to explore differences created by social position, personal agenda and so on, in enacting a specific scenario, for example, in a dentist's chair where the patient is of higher status than the dentist; then repeating it where the patient is of lower status.

Psychodrama

Psychodrama usually involves more participants than a role play, and recreates a whole scene (eg, a classroom) rather than an interaction between two people (though there are various individual humanistic/personal development exercises that are also referred to as psychodramas). There is a 'director' who can call 'Cut!' and freeze the action. Participants can then be interviewed about their feelings, what they really want to do or say, etc. These revelations are heard in public and then the director calls 'Roll!' and the action continues. Psychodrama is particularly useful for examining what is going on in a situation familiar to the person who is the focus of it.

Alter ego

Each participant in the role play has another person standing behind them (possibly with hands on their shoulders) acting as the person's alter ego. The alter ego says out loud, and during the role play, what he or she thinks the person is really thinking or feeling, for example:

Participant: 'Oh hello! How very nice to see you again.'

Alter ego: 'Bloody hell! Not him again!'

Changing places

A variant of the alter ego device occurs when one of the observers chooses to take an active part in the role play (this procedure having been agreed beforehand) by tapping one of the players on the shoulder and taking his or her place. This can be useful where it is becoming obvious that someone is getting 'bogged down' or there seems to be another way of handling the situation in the role play.

Fishbowl

All games and simulations, but especially role plays, may be run by a small group with everyone else watching or with a set of small groups all running simultaneously. Sometimes it may help to enact a role play in a fishbowl situation before inviting small groups to follow suit.

Role briefs

Briefs are valuable in enabling inexperienced 'players' to get into role; they may not be necessary where players are familiar with the simulated situation and its *dramatis personae*. Briefs should not be over-elaborate or caricatures. Extreme or clichéd personality traits allow too little scope for personal interpretation or unpredictability of outcomes. Too much detail makes the role too difficult to play and constrains outcomes. Briefs should contain some information about what it is reasonable for the person to know (and feel) about the other roles in the role play.

Role perspectives

Often we are not looking so much at how individual role players perform as understanding issues and weighing the odds. Here, groups in the class are asked either to take the perspective of particular groups or to identify with one of the players, following which they may elect a spokesperson or simply ad lib their interaction with the other groups. This approach may also be used to rehearse role players in preparation for a role play in the round (see Fishbowl).

Scenario

It is the scenario that turns a disembodied role play into a simulation role play. Such contextual information is valuable and can substitute for detail in role briefs. Some scenarios about the motives of the 'players' and the nature of the social processes or practical procedures operating can be very useful. Again, too much detail can be counter-productive. Extensive scenarios emphasize the simulation/case study aspect at the expense of personal involvement in the role play.

Role reversal

When a role play is to be used to look at a problem situation presented by one of the participants, it can be useful to invite that person, having described the situation, to play one or more of the other parties, especially those he or she is having most difficulty with. Presenters of the problem thus have an opportunity to experience what it might be like to be the other person coping with them!

Presented roles

Rather than presenting a problem in the form of a written case study, it can be performed by a well-prepared, role-playing contributor so that it can be viewed more holistically. The use of simulated patients at MacMaster University is a well-known example of this genre.

Concurrent role plays

Rather than everyone performing in public view, role plays can be organized to occur simultaneously in a set of groups, each one having clearly delegated responsibility for keeping to a time schedule and with the possibility of repeat enactments as roles are rotated in each group. For example, in role play involving job interviews, one could have groups of four: two interviewers, one candidate and an observer/timekeeper, working on a schedule of 5 minutes preparation, 15 minutes interview and 10 minutes debriefing, rotating roles every 30 minutes.

Behaviour roles

Very often in real-life situations people find themselves inexorably drawn into a particular role or behaviour pattern vis-à-vis others, for instance in a team meeting where one person might always leave it to others to decide, another may always feel responsible for what happens, etc. With behaviour roles people are asked to adopt a different, specified role (eg, clarifier, leader, questioner, challenger, ideas person) possibly allocated randomly via cards; and of course they can choose not to reveal it to the others. This can be particularly useful training for an under-functioning team.

Observers

Observers can use checklists: either related to general models of skill development (eg, Rogers' (1983) principles of non-directiveness) or related to specific issues to do with the content of the role play (either agreed upon or provided by the counsellor). Observers can time and stop role plays. Observers can be assigned to each participant in the role play, or each have a different observer brief. Observers can chair debriefings.

Time out

Any participant can temporarily halt a role play – because they are stuck, distressed, or because an idea has struck them that they want to explore immediately. Everyone could move in clusters to a physically separate space and discuss the issue or problem. All then return to the role play, either starting from the point at which time out was called, or from an earlier point. Time out can be used to review strategies, to try different ways of approaching a particularly difficult moment, or to give different people the chance to cope with this moment.

Structured debriefing

When the students work in autonomous groups, the debriefing can be held in the separate groups, with the tutor handling only the final discussion:

1. All reflect in silence and prepare comments.
2. The 'client' makes uninterrupted comments.
3. The 'counsellor' makes uninterrupted comments.
4. The 'observer' makes uninterrupted comments.
5. All discuss the role play.
6. Reality exercise – what has all that to do with the real world?
7. All discuss general conclusions without referring to details of the role play.

De-roling

It is important for the tutor to de-role participants thoroughly before debriefing, lest they be left unsettled and anxious, especially if they have been deeply involved in the experience. There are three necessary steps for getting out of the character. Each person in turn involved says:

1. As (the role-played character's name) I was . . . (the qualities you portrayed).
2. As (own name) I am like (the character's name) in this respect . . .
3. As (own name) I am . . . (all different qualities from the character).

Role play when watched by others can sometimes be a bit threatening to participants. In a sense they are on stage and the rest of the group or class is watching them. Gibbs (1984) describes a peer learning method in which participants, working in tutorless sub-groups, take full responsibility for their own role play and debriefing. For the scenario described above, for example, the roles of tutor, student and observer(s) would be designated and rotated in groups of three for as many cycles as needed. The observer(s) would be responsible for the time boundaries and the debriefing.

Simulations in context

It is sometimes said that games and simulations are manipulative in that they constrain people to behave according to the designer's model of reality, with all its attendant values. This is an indisputable danger, but can readily be countered through a proper debriefing in which such issues are brought out.

Games and simulations can, as may already be apparent, be used within a scheduled group meeting or at a specially convened, extended, session. As such they can be of great value as a stimulus for further discussion or in illuminating particular issues. Alternatively, they may be used to bind together the disintegrated elements of a course either in the form of a grand finale or by constructing the whole course as a 'partial' simulation in which students participate only at certain scheduled times and otherwise work on tasks demanded by or related to the simulation. For the imaginative teacher there is no end to the possible variations in the style and scope of games, role plays and simulations.

Benefits

- experience is first-hand and concentrated;
- motivation intrinsic to activity, learning well retained, high level of interest;
- removes teacher/student polarization;
- learning occurs at sundry levels.

Drawbacks

- time-consuming, can demand a lot of preparation;
- some students don't or won't participate, colleagues regard games as trivial;
- materials often expensive, learning unpredictable and difficult to evaluate;
- dangers of hurtful stress in some, especially where not carefully handled by tutor.

As a footnote, readers may like to know that three publications, Lewis and Mee (1981), Jaques in Cryer (1982) and van Ments (1983) give clear counsel to tutors in the handling of role play and similar 'experiential' exercises.

Case studies (L)

A standard technique of teaching in management and business studies, the case study is in a sense a kind of simulation of a real-life situation in which the experience is second-hand and probably condensed. The important merit of the case study is that it allows a problem to be studied in a complex form, including elements of real-life events it might be impossible to reproduce in the classroom. Typically the students are provided with case notes in advance and are expected to prepare their own solution to the problem or problems presented. Case studies open up opportunities for role play, where it becomes necessary to shed light on particular encounters rather than general issues. In some ways, case studies have the edge on simulations in that students are not tempted to trivialize;

there is, however, little of the sense of risk-free competition and personal involvement that appears to be an inherent part of games and simulations.

The main virtue of case studies is the way in which they can efficiently integrate a wide diversity of subject matter. They are mainly used in applied social sciences, but there is no reason why they should not be used to advantage in science and engineering, for instance in respect of socially related issues and design failures. The Open University 'Open' files of written material on their technology foundation and man-made futures courses are excellent examples of this approach. Case studies can also be used as examination questions in order to test a student's power of synthesis (Easton, 1982).

In problem-based learning, case studies are the driving force behind students' independent study: their learning is to a large extent dependent on the quality of cases presented to them. Dolmans *et al* (1997) propose seven principles for the design of case studies:

1. The contents of the case should adapt well to the students' prior knowledge.
2. A case should contain several cues that stimulate students to elaborate.
3. If possible the case should provide a context that is relevant to the future profession.
4. Relevant basic sciences concepts should be presented in the context of a clinical problem to encourage integration of knowledge.
5. A case should stimulate self-directed learning by encouraging students to generate learning issues and conduct literature searches.
6. A case should enhance students' interest in the subject matter, by sustaining discussion about possible solutions and facilitating students to explore alternatives.
7. A case should match one or all of the faculty objectives.

They have based these principles on findings from research on learning and cognition and argue that 'the design of cases should no longer be exclusively centred on experience-based knowledge, but can and should also be centred on evidence-based knowledge'.

Benefits

- integrative – encourages a 'broad view';
- develops a sense of objectivity;
- demands tolerance of several points of view.

Drawbacks

- requires some maturity and prior experience of students;
- makes heavy demands on the tutor in holding the discussion together;
- can be time-consuming.

Independent learning in groups

Syndicates (L)

A dilemma that commonly faces tutors in seminars is how to exercise control over the content while at the same time giving students room to express their own ideas in their own terms; to a great extent this is resolved in syndicate learning. The technique is described by Collier (1968, 1969, 1983). The students in small tutorless groups (five to six members in each) are given joint assignments that require reading, discussion and written work. The tutor's first task is to prepare the assignments; these may cover the same ground as a lecture course and comprise a developing sequence of questions and references. Here, by way of illustration, is part of one of the assignments Collier describes as it is presented to the students.

Organization structure: principles of interpretation

1. What are the characteristics of the 'organic' and 'mechanistic' forms of organization described by Burns and Stalker? In what circumstances does each have advantages?
2. What features of the organization of Plant Y under Messrs Stewart and Cooley's methods of administration do not come within Burns and Stalker's analysis? See:
    - Burns and Stalker: The Management of Innovation, Chapters 5 and 6.
    - Revans: Standard for Morale, Chapters 1, 8, 9 and 10
    - Guest: Organizational Change, Chapters 2 and 5
    - Thelen: Dynamics of Groups Work, Chapter 4.

Some assignments may be considered sufficiently important to be worked on by all the syndicates on behalf of the class as a whole. The students distribute the reading, discussion and writing tasks among themselves with the groups, and meet during what would otherwise be a lecture period to work on the tasks, while the tutor circulates among them. Plenary discussions are held at various points during the course. The collection of student views emerges in either a written or an oral report; dissenting opinions, where they arise, are included. The tutor summarizes the reports in a formal lecture, suggesting any changes and improvements in the work produced and extending ideas beyond the students' material where appropriate. A final plenary session follows.

The students are thus given both the security of specific content and a clear task, and the freedom to exercise their own skills and judgement in analysing and synthesizing information. Collier claims that syndicate learning cuts across any of the fundamental assumptions about teaching and learning that the educational system may have established in the students. The students are placed in a situation where, in the first instance, they form views derived from their reading and experience and from discussion with their peers, rather than from the teacher. The students form bonds within their syndicates, which give them some support in the face of the teacher's authority. The relations are no longer controlled by the naked confrontation of the teacher with a number of separate individuals and can thus become more easily personal and informal.

In this way, whereas the tutor's authority in respect of discipline and procedures within the group is either ignored, or rejected, his or her authority as subject expert is, if not intact, a separate issue to be treated on its own merits. This may of course raise problems for some students who find it difficult to function in groups without the guiding hand of a tutor, but it is equally possible that it is liberating to those students who have problems in expressing themselves freely in the presence of a tutor. Syndicate learning also appears to combine the two ingredients of high motivation – competition between groups with the consequent cohesion and purpose within them. There is nevertheless a tight prescription of task, and the boundaries of knowledge are firmly controlled.

Benefits

- combines control of content with freedom in discussion;
- authority is clearly delegated, groups take pride in achievement, work harder;
- disparate knowledge is integrated.

Drawbacks

- not all students able to cope in tutorless groups;
- discrepancy between kind of learning and assessment methods;
- overall control of what is learnt tends to be non-negotiable.

Peer tutoring

It is clear that a lot of teaching is done in courses by the students themselves – perhaps more than many teachers would wish to recognize. In laboratory groups, for example, it is quite common to see students explaining points to each other and helping one another over basic misconceptions and more advanced problems. Not quite so apparent is the mutual help and support that exist outside the curriculum in the refectory, the halls of residence or in the library.

Peer tutoring is a way of harnessing these valuable processes within the bounds of the curriculum. According to Goldschmid and Goldschmid (1976), it can be supported on the following grounds:

- socio-psychological – it offers close personal contact in an otherwise remote environment;
- pedagogical – students are active as learners, teaching enhances learning for the 'student tutor', and there is increased cooperation, motivation and self-esteem;
- economic – a saving on staff time and energy;
- political – it helps students effectively adjust to the curriculum as a 'system'.

Examples of different models of peer tutoring are:

- senior students acting as regular seminar leaders;
- 'proctors' who help test and guide more junior students through a programme of individualized instruction;
- self-directed student groups;
- the learning cell, in which students in pairs alternately ask and answer questions on commonly read material;
- 'parrainage' (or sponsorship), where older students counsel new students, firstly over practical matters to do with settling in, and later over study problems.

Because they have long been trained in the passive 'reception of information' and in 'success through competition', students may need to be inducted to the academic and social skills necessary for peer tutoring. Moreover, not all students will be suited to the role of peer tutor and in some of the above schemes care may have to be exercised in both role choice and training. In others, everyone will perforce be involved in the operation. For further reading on peer tutoring see Boud (1981) and Cornwall (1979).

Students can also practise a form of peer tutoring in learning teams – groups of four to six, which have the following tasks:

- to maximize the learning of its members;
- to provide the incentive, the opportunity and the ability for its members to learn;
- to learn about teamwork through the conscious experience of working in a team;
- to develop the ability of its members to work in a team;
- to organize tasks and roles for each learning activity within an agreed set of rules;
- to rotate tasks and roles so that each member has a range of experiences;
- to monitor, and report on, their individual and collective progress.

The role of the teacher with learning teams is to negotiate appropriate rules to provide team training for the sharing of group tasks and opportunities.

The activity of learning from each other does not, of course, have to be initiated by a tutor. Donaldson and Topping (1996) have written a do-it-yourself manual for students who do not have, or do not want 'peer-assisted learning' to be organized for them, but are interested in the benefits of it in an informal, self-managed way.

Benefits

- students actively involved – learn by teaching;
- integration of students into course facilitated;
- inexpensive.

Drawbacks

- students require training – needs regular monitoring;
- not all students good at it;
- may demand constant staff supervision for success.

Computer-mediated discussion

The nature of discussion through computer-mediated communication, whether on an e-mail list server or through a Web bulletin board, is that the interaction is 'asynchronous', and that responses are not necessarily spontaneous and usually receive a little editing as they evolve. This may suit some people more than others, especially those who find it difficult to contribute in a face-to-face group or to improvise their ideas as they talk. As for all group work there has to be a demand for cooperative work built into the course. Sometimes the demand can be force of circumstances such as described by English and Yasdani (1999) – a distance learning module for which e-mail was the only medium through which the students could communicate, or where it is part of a process of collaborative work in writing group reports for assessment. Where students have regular daily contact they are likely to view it as an added extra.

The role of the tutor can be critical to the success of the group: individual members or the whole group can just 'fade away' without any evident reason. Typically the tutor would oversee and regularly monitor the discussion and make stimulating and supportive interventions, as well as mediating when things are not going as they should be. Equally it may be necessary to assign team members with specific responsibilities (Parry and Dunn, 1999).

The timing of discussion can be a significant factor too. The groups can agree to 'meet' to discuss a topic at a specified date and time and submit their comments within a particular time frame, or the discussion can run for weeks with students and tutor opening up whenever is convenient to them (Toohey, 1999).

Benefits

- students are unable to see each other and are less likely to make biased judgements of others' opinions based on age/appearance/cultural background, etc;
- shy members can join in without being identified or feeling threatened;
- there is time to reflect during a 'conversation', thus helping to clarify and sharpen thinking;
- it can help improve writing skills as well as providing more ready-made material for written assignments.

Drawbacks

- it is easy to misconstrue what others intended to communicate because body language and sub-verbal communication is not accessible;
- it favours those who can type quickly if there's live dialogue going on;
- writing may not come so easily for some as talking spontaneously.

Projects

Put simply, a project is a learning task in which the students have a choice of topic and direction and whose outcome is therefore unpredictable. It demands initiative, creativity and organizing skills of the students: they are required to produce a report, plan or design that comprises the solution to a problem. In pursuit of this goal the students have a considerable amount of time to develop their own learning strategies according to where the project takes them and generally rely on a supportive relationship with a tutor/supervisor.

Projects thus involve a comprehensively different philosophy of learning from that of the traditional group discussion method. Students are responsible (to a greater or lesser extent) for the direction and range of the work they undertake, which may carry them beyond the tutor's own area of subject expertise either in breadth or depth. Consequently projects are likely to create all manner of anxieties in both tutor and students as to direction, progress and personal competence. Various studies of project work (Jaques, 1980, 1981; SRHE, 1975) show a fairly consistent pattern of events. Goodlad (1978) summarizes these in *Improving Teaching in Higher Education*:

> *Firstly, students should be actively involved in the choice of the subject; this increases their involvement with the task. Secondly, the student should be encouraged to discover for himself the implications of the constraints of conceptual fruitfulness in the discipline, availability of resources (library information) or institutional arrangement. It is a delicate task for the tutor to strike a balance between over-direction of a student's work (which can destroy the distinctive benefits of project methods) and under-direction (which can lead the student into muddle and frustration). Thirdly, some teachers have found that student's enthusiasm is closely related to the production of documents – high at the beginning (when an outline and bibliography are being prepared) and at the end (when the final presentation is being fabricated), but low to the point of despair during the period of gestation. It has been found wise to arrange an input of teaching (presentation of ideas at a seminar, brainstorming sessions, simulations, discussion of rough draft, etc) in the middle of the lifespan of a project and just at the beginning.*

Group projects present students with two additional problems. One is that the choice of partners is often confused with the choice of topic and tutor, and this may be too much for students to unravel – a bit like choosing who to marry and where to work at the same time! It is not unusual to find a group project resolving itself into a collection of individual, if related, tasks.

One procedure for tackling this problem was operated at the City University, in electrical engineering (Edwards, 1980), where groups are organized as follows:

1. Topics of interest to the class are listed.
2. The topics are whittled down, through discussion, to a small number.
3. Each student ranks the topics in order of personal preference.
4. The course tutor then allocates topics to students according to these preferences: the groups are thus constituted.
5. Tutors' names are not revealed or allocated till the groups are established.

On the other hand it might be preferable to allow the project to emerge as an expression of the combined interests of pre-selected groups. The tutor in this case might, having formed the groups, give them a file of papers covering a range of issues and then assist them in the formulation of a problem to be solved. Of course this presupposes there is no 'hassle' about who teams up with whom. Either the grouping must be done arbitrarily according to some principle (eg, random selection or heterogeneous mix) or the students must take part in a team-building exercise.

The second problem about group projects arises both logically and psychologically out of the first. Notwithstanding the use of a clarifying procedure for selecting topics and projects, it may in many circumstances be too much to ask a group.

Several 'Files' or 'Case Studies' have been produced by the Open University on problematical issues, as 'supplementary' material to their course units. They allow students to handle both the uncertainties of project work and the problems of working in a team concurrently. Tutors at Delft in Holland offer their project students in town planning a prior training course in group dynamics and teamwork. However, prior training has to be followed up with procedures for monitoring the unfolding progress of the group if it is to be of enduring benefit. If learning about teamwork is one of the critical aims of the project then students might learn much through monitoring the group process, not merely about the personal and collective problems of teamwork, but of their priorities as individual learners. Various checklists and exercises in Chapters 9 and 10 should be of help in this respect.

Gibbs (1995), in three manuals entitled *Learning in Teams*, provides a stack of useful exercises and guidelines for both tutors and students involved in project teams. He particularly emphasizes the importance of team building, organizing the schedules, allocating tasks, monitoring progress and for students to accept that teamwork is never easy. The section headings pretty well summarize all that needs to happen in effective group projects:

> What it's all for
> Forming a team
> Developing a team
> Sharing and organizing the work
> Making meetings work
> Being creative
> Spotting and sorting out problems
> Reporting
> Planning your next team

How the group organizes itself and, in may ways as important, how it communicates with the tutor has been addressed by Yamane (1997), who tackles problems in a project group by assigning members one of four possible roles:

1. President/discussion leader who keeps the group on task by developing an agenda and using it to structure meetings.
2. Scribe/recorder who keeps minutes of each meeting (paying particular attention to work assigned to members) and distributes the record to the rest of the group.
3. Coordinator who considers each student's submitted work and class share deals, as well as ongoing conversation with them to identify regular meeting times and places.
4. Intermediary who periodically meets one-on-one with the tutor to report on his or her group's progress and to answer instructor questions about how the group is working as a team.

The keeping of a group diary or logbook could also help in forming the basis of a commentary on the work of the project to be submitted, but not assessed, with the project report. If, on the other hand, the students are being asked about teamwork issues 'the hard way', one may wish to give them some help with their programming of the work – it is all a matter of time and priorities. A more elaborate form of the diary idea is the portfolio: 'a permanent record of a personal journey' and 'a basis for continuing reflection' (Boud *et al*, 1985).

The portfolio can include ideas, pictures, cuttings and reflective comments on these. It works best when treated as confidential or when students are permitted to withhold those parts they wish to keep confidential.

Projects offer students a unique chance to develop skills and capacities that might never be apparent in other kinds of learning. They give students feedback on their ability to handle freedom in relation to the constraints of the outside world, to cope with real problems and, if all goes well, to build up a continuing interest in them beyond the completion of their studies. The learning potential of projects is therefore enormous. Group projects add the further benefits of pooling resources, division of labour and the enjoyment of interpersonal learning.

The economy of supervising a group can be another bonus for the busy tutor: four students seen as a group can take much less time than meeting with each individually, as of course does the marking of one report rather than four. But even better for educational and not just time management purposes is for groups to supervise each other, possibly with a list of starter questions, and to provide a record of these meetings in their final report. The learning potential of peer supervision for both groups is of course vast.

However, assessment, yet again, presents a problem. It is very difficult to compare one student with another when the report is the result of a group effort. Students differ in their skills, their rates and levels of working, and their styles of learning. Who is to say the student who held them together and constantly inspired the group yet contributed nothing to the report should receive no academic reward?

Two assessment schema in use for dealing with this problem are shown in Chapter 9. It makes sense for a group project to be assessed according to criteria that demand a cooperative effort and that these criteria should be clearly negotiated with the group near the start of the project or, at the very least, before irrevocable decisions are made. Gibbs and Habeshaw (1989) give a clear example of an assessment pro forma that requires a project group to distribute its tutor-determined grade to members of the group according to their individual contributions. (This is explained in more detail in Chapter 9.)

A clear step forward in clarifying goals, relationships and responsibilities in project work is the use of a learning contract. Knowles (1975 and 1986) describes contracts for self-directed learning that are evolved through a set of class discussions. The contract comprises learning goals, strategies and sources, evidence of accomplishment and criteria and means of measuring accomplishment. Heron (1981) proposes a scheme for self-monitoring and assessment which, though less clearly prescribed, is clearly worth considering in projects where one of the critical aims is for students to learn about themselves as learners. The tutor's (as supervisor's) role in promoting group experiences in project work is of course considerable. If students are to gain full benefit from working together there must be a demand in the project design for collective effort, training opportunities for the students in teamwork, a clear monitoring of the students' team dynamics and an assessment that emphasizes group effort. Each of these features requires leadership from the tutor, but external to the group: in other words a clear definition of authority and boundaries (see Chapter 1). Further reading on the role of the project tutor may be found in Jaques (1987, 1989).

The kind of learning that can be achieved in project work, given commitment, energy and imagination from all concerned, is potentially vast in both variety and depth. Our understanding of the processes and their scope, nevertheless, has a long way to go.

Benefits

- freedom to study in depth and breadth;
- chance to tackle real problems, provide solutions that can be tested in 'real world';
- learning active, comprehensive challenge to students.

Drawbacks

- things can go radically wrong;
- challenge and freedom may prove too much for some students – some tutors not able to function in non-directive role or outside area of subject expertise, assessment may be a problem.

Why have variety?

The methods we have discussed are certainly far from comprehensive and new frameworks and variations are being created every day in the life of an active group; yet they do embody a multitude of principles and procedures for group work, many of which might be combined or used in sequence. Their inclusion within the repertoire of a tutor may prevail. Yet, if for the following reasons only, the value of acquiring a repertoire of tasks and group activities seems compelling:

- Students' learning styles vary, and implicit in each of the activities described is a different approach to learning (Gardner, 1993; Ramsden in Marton *et al*, 1984).
- Most students need variety of stimulus and experience because of spans of concentration, as well as activating the various learning modalities in each.
- As students develop intellectually and emotionally, a change in their relationship to knowledge and its 'agent', the teacher, is necessary (Perry, 1970).
- It is possible to cast the teaching and learning net over a wider range of learning outcomes than would otherwise be feasible.
- Students who have experienced a variety of approaches to learning and to human interaction are more likely to achieve increased choice and awareness in ways of working in later life.
- It is impossible to predict the way any teaching/teaming interaction will go: a tutor therefore needs to be adaptable and resourceful to maintain interest and momentum.

■ In making choices and exercising a wider range of skills the tutor becomes more alert.
■ Evaluative feedback is easier: students can make critical remarks with less embarrassment when the tutor is not too closely identified with any one procedure.

Many of the various methods proposed in this chapter can of course be combined, embedded or linked with each other. Two project groups could 'fishbowl' on each other; a seminar could open with a round or a buzz group; a role play could take place in a 'fishbowl' format. In order to make such combinations work, tutors and students have both to be 'planful' and flexible: ready with the resources and techniques to ensure an activity is possible and flexible enough to introduce it at a different stage than intended or to modify it to suit the occasion. Becoming skilled in a variety of tasks and learning activities is as important as being resourceful in any specific situation, and that involves a few process skills. How do we handle the knotty problems? Can we recognize the part we are playing in any interaction? Are we able to find time, space and a clear head to make decisions about what to do and when to do it? We shall make some progress towards answering these questions in the next chapter.

Exercises

1. Arranging the furniture

Figure 6.13 shows several possible arrangements of furniture in a classroom. Each chair with a 'T' in it represents a tutor.

1. Working individually for five minutes, each person thinks about the configurations and ask themselves:
    – What kind of interaction might these promote?
    – What task might you give the participants?
    – How do you think they might respond?
    – What improvements or alternatives can you suggest?
2. Now, groups of three for 15 minutes, take each configuration in turn and discuss each person's ideas for it.
3. Now, groups devise one new configuration with a suggested task and each person draws a sketch of it, possibly on a flipchart.
4. Finally, either in a plenary forum with a flipchart or through crossover groups, each group's idea should be presented, with any provisos.
5. Finally, each person completes the following sentences in a group round:
    – One arrangement I could use is . . .
    – I could do the following things with it . . .
    – I think the problems of using might be . . .
    – I reckon I could overcome those by . . .
6. Reverse the inner and outer groups for a re-run as needed.

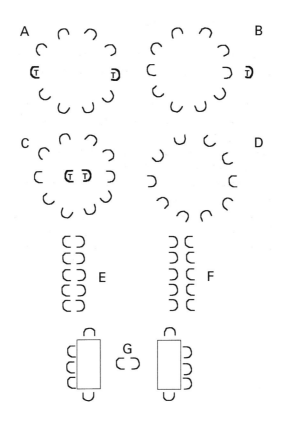

Figure 6.13 *Arranging the furniture*

2. Group activities

Choose five of the group activities described in this chapter and indicate what problems these might address. Use Table 6.1 to mark each 1, 2 or 3 according to how confident you feel in running it and add comments in relation to that.

3. Problems in groups

Problems in groups are notoriously difficult to pin down, but if they are not dealt with speedily they may become part of a pattern of the group culture that is hard to shift. What can you do to anticipate or tackle them as they arise? This exercise is designed to pick out some of the common problems and develop solutions from your own resources.

Task 1. Working by yourself, write down in the left-hand column as many problems or tricky situations that seem to occur in your groups. Do not at this stage fill in the right-hand column. (3–5 mins)

Confidence

Problem	Group activity/task to be tried	1	2	3	Comments

Task 2. In groups, conduct a group 'round' to share what you have written down: one item per person in turn on a 'top-slicing' basis (each takes the top of the remaining items on the list each time round).

Task 3. Plenary session: each group in turn calls out a problem/incident to be listed on the board/screen (this can be omitted).

Task 4. In groups, each person chooses a particular problem/incident to address and has a five-minute slot in which to solicit the help of the group in coming up with solutions. This requires one or two members of the group to act as 'consultant' to each 'client' in turn, which will mean listening, clarifying and helping the client to come up with solutions of his or her own. Others may act as timekeeper and peer assessor. The facilitator may wish to model the consultant role, and also remind participants of Task 6.

Task 5. Plenary session: each group contributes, in turn, a chosen problem and the proposed solutions, a different group member contributing each time round. *Or* each group receives and reads the list of possible solutions and the facilitator checks out any unsolved problems.

Task 6. Group 'crossover', ie each group numbers its members and all the ones, all the twos, all the threes, etc, get together so that there are new groups with a mix of members from the previous groups. The task now is to conduct a self-assessment, completing the sentences: 'What I did well as a consultant . . .' and, 'What I could improve on . . .', then to compare this with the peer assessment.

Problem/incident	Possible solution/intervention

3. Non-verbal communication

Organize the group into a fishbowl, the outer group to observe the inner one. Give the inner one a suitable task, eg discuss what you think this group is best suited for or agree an appropriate slogan for the group. For a given time (eg, 20 minutes) the outer group is asked to watch for and record non-verbal behaviour in:

- getting attention;
- expressing agreement;
- expressing disagreement;

- emphasizing;
- showing puzzlement or confusion;
- stopping someone;
- cutting in.

They should also look for any variations according to sex, order of speaking, position in the group, etc.

The outer group, still in position, then feeds back what they observed, particularly picking out differences between members. They should be especially conscious of the need for sensitivity in giving this feedback and of the principles described on pages 66–67.

Discussion points

- List as many group tasks as you can that might encourage people to understand and apply the ideas in this book.
- Draw up a chart of the various learning activities described in this chapter according to aims, tutor's role, special skills, etc.
- What would you look for as evidence of success for each of the techniques described? Why?
- Take the group methods described in this chapter and list the principles of group behaviour that each seems to embody.

7 | The tutor's job

He asks us questions and then answers them himself. At the beginning of the course we all waved our hands in the air like fools. No more. We get in there, put on our pleasant masks, and go to sleep.

(Tiberius, 1999)

By the end of this chapter you can expect to feel better prepared for leading a group and have a wider repertoire of effective interventions in promoting lively group discussion.

Whatever good intentions we may have, they are often difficult to put into effect even where we know what is necessary to achieve them. In the process of realizing our aims we may find ourselves stuck in patterns of communication and interaction that fail to unleash the full energy and potential of a group.

To write about the practice of skills in groups is in some ways self-contradictory in that it is making 'content' out of 'process'. Nevertheless, in this chapter, I propose to offer some specific ideas about what the tutor, and in turn the students, might positively do to enhance the effectiveness of group learning. In some cases the tutor may choose to keep a low profile and merely respond to the ferment of discussion at suitable times.

While many of the variables affecting behaviour are ephemeral and even capricious, there are some that the tutor can influence, if not control, by decisions taken before the group actually meets. In acting in this more strategic way, knowledge and understanding of group dynamics and of the characteristics of the particular group may suffice. For tactical purposes, however, the more elusive qualities of skill and sensitivity are demanded, and these cannot be acquired without some training, practice and reflection.

Preparation

As the organizer of a group meeting or a series of meetings, the tutor has an opportunity to influence the course of events in at least three areas of decision: group size, group membership and the physical conditions in which the group meets. The tutor might also wish to plan for possible exigencies and prepare a small list of self-questions to ask such as, 'What am I trying to achieve and what do I have to do to achieve it?' (see Chapter 5) and 'What courses of action should I be prepared for?' (see Chapter 6 for some possibilities).

Though we often tend to make such decisions alone, there is a lot to be said for drawing on a friendly colleague's help to check out our thoughts. If this can be done happily and on a reciprocal basis, then so much the better. Care taken in the preparatory work can reap many later rewards and pre-empt several of the common problems of learning groups.

Group size

The number of students in each group has a profound influence on the kind of interaction that can be attained. The smaller the size, the greater is the likelihood of trust, close relationships and consonance of aims among members. These advantages may, however, be offset by the lack of variety and the greater probability of a 'poor mix'. In the larger group, although a better mix and a more favourable student/staff ratio may be achieved, a sense of competition and a greater differentiation of role might be expected to occur. Not only does the opportunity for each member to contribute diminish in inverse ratio to the number of people in the group, but the discrepancy in level of participation between high and low contributors is disproportionately greater. There are thus quite significant differences in the style, frequency and length of spoken contributions, not to speak of non-verbal behaviour in groups of three to six compared with those of 12 to 15 students.

If timetablers and course tutors have not already determined the size of group for us, we might ask ourselves the following questions:

- What is the optimum range of group size, socially and educationally, for a given set of aims and tasks (assuming we can predict these)?
- What, apart from learning outcomes, do I hope the groups will achieve socially?
- What mix of sex, nationality, age, etc, do I want to have?
- Do I intend or need to be present as tutor with all the groups all the time?
- What limitations does the meeting room(s) impose on the total group size and the kinds of activities possible?
- How does it all fit into the scheme for the whole course?

Figure 7.1 may give some indications of the dimensions to be taken into account.

Although decisions about group size may be predicated upon several variable factors, more often than not the tutor will be stuck with two fixed ones: the total number of students and the room in which they meet. However, with a little initiative, we can, whether with six students or 96, create a variety of group sizes for different purposes. For instance, it is possible by pairing the students, to encourage the sharing and development of half-formed or tentative ideas, the airing of anxieties, or merely to provide a break in the pattern of participation.

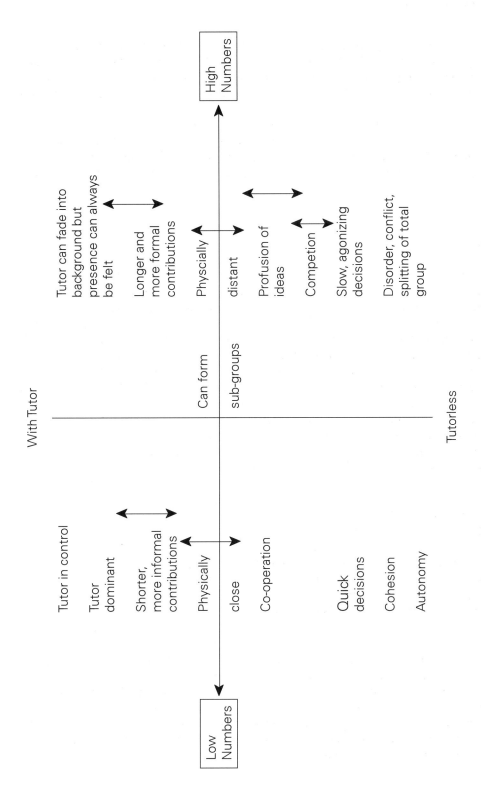

Figure 7.1 *Characteristics of groups in relation to size and tutor's influence*

Note: The short arrows indicate possible variations of that characteristic on the chart

In many ways the size of total group most amenable to a variety of aims and techniques is 20 to 30. In recent years this sort of number has achieved popularity in management and teacher training as the most suitable for workshops. Workshop formats allow a variety of group techniques to be practised. Apart from the universal facility of organizing dyads, they provide for either three to five groups of 6 to 18 with or without a tutor, or plenary sessions; workshops thus combine the advantages of small and large group experience.

Group membership

The way in which students are assigned to groups likewise depends on the purposes, both educational and social. As a general rule a heterogeneous mix of students in each group provides the best chemistry for interaction and achievement of task. Such qualities as age, sex, nationality and personality can be taken into account. One procedure for accomplishing effective mixes is as follows:

1. Divide the total number of students by the possible number of groups to estimate the rough size of each group.
2. Decide on criteria that might be used to differentiate one student from another, for example sex, age, background, expressed interest, exam results, nationality.
3. Go through all the notes and assign a code to each according to these criteria – A, B, C, etc.
4. Then, starting with group 1, take one person from each of A, B, C, etc, until this group's complement is made up. Repeat this if the complement is more than the number of qualities. Do the same for the other groups. Finally, check that each group has a similar mix and adjust if not.

Intellectual differences may also be taken into account. If the main purpose of discussion is to solve problems or to clarify or elaborate matters that have already received attention, then there are both commonsensical and research reasons (Amaria *et al*, 1969) why it may be wise to mix the better progressed or more quick-thinking students with those who are either behind with their work or slower thinking. Provided the given task demands cooperation, the former will find themselves teaching the latter. In this way we can kill two birds with one stone: the quicker students learn the subject matter themselves and the slower ones are provided with the opportunity to query misconceptions without embarrassment. Suddenly there are as many 'tutors' as students.

It would be a mistake, however, to think of group composition solely in terms of individual qualities. Of equal concern is the sociometry or likely pattern of emotional links among the members (where these can be known beforehand). In every group, personal likes and dislikes for fellow members soon begin to grow and can have an important influence on the way the group functions. Again, research and common sense tell us that people tend to agree with the individuals they like and disagree with those they dislike, even though both might express the same opinion.

Cliques may present another problem. There are good reasons for separating groups of students who have such close affinity with each other that they form an exclusive sub-group that could easily destroy the cohesive fabric of the larger group. On the other hand, there may be pairs or threesomes who somehow trigger or inspire each other in more productive ways. The tutor needs considerable skill and sensitivity in watching out for cliques and taking appropriate action which, though an extra chore, can deflect so many subsequent problems.

If the choice of group partners is to be left to the students (as happens often with projects) it is advisable to adopt a scheme that allows them to find partners with whom they prefer to work yet avoids the risk of some feeling left out or not chosen. A sociometric device suggested by Stanford and Roark (1974) is as follows:

> *Give each student a card and ask them to write their name in the upper left-hand corner. Then ask each to list two members of the class with whom they would like to work. If a student can think of only one or wants to list more than two, that is perfectly acceptable. The cards are then handed in to the tutor who uses the information on the cards to assign students into groups containing at least one colleague for whom they expressed preference.*

Even with preparation like this, the tutor may need to be alert to the dangers of friends falling out or of exclusive cliques developing as the life of the group develops. What the tutor might subsequently do about such happenings is suggested later.

The elegance of the workshop format described on page 158 is the facility it offers for varying the mix of people and affinities in groups while still allowing for planned changes of group membership both for the sake of variety and in order to monitor the progress of each group (though any such decision must be tempered by knowledge of the disruptive effect of breaking up groups).

Physical conditions

It is in the physical arrangement of chairs that many of the most basic yet influential problems in group discussion can occur. Who sits where and at what distance from whom will affect the social roles and relationships pursued by members. The cardinal rule is, if you want full and democratic participation, play down any prior differences of role and reduce the likelihood of their becoming firmly established. A closer sense of sharing in a common task is thus more readily achieved.

A starting point in organizing the physical arrangements is to ask:

- What associations does the room have in the minds of the students?
- Is it the tutor's room, a classroom, a 'neutral' room?
- Is the room a regular venue, is discussion vulnerable to noise or interruption?

Then it may be sensible to consider the seating arrangements:

- Is everyone equally spaced?
- Does anyone have a special position, eg behind a big desk, at the head of a table?
- Can everyone make eye contact?
- How possible is it to rearrange the groupings of chairs and tables?

It is remarkable how often tutors maintain an evidently dominant position for themselves by sitting behind their desk, with students grouped round in front, without being conscious of the effect it has on participation. Figure 7.2 indicates some of the layouts commonly used in tutor-centred discussion groups. I leave the reader to judge the level of participation and the sort of communication pattern likely to occur in each case.

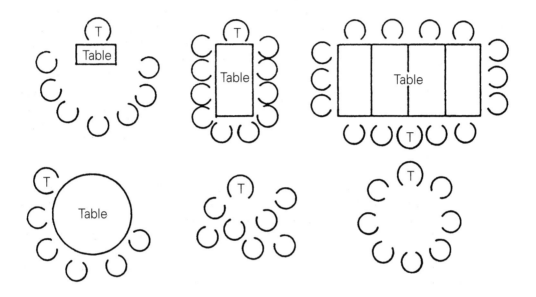

Figure 7.2 *Optional arrangements of furniture in the classroom*

Although an awareness of the effects of the physical position of students and tutor may be highly desirable, there may nevertheless be a limit to the amount of self-conscious juggling of furniture that a group of students will be prepared to undertake. Sometimes there is a sense of, 'Why can't we just stay as we are?', and perhaps the tutor should bow to this feeling rather than make a self-conscious effort to 'structure the environment'. If the configuration of chairs and tables is strange to the students, the tutor may have to explain the rationale, particularly when the students themselves are invited to help in the operation. An obsession with rearranging the furniture can indeed unsettle students.

Even in such an apparently 'impersonal' task as arranging furniture, some sensitivity to the underlying feelings of students may be necessary. Students can become oddly unsettled by unexpected and unexplained changes in the physical environment of the classroom.

The physical scenario of teaching requires careful handling and its effects are not always predictable. As with all manoeuvres connected with group study, however, the need to reveal reasons and to be attuned to the resulting feelings cannot only make things easier but be of unforeseen benefit to the learning process.

Planning what to do

It is never easy to decide in advance what will catch the imagination of a group of students or to anticipate what kind of learning might occur through a one- or two-hour session. To some extent, the learning may be gauged by the level of subject matter implicit in the prior reading.

Nevertheless, to rely on a factor external to the dynamic of the group and its stage of development might have a stultifying effect. Theory and research inform us that both the evolving dynamic of a group and the intellectual growth of students require that the sophistication and the spectrum of aims and tasks should change and develop within each meeting of the group and as the group progresses through a course.

The choice of aims and tasks will be largely predetermined by what is feasible for a particular group and its physical environment, and also by its state of preparedness. Prior reading is a clear case in point: group discussion frequently falls down or lapses into a mini-lecture as a result of inadequate preparation by the students. If this is likely to happen, the sensible tutor will have some alternative strategy in readiness. Here are three possibilities:

- Have copies of a few seminal paragraphs, discussion points, or critiques related to the text that the students can quickly read in the group (for the tutor to talk through what the students have not read puts the tutor in a lecturing role).
- Discuss with the students why the work has not been done and perhaps agree a firm contract henceforward on preparatory work.
- Cancel the meeting on the grounds that nothing useful can take place until the students have fulfilled their part of the (implied) contract.

As we saw in Chapter 5, specifying aims in group teaching carries with it several hazards, mainly because of the unpredictability of the outcome. Nevertheless, depending on the overall purpose of the group meeting, there are good reasons for improving our capacity to understand the tutor's job better through a process like the one shown in Figure 7.3. It indicates how we as tutors might take time out to anticipate, monitor, reflect and revise procedures.

As with all cycles, one can engage in the process at any point, though logically one might be expected to start at 'before'. The proposed activities under each stage are:

Before:

- consider what you want to achieve (aims);
- decide on how you might do so (techniques/tasks);
- write some notes on these to refer to after (read up any notes on previous sessions);
- try to anticipate incidents or developments that might occur (start with 'the worst thing that could happen is . . .');
- imagine what you might do to meet such eventualities;
- decide how you might monitor what happens in the group during its progress.

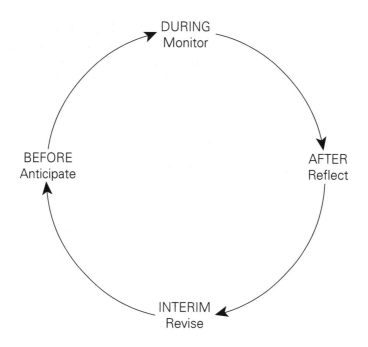

Figure 7.3 *Monitoring strategy for group tutors*

During:

- monitor what is happening; this will at the very least require you to set yourself slightly apart from the discussion at times, even when you are directly involved;
- ask yourself how your intentions compare with what you observe happening and what that implies;
- whenever the opportunity occurs take 'time out' either by yourself or collectively to take stock of progress.

After:

- check back with the notes you wrote before the session;
- review the session – if possible with a colleague – and in any case jot down further notes on what you want to do differently next time;
- look at any other information you have gleaned, eg video or audio tape, questionnaire, informal chats with students outside.

Interim:

- mull it over;
- read books like this one for new ideas;
- revise as you see fit;
- prepare new material.

While this model can be viewed as a 'macro' cycle of thought processes and experiences, most reflective tutors will be carrying out a series of 'mini' cycles in which the processes of anticipation, decision, action and assessment are quickly, if not subliminally, rehearsed during the group session. A more representative diagram might therefore be that of Figure 7.4.

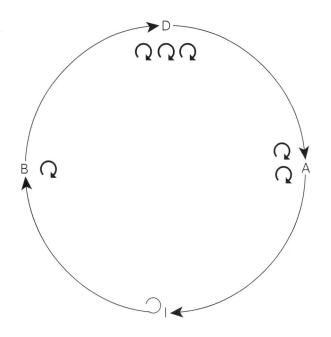

Figure 7.4 *Modified strategy for monitoring*

This whole procedure may strike the busy tutor as far too self-conscious and elaborate for practical purposes. Yet it is merely making explicit a process of thinking that commonly exists at a subliminal level which, because it is conducted unconsciously, is prey to the vicissitudes of emotional blocking and denial. In other words it is an attempt, as is much of this book, to apply academic canons and procedures to our everyday practice: and by and large we are notoriously poor at doing just that!

The practical value of any of these catechisms is probably as great as those of a more religious intent: they depend on some commitment to the faith and on a kind of dedication to the task. Yet they do require honest checks against first-hand experience. A 'meta' cycle might therefore be added – a check on the whole procedure and its revision or replacement according to personal needs.

The simplest adaptation might be to reduce the 'catechism' to two simple questions which, though self-evident, are most helpful to ask oneself prior to each meeting with a group of students: What do I want to achieve? What do I need to do in order for that to happen? It is to the second of these questions that we now turn in looking at the tactical aspect of tutoring.

During discussion

Roles

As soon as tutor and students encounter each other at any meeting, mutual sets of expectations about personal behaviour begin to hold sway. As explained in Chapter 6, the tutor, like it or not, is invested with some of the authority of the institution in as much as it defines the rules and requirements of courses for the students, and this is compounded by the tutor's authority as judge and assessor of the students. In this sense the tutor will be an authority figure no matter how he or she may try to minimize it.

However, one must distinguish between being 'in authority', being 'an authority' and being 'authoritarian'. As tutors we are in authority for the reasons described above and because we have ultimate responsibility for the time and space boundaries in the meeting: that is, we are (usually) deferred to over questions of starting and finishing, and who may join or leave. We will also be perceived as an authority in respect of our expertise in the subject matter. When either of these aspects of authority is challenged there is a possibility that we will fall into an authoritarian style of leadership in order to preserve the only image or role we are able to conceive of ourselves. What sort of threat such a challenge poses depends on either our point of view or on how we personally experience the problem. Fears of losing control or (at the level of unconscious fantasy) of being destroyed, are common in such situations.

The virtue of acquiring a repertoire of options is again evident. The authority role is not the only one available to us. We can adopt one or more of several roles according to how we define the need and the educational aims. The following set of leadership roles presents some options for the versatile tutor.

Leader/instructor

This is the traditional role, which is easily adopted through the preconceptions of both tutor and students, though it frequently leads to dissatisfaction on the part of both. Typically, the tutor initiates proceedings and demonstrates control over content and process with a short statement or summary and then tries to draw out students' thoughts, periodically linking them together and redirecting the content of discussions as appropriate. Often the tutor's task in providing the initial stimulus is taken by a student, but in a sense only as an 'alter ego' for the tutor. There is a great danger with this role that the students may become over-dependent and feel constrained by what the tutor demonstrates as acceptable knowledge, ways of thinking and academic standards. In educational terms, at least, the tutor may thus establish an authoritarian or autocratic atmosphere. Sometimes students behave as if this atmosphere existed, even though they would hotly deny it.

Neutral chair

This is a variation of the leader/instructor role in which the tutor controls procedure but does not contribute to the content in any determining way. It is thus possible for the tutor to create a 'democratic' atmosphere (see page 32).

Facilitator

This is a difficult role for the 'traditional' teacher in that it involves careful listening and eliciting rather than giving of one's own knowledge. Both tutor and students may find this regime difficult and even painful to adapt to. It should not be supposed that the facilitator role represents a 'laissez-faire' style of leadership: rather, there is a sense of shared or developed responsibility for learning. It usually requires that the tutor be student-centred, helping students to express what they understand by respecting them for what they are rather than what they 'should' be.

Counsellor

If the personal or social needs of the students demand it, or if a tutorial is designated for such purposes, the tutor may wish to draw out some of the students' emotional problems on the grounds that sharing anxieties can be both relieving and reassuring, and may provide valuable feedback for the tutor. The tutor may also have some tentative suggestions for tackling the problems. Small, more 'intimate' groups are of course preferable for these purposes.

Commentator

The tutor sits outside the perimeter of the group and comments from time to time on the dynamic of the group interaction or on the kinds of arguments being used by members. In this way, though students may be aware of the tutor's presence and influence, they are not constantly using her or him as a reference point or focus of attention in discussion.

Wanderer

Where the total group is split into sub-groups (as in a workshop) who are working on a set task, the tutor can helpfully infuse influence by circulating round the groups to:

- check their adherence to the task and identify any teething problems;
- help them out of any unproductive patterns of thinking or interaction they have got into;
- pick up trends in the discussions for use at any subsequent plenary discussion.

In this way we may, as tutor, perform several roles in our travels according to what is currently taking place in any group we happen to drop in on. Here again, the tutor's authority is in general evidence but should not be obtrusive within the groups.

Absent friend

Many of the best virtues arise from necessity: tutors who find it necessary to absent themselves from the group for reasons of nature or administration are often surprised at the intense buzz of conversation that greets them on their return. It is an interesting test of the effect of one's authority to make a video tape before, during and after one's temporary absence from a group. The essence of this 'role' is physical withdrawal from the room, and this applies equally to situations where sub-groups have been formed as to the integral group. For instance, it is not unusual for a tutor to sense that his or her presence is causing some sort of 'stuckness' in the group, especially where students are being asked to make a decision that requires them to reveal some of their doubts and uncertainties. There is a danger nevertheless of the group(s) disintegrating unless a task (implicit or explicit) is generally agreed for the duration of the tutor's absence.

The choice of role for the tutor may be determined by:

- the declared aims and objectives of the meeting or the course;
- the kind of task undertaken; or
- a summary assessment of the dynamic of the group.

Clarification of the role can help polarize activities more purposefully than is typically the case when the relationship between students and tutor is tacit and obscure. Several of the roles could be combined and varied over time. With a project group, for example, the tutor may first act as a chair, then as a facilitator, followed by consultant and, because of the students' withdrawal to work on their project, an absent friend.

It is arguable that as competent tutors, we are in and out of these roles continually and the above discussion merely confirms established modes. That is possibly so, but the muddled and often uneasy nature of some teaching relationships may need sorting out at times in order to make the transactions more straightforward and explicit. Students can thus reorient themselves to what the tutor offers and respond accordingly.

While the spelling out of roles may seem in general to be valuable there may be occasions when, for good reasons, the tutor may wish to leave things opaque; when, for instance, the aim is to examine the students' response to the tutor in the traditional leader role in order to dig out some of the deep-seated assumptions they may have about teaching and learning. Richardson (1967) describes the resounding silence that frequently followed her proposal to a group of students that they decide for themselves the form and content of the discussion. She claims it is important to discuss this reaction on the road to achieving a better comprehension of crucial relationships in the group and particularly the most problematical one, that of authority.

If we look again at this question of authority in the group, it may now be apparent that some aspects of it are an unnecessary encumbrance to the creative tutor who may decide to devolve the leadership role among the members. Hill (1977) proposes a set of roles and functions that enable this devolution to take place. As the lack of satisfactory experience of democratic discussion makes it difficult for students to adopt such roles readily, he proposes a list of criteria for gaining a common understanding of what effective discussion can be like. These criteria are that:

- a happy, non-threatening atmosphere prevails;
- learning is accepted as a cooperative exercise;
- learning is accepted as the object of discussion;
- everyone participates and helps others to take part;
- leadership functions are distributed;
- material is adequately covered;
- members attend regularly and are prepared for the discussion;
- evaluation (assessment) is accepted as an integral part of the discussion group.

In respect of learning groups, there are more particular functions for both the tutor and, where the occasion demands it, for group members to perform:

- initiating – starting the discussion, proposing new ideas, activities, resuming it after a lull;
- giving and asking for information;
- giving and asking for reactions;
- restating and giving examples;
- confronting and reality-testing – restating others' messages and checking their examples;
- clarifying, synthesizing and summarizing;
- timekeeping and holding groups to discussion plan;
- encouraging participation by others.

Readers will notice the similarities with Knowles' list of functions for group maintenance and task (page 28), though here the maintenance roles are somewhat underplayed. Obviously, these functions are not required at all times or in equal measure in a group. Indeed, as Knowles remarks, if a function is performed inappropriately it may interfere with the group's operation. But it can be helpful when a group is working unsatisfactorily to pause and consider which of these functions might be lacking and to remedy the situation before moving on.

Whether the functions should be allocated to individuals or shared and used as necessary by the group as a whole is a moot point and will depend on the skill of its members. What is fairly certain is that members should be discouraged from playing just one role at every meeting, lest they become stereotyped in it. If possible, roles should be reallocated as and when individuals feel able to perform them adequately. One might expect the competent tutor to realize all these behaviours in the leadership role, yet the value of sharing them round the group can be immense as then students are able to learn the skills for lifelong participation in groups. These positive or helping functions would, however, be of little use if due recognition were not also given to some of the 'negative' behaviours, which Hill (1977) lists as:

aggressing (being aggressive)	blocking	self-confessing
seeking sympathy	special interest pleading	playing around
status-seeking	withdrawing	dominating.

The appearance of these behaviours in individuals tends to be irritating to other members. They may be tackled most constructively through regular reflection on, or evaluation of, group process, but always bearing in mind the need for a consistency between them and the group task.

Norms or rules

Whereas roles describe the positions taken by individuals in a given context, norms or rules define the context. Norms, except in particularly formal settings (eg, committees), are internalized, implicit and generally unstated. Nevertheless, it is usually clear when they are broken: if disapproval is not openly expressed, the 'offender' may feel a sense of exclusion.

In general, the norms of everyday interaction work for groups as long as they appear to be productive, or evidently maintain stability. Yet from our understanding of some of the unconscious processes to which groups regularly fall victim, it is apparent that in some cases the unexpressed needs of members may be satisfied only through somewhat destructive behaviours. Everyday norms are often more ambiguous than many would like to believe, and there may be hidden disagreement about them anyway.

Many of the problems that students feel in expressing themselves in groups stem from either uncertainty about what the 'rules of the seminar game' are, or from their feeling overly constrained by assumed rules to do with authority and competition. For instance, it is frequently assumed that it is the tutor's job to fulfil most of the roles listed on page 167 and it is not for the students to propose objectives, topics, changes of direction, or procedures. Often there is also a norm against expressing one's inner feelings or against interrupting anyone making a presentation. Several of the rules of behaviour in seminars are drawn by students from their school experience and have no great relevance in tertiary education. It is sometimes important, therefore, for a tutor to formulate with the group members some explicit ground rules which, though they may appear more constricting in some ways, can generate a sense of freedom as students begin to understand what is and is not 'OK', with the added knowledge that they are free to propose changes if they wish. It is the very fact that such ambiguities and confusions are hidden that leads some tutors, and more especially 'growth group' facilitators, to propose ground rules for discussion.

Ground rules

As we have already seen, the kind of hidden rules or norms that often determine behaviour in groups can be made more explicit in order to understand some of the undercurrents and to increase awareness of group dynamics. However, for most groups this can be bypassed with the introduction of ground rules, and very often discussion of these can be sufficient in itself in improving group process.

There are some that the tutor can introduce from the very start, for example:

■ the group will always start at the agreed time (even if not everybody is there) and will finish at the agreed time;

- anyone has the right to suggest what the group should do next;
- when anyone speaks they are addressing the whole group and not just the tutor;
- everyone has some responsibility for the process; therefore it is up to every member of the group to bring in other members and is not just the tutor's responsibility.

After one of two meetings of the group the tutor can invite members to propose their own ground rules. This is best done by asking them to work in pairs to discuss what problems they have experienced in the group and each to develop a list of rules that would improve group communication. These rules should embody both rights and responsibilities. Brookfield and Preskill (1999) gives a full account of the generation of ground rules.

It is clear that the more ground rules that are introduced, the nearer the discussion gets to a game and many students may take legitimate exception to that as a regular feature. However, there is a lot to be said for encouraging a group to explore its own norms and to consider which of these it means to keep and which to change, in order to determine whether any improvement in the group climate takes place.

Leadership interventions

Of a good leader, when his task is finished, his goal achieved, they say, 'We did it ourselves.'

(Lao-tse)

Encouraging interaction

For several of the reasons already described, students are often strangely inhibited in discussion and at best seem prepared to make only rather formal contributions. As one student remarked:

People ask questions and this stimulates the group. I feel we don't mind if a friend asks a question, but if a lecturer asks you, you dry up. A member of staff will always have the answer at his fingertips. I've always resented making an idiot of myself.

Students who are remarkably talkative outside classes are often reluctant to contribute to group discussion when a tutor is present, and we have already noted how a tutor's leaving the room quickly stimulates a resurgence in conversation among the group, even on academic topics. What can a tutor do while present to induce a similar sense of open discussion among students without abdicating a leadership role? The necessary skills or behaviours are not difficult to acquire, though it may not be easy to produce them always when most wanted. They are nonetheless worth including in our repertoire even if we do need to perform them self-consciously in the first instance.

Glancing round the group. It is generally considered rude not to look at somebody when they are talking to you. Yet to do so as a group leader will quickly create the sort of communication pattern illustrated in Figure 2.1 (a) – see page 24. It is not easy to pick up the habit of scanning the group when we are talking, let alone when students are contributing. Though we will want to catch the eye of a student as he or she talks from time to time we can, by looking around, encourage others to follow suit and so cause the whole group to give that person more attention, thus discouraging the common tendency for discussion to drift into a series of one-to-one duologues.

Looking for signals. If, when one student is talking, we glance round the group, we will find ourselves picking up cues from others who are puzzled, or anxious to check something. As the contribution ends, we will be in a better position to draw in some of the less vocal students.

Often the cues are not more than an indrawn breath, a snort of frustration, a shifting of position, or a puzzled frown. To have noted them and to be seen to have done so, is usually helpful to us in the role of tutor in deciding what to do or what not to do at the next stage in the proceedings. We will also be better apprised of the group climate. In fact we may even be contributing to a more positive climate through the very act of glancing round the group.

Using non-verbal communication. Sometimes it may be difficult to interrupt a discussion without sounding critical or punitive. A non-verbal intervention can work wonders in this situation. On some occasions, this might consist of catching a student's eye and giving an encouraging smile, or an invitation to speak by raising your eyebrows. On others, the connection may be through gestures – an extended palm to suggest, 'Would you like to come in now?', or using two hands to indicate, 'What does everyone else think?'. Of course, these non-verbal signals are natural partners to verbal invitations but are generally less intrusive and just as productive.

Two non-verbal gestures that are often used but seem to work effectively are the 'traffic cop' signals designed to bring students into a discussion and to block them out (see Figure 7.5.)

Bringing in and shutting out. The gestures in Figure 7.5 highlight two complementary purposes. In order to encourage a student to talk, it may be necessary for the tutor to invite him or her into the discussion, either verbally or non-verbally. By the same token, it is sometimes necessary to exclude more vocal members or to stop them before, as often happens, both their less vocal colleagues and they themselves have become fed up with what they are saying. This becomes a sort of 'rescue operation'.

Sometimes a verbal stimulus is also needed. For example, when a student silently smiles, looks puzzled, or rolls his or her eyes you could say, 'What are you thinking Liz?' or 'You smiled, John'. This usually has the desired effect of drawing a student into discussion. However, the opposite problem may prevail: how to shut out someone who constantly talks or interrupts. Provided we can do it supportively and straightforwardly – 'Could you just hold it there Brian, it would be interesting to know how the others respond to that' or, 'Let's put that on ice for the moment, Gill, while we hear what everyone else has to say' – the student should not feel unduly put out. The problem is rather on the tutor's side, as it can feel extremely awkward consciously to interrupt someone in the sure (but often erroneous) belief that one could be hurting his or her feelings, and we may well feel that the risk is too great to take in a group of students. Should this be so, the solution might be to practise these skills within the safer company of colleagues in a training group.

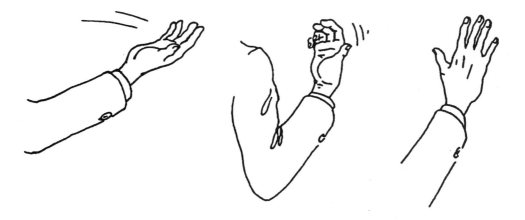

Figure 7.5 *Hand signals for bringing in and shutting out*

Turning questions back. Of the many temptations open to the unsuspecting tutor, one is the supplicant question from students that places us on our authority pedestal: 'Can you tell us what you know about . . .?' or, 'What should the answer be?', for example. The question can simply be turned back with: 'Well, what do you think?' on the grounds that the student probably has an inkling of the answer anyway or would not have asked the question, and it is usually better to get students to formulate their own ideas in the first instance.

This is not to say that there are not many occasions when the tutor may be the only person present who could possibly know the answer to a particular question or where a refusal to answer could slow down proceedings. The judgement in all these situations must be based on a recognition of the dynamic and the learning needs of the group.

A very useful and more comfortable variation of 'turning questions back' is to redirect or deflect them. For instance the question from a student: 'I don't understand what the author is trying to say. What does it all mean?' could be met with, 'Well, what does anybody else think?' or, 'Does everyone else have the same problem?' or, 'Do you have any ideas about what it means?'.

Supporting and valuing. Thus far we have considered some very quickfire, though not always easy tactics for the tutor in a leadership role. However, it is easy to overlook an important ingredient of effective group discussion: the creation of a feeling of security and belonging; an atmosphere of trust and openness where people are valued for what they are and have no need to fear making a fool of themselves. Now this is easily said but not so easily done in the thick of a hectic term's work where teaching and assessing become an almost undifferentiated continuum. The temptation to correct discussion contributions in the same way as one might write comments to an essay is great. Perry (1970) describes how tutors typically view the discussion as 'an opportunity to develop initiative and scope in their own thinking', at least initially.

No sooner do the students get started, however, and some error or inexactness is voiced, than the older form of responsibilities imposes on the tutor – the imperative of 'correcting'. Three to five corrections of this kind appear sufficient to defeat the students' initiative for search and flow in their exploration. The initiative for conversation then falls back on the instructor who finds himself in a monologue or lecture, with the sensation of being somehow trapped, compelled by powerful forces in himself and the students, to do what he had never intended to do.

This is not to say that the correction of 'errors' is an unacceptable sin. The question is not one of 'whether' but rather of 'when' and 'how'. To reject or correct the first contribution a student makes would generally be counterproductive. Apart from inhibiting expression, as in the above quotation, it is likely to lock the students into the first four stages of Perry's scale of intellectual development. Nevertheless some kind of corrective action may be called for – but this can be achieved in a less inhibiting and intellectually more elevating way:

> 'Is that really so?'
> 'Could you think about that again?'
> 'Let's just took at that more carefully.'
> 'How does that tally with what you said before?'
> 'Would anyone else like to comment on what George just said?'
> 'Uh-huh!'
> 'OK, so what does everybody else think?'

Students will doubtless pick up that they have said something irrelevant or inconsistent but be encouraged to discover their own way out.

Checking and building. Students (not to mention tutors) are not always as lucid as they would wish to be when formulating ideas for the first time. Some of the most imaginative contributors to a discussion may find it difficult to express their half-formed ideas clearly at first. Lest the whole group continue in a state of confusion, the tutor can quickly check for understanding by simply asking: 'Let me check that I understand you. Are you saying . . .?'. The student is often grateful for the clarification. What the student does say may well relate to a line of argument pursued earlier in discussion or contradict something he or she has said earlier. In each case, the tutor can help to make links with comments such as: 'That ties in with what you were saying before – it sounds as though you have a coherent view of it' or, 'Does that contradict what you said a few minutes ago?' or, 'So it would be fair to say that while you disagree with the functionalist view, you have not yet . . .'. Ideally, it would be preferable if the students were left to make the interpretation for themselves: 'How does that connect with what you said before?', 'Is Renata being consistent there?'.

Sometimes the tutor may go further in putting several emerging themes together and formulating a new coherent picture of the topic under discussion. But again – how much better it would be to allow the students to do so for themselves.

Re-directing. The initiative required of a tutor in acting on the physical environment, which we discussed on pages 159–60, is just as valuable when it comes to changing the social interaction. Again it is a matter of knowing when it is important to act and when the prevailing climate is too good to destroy. It is never easy, especially when the tutor has a planned schedule of discussion, to decide whether students would be glad of a change in the direction of the discussion or would feel cheated of a rewarding line of interest. Yet sometimes it is necessary to take command and say: 'Hang on to that but let's switch our attention to another aspect . . .' or, 'I think we've reached the point where we could turn our attention . . .'

More often than not, it is difficult to be sure of the climate and also of one's own motives. A safer way of approaching the problem may once again be to test the group: 'Are you ready now to . . .?', 'Do you think we've worked on that one for long enough now?'.

It may be even more valuable to check the process as well as content: 'Could we stop at this point and check whether we're going about this the right way?'. This intervention is almost identical with the basketball term 'time out' in which teams take a break from the game to review progress and discuss tactics.

There is nothing unusual about all these leadership interventions. They are practised quite frequently in everyday life but are somehow forgotten in the culture of a discussion group. We must, however, use them with discretion, not in pursuit of our own needs, but in response to what our growing awareness of the group process tells us.

Asking questions

Supposing a tutor were to open discussion with:

> *Do you think the assassination of Archduke Francis Ferdinand was intended as a precipitating factor for World War I, even though none of the schemers, if schemers they were, could have had any notion of the consequences in terms of both the extent of hostilities and the degree of suffering that resulted?*

Pause. Ten seconds' silence.

> *Let me put it another way. On the evidence we have, was the war a typical example of intentional cause in international conflict? Or was World War II a better one?*

Pause. Another 10 seconds' silence.

> *Did nobody read the papers I asked you to look at last week?*

What, if anything, went wrong here? Were the questions too complicated? Did the tutor wait long enough for an answer? What sort of answer was expected? This imaginary dialogue (based on two real transcripts) is intended to demonstrate at least one of the common traps in asking questions: posing a multi-part, highly academic and leading question at the start of a session, not waiting long enough for a response and then rephrasing it as another question. We all do this sort of thing from time to time and we usually wish we could 'unask' the question rather than become more deeply enmeshed through our own wish to appear clever. Yet having got ourselves into this fix, perhaps we could learn from this tutor by waiting a little longer for a response, using our 'third ear' to reflect on the way the question came out, and possibly checking with students: 'Do you want me to rephrase that?' or, 'Was that question too complex/obscure/involved to answer?'.

Questions serve at least three purposes in discussion: to test the students' knowledge, to clarify information, and to stimulate students into expressing ideas and constructing arguments. Very often the same question can satisfy all these purposes, though that will depend on the group climate and any underlying message in the question.

There is perhaps a further purpose served by questions: the opportunity they give the tutor, or anyone else in the group, to make a link between what they and the others are thinking. The choice of question will depend very much on when it is put and the purpose of the discussion. If, however, we take the above three purposes of questioning, we can look at the different types of questions that relate to each and leave the decision as to their practical application to the reader.

Testing questions

These will mainly begin with words like 'what', 'where', 'when', 'which' – and will therefore be essentially convergent as they are intended to elicit specific information. They are concerned with:

- checking knowledge – 'What is the best catalyst for . . .?', 'Which critics have described Godot as a comedy?'
- comprehension – 'How do you justify that . . .?'
- application – 'How do you predict that would work in . . .?', 'What relevance does that have in . . .?
- analysis – 'What qualities do these have in common?', 'What would happen if . . .?'
- synthesis – 'How does that connect with . . .?', 'Could you summarize what we've discussed so far?'
- evaluation – 'Which do you think is best?', 'How do you feel about that?'

Such questions are clearly linked with Bloom's taxonomy (see page 88) and the accompanying list of verbs might prove a helpful reference. However, they can, as part of a probing exercise (Hedley and Wood, 1978) be combined in a way that is searching and vigorous.

Clarifying questions

Whether a question is defined as a clarifying or as an elaborating one will often depend on the expression on the questioner's face and what has preceded the question. However, these sorts of questions could be used to clarify:

- 'Can you rephrase that?'
- 'What did you mean by . . .?'
- 'Can you give me an example?'

Where the last question fails we might follow it up with: 'Might this be an example . . .' and provide one of our own.

Elaborating

Elaborating questions are essentially a gentler way of enquiring than the other questions we have discussed. They are concerned with helping students express themselves more fully, both in thought and feeling:

- 'Can you tell me more?'
- 'Could you elaborate on that?'
- 'Uh-huh, what else?'
- 'How does that make you feel?'

Echoing and selective echoing

Echoing and selective echoing (see page 16), while not strictly a form of question, have an important place here. For example:

Student: 'I've been thinking that, if you take the phenomenological argument to its limits, then you end up with nobody helping others to make sense of their own world. There would be no point in teaching, for a start.'

Tutor: 'No point in teaching.' (Echoing)

or

Tutor: 'Take the argument to its limits.' (Selective echoing)

It is easy to see how, with a little inflexion, these 'echoes' could sound like quite threatening questions. It is essential, therefore, that they are said in a neutral tone as though one was ruminating over the particular phrase.

There are also questions that are intended to rouse the curiosity or the imagination. For example: 'I wonder if that really would happen?' or, 'If you were in that position, what would you do?' Often, questions like these are best kept ambiguous, though this could be very threatening for a new group.

Let us not forget, too, the principle of personal relevance mentioned already in the section on communication. A question like: 'How did it seem to you?' or, 'What did you like about it?' is much more acceptable as a starter than: 'What is your assessment of Y's theory?'.

It is clearly not in the best interest of discussion that the tutor should spend most of the time asking questions: this would quickly set up a focal pattern of communication. The more students can competently take over the task of asking each other questions, the more responsibility they will be taking for their own learning. However, it is quite properly the tutor's job to explore and probe further into students' understanding of issues.

Opening questions

In the case of large groups (say 20 to 40 in number) the importance of questioning as a spur to discussion becomes much more evident because of the increasing level of tension and sense of risk, described on pages 7 and 8. An article in the *Teaching Professor* (1995), outlines how one tutor manages discussion in large classes:

I first go over the material assigned, trying to identify the ideas and passages that seem most important, both for me and the students (and he begins to select clusters and themes on the basis of which he prepares opening questions for each area).

   Do I want to open with a shocking question designed to surprise the students into really imaginative thinking? Or should I choose instead a much more predictable beginning:

How is this work like . . .?

or

What in this work did you find confusing, important, or notable?

Should I perhaps open the discussion in a low-key way by simply asking what issues the students want to talk about, what questions they want answered?
   Should I focus on a particular moment in the text or use it as a way of discussing crucial themes or problems?
   Should I begin with a context-specific question that has important sub-textual ramifications?

As we have noted, the group or class tutor must give more attention to the process than the lecturer, in order constantly to 'monitor the ebb and flow of ideas'. In focusing on the process, the tutor might have ready, or might be asking him- or herself, Huston suggests, a regular subtext of questions:

- Who is prepared?
- Is the material interesting most of them?
- Do they understand the reading?
- Who wants to participate?
- Who's carrying the discussion?
- Should I call on one of my best tunes to give the class a lift? Or can the person shine on this issue?
- Am I tending to all parts of the room?
- Should I try the topic from a different angle?

It is thus a constant balancing act (as the article reminds us) between the content being discussed and the processes being used to discuss it.
   For Huston, this attention to questioning is well worth the effort:

teaching an effective discussion class is for me a deeply human and humanizing activity, a process built both on community and on communication, in which all of us work together – questioning, listening, examining, qualifying, challenging, explaining and elaborating – to build something more imaginative, more interesting, more satisfying and ultimately more enduring than any of us could build alone.

Effective questioning technique

Several research-based recommendations for effective questioning in discussion have been noted by Wilen (1986, quoted in Bonwell and Eison, 1991). Plan key questions to provide structure and direction to the lesson. A useful sequence might be:

- What are the essential features and conditions of this situation?
- Given this situation, what do you think will happen next?
- What facts and generalizations support your prediction?
- What other things might happen as a result of this situation?
- If the predicted situation occurs, what will happen next?
- Based on the information and predictions before us, what are the probable consequences you now see?
- What will lead us from the current situation to the one you've predicted?

In using this approach, some spontaneous questions will naturally evolve from students' responses, but the overall direction of the discussion has largely been planned.

- Phrase questions clearly and specifically.
- Adapt questions to the level of students' abilities . . . using vocabulary that is appropriate for the students in the class.
- Ask questions logically and sequentially – random questions confuse.
- Ask questions at various levels (for) cognitive memory to establish an initial base; higher level questions can then be posed to illustrate the . . . objectives.
- Follow up on student responses . . . Teachers can elicit longer and more meaningful statements from students if they simply maintain a 'deliberative silence' after an initial response. Too often teachers ask rapid-fire questions, one after another, a circumstance more like an interrogation than a discussion . . . Invite the student to elaborate, make a reflective statement giving a sense of what the student has said, declare perplexity over the response, invite the student to elaborate, encourage other students to raise questions about the issue at hand, or encourage students to ask questions if they are having trouble.
- Give students time to think when responding. The single most important action a teacher can take after asking a question is simply to keep quiet. An analysis of the patterns of interaction between teachers and student in hundreds of classrooms found that teachers averaged less than one second of silence before repeating or re-emphasizing material, or asking a second question. Under such circumstances it is no wonder that students remain silent. Training teachers to wait silently for three to five seconds after a question achieved significant benefits: the length and number of appropriate but unsolicited responses, exchanges between students, questions from students and higher-level responses all increased, while the number of students' failures to respond decreased.
- Use questions (and techniques) that encourage wide participation from students . . . Frequent individual successes will ultimately empower even the most hesitant students to jump in.
- Encourage questions from students. Create a supportive environment that allows risk taking and then encourage student to ask questions. They will respond.

The central task of the tutor is to model the behaviour and demonstrate the techniques that will enable students to be more productive members of the group. These principles are exemplified in a US college catalogue. Tutors should:

be good questioners, able to raise important issues that will engage the intellectual and imaginative powers of their students. Next, they must be good listeners, able to determine the difficulties of their students and to help them to reformulate their observations and examine their opinions. The tutors should be ready to supply helpful examples and to encourage students to examine the implications of their first attempt at understanding. In summary, the role of the tutors is to question, to listen and to help . . . but first of all the tutors will call on the students to try to help themselves. (Myers, 1988 in Bonwell and Eison, 1991)

To end this chapter it may be helpful to return briefly to Chapter 2 in order to put all the above into the context of the developmental sequence for a learning group proposed by Johnson and Johnson (1987). The tutor's job, in relation to the seven successive stages, is to:

- introduce, define and structure the group;
- clarify procedures, reinforce members as they assimilate the rules and procedures, and help them become better acquainted;
- stress, and help model, the need for cooperative interdependence and encourage the development of mutual trust;
- accept the rebellion and differentiation between members as a natural developmental stage and use constructive confrontation and negotiation to affirm their right to independence from each other and the prescribed procedures;
- enable the group members to commit themselves to take ownership of the group goals and procedures, as well as for other members;
- act as a consultant and resource to enable the group to function effectively;
- signal termination and help members to move on to future groups.

Exercises

1. Teaching small groups – checklist

Read the following list of statements and tick the box that describes your own teaching best.
　　Add four statements of your own.

1. I find it easy to learn students' names　☐ ☐ ☐ ☐ ☐　I find it hard to learn students' names

2. My sessions start working slowly　☐ ☐ ☐ ☐ ☐　My sessions start working quickly

3. It is easy to get students to contribute　☐ ☐ ☐ ☐ ☐　It is hard to get students to contribute

4. Most students prepare well   ☐ ☐ ☐ ☐ ☐   Most students prepare poorly

5. It is easy to keep discussion   ☐ ☐ ☐ ☐ ☐   It is hard to keep discussion to
    to the point   the point

6. It is easy to keep discussion   ☐ ☐ ☐ ☐ ☐   It is hard to keep discussion
    going   going

7. I speak more than I would   ☐ ☐ ☐ ☐ ☐   I speak less than I would like
    like

8. I find myself talking to one   ☐ ☐ ☐ ☐ ☐   I find myself talking to the
    or two students   whole group

9. My sessions lack structure   ☐ ☐ ☐ ☐ ☐   My sessions are well structured

10. My students seldom express   ☐ ☐ ☐ ☐ ☐   My students freely express their
    their own views   own views

11. ....

12. ....

13. ....

14. ....

Now write a statement of what you intend to do to deal with problems implied by this checklist.

2. Tutor interventions

Knowing what the problem is in a group does not necessarily mean that we have the resources to solve it. The incidents in the following list are typical of many student groups. What interventions might you use if you were the tutor in the situation? List as many possible ways as you can think of to deal with it. Add more incidents from your experience and describe how you have, or could have, handled them.

Incident   **Possible action/
                                                       intervention**

Group silent/unresponsive
Individual(s) silent
Students not listening to each other/not building/point scoring
Sense of group secret/private joke/clique
Sub-groups form/pair starts conversation
One or two students dominate
Students look for answers from tutor/too deferential

Incident	**Possible action/ intervention**

Discussion too abstract
Discussion goes off point/becomes irrelevant
Attendance is poor
Distraction occurs
Preparation not done
(Add more from your own experience.)

Possible solutions to these may be found in the Appendix.

Discussion points

- What prior planning is done in order that the groups to which you belong run successfully?
- What assumptions lie behind the various interactions, roles and rules described in this chapter? To what extent might students employ them?
- Write one or two ground rules that might improve interaction in your group.
- Invite the group to try them out in order to gauge their value.
- Make a note of the number of times you exercise the functions on page 167 in your group. Invite others to do the same and compare notes.

8 | Learning groups in context

Like all living systems, organizations establish and maintain themselves through communication with their environments and amongst their parts.

(Lee Thayer, quoted in Myers and Myers, 1982)

> By the end of this chapter you can expect to be better able to recognize and analyse some of the relationships between the parts in a teaching and learning milieu.

The learning milieu

Although the institutional setting in which a learning group occurs may not be seen by the group itself to have a significant influence over their deliberations, it is evident that students can be profoundly affected by aspects of institutional life outside the formal curriculum. Parlett (1977) contrasts the educational foreground of lectures, tutorials, courses, examinations and so on with the relatively unchanging background of buildings, traditions, local customs, geographical features, etc.

While students are concerned – inevitably and properly – with attending to the foreground, much of what they do and think about while in the institution is governed by the background. That this is ever present, 'taken as read' and rarely examined systematically, is no guarantee it is educationally insignificant in its long-term impact.

The view that a department has of itself is a kind of foreground that may conflict with the background of learning norms among students. Indeed the more loudly trumpeted the self-image, the more likely is the presented picture to be a false one, with consequent disillusionment for students. Self-image is often revealed at induction talks designed to orientate students to their studies. Parlett reports one department that adopted a tough and austere image, warning the students of the hard work ahead, that some would fail and that the control of knowledge and its dissemination lay firmly with the department. Another conveyed a more open attitude to learning; the department chair talked about university as: 'a time during which you should take a critical look at yourselves and rethink things – it should be a most stimulating time', and later broke the meeting into small groups to discuss the course. He cautioned: 'Don't let the work get on top of you.' A third department set the tone by immersing students in their work from the start with experiments involving measurements of each other, while staff circulated and instructed students on techniques.

Nevertheless, it is more than possible for student norms to prevail in spite of staff intentions. Students can be reluctant to discuss academic matters outside the organized class – there is often a taboo on it. Further, there may be strong disinclination among students to follow what they agree are desirable educational goals but which conflict with more immediate pressures to do with assessment. In physical sciences for instance, some students are likely to look for 'correct' answers to tutorial problems rather than engage in a more open intellectual discussion, even though they may accept this as valuable in a more professional sense. In other words, they can remain firmly glued to surface approaches to learning or the dualistic stage of Perry's scale (Chapter 3), a reality that may be either sustained or readily permitted by the system of teaching and assessment. Many of these features of student life become part of the folklore that is passed on from one influx of students to another. Folklore can, as Parlett suggests, support the status quo so much more powerfully when the departmental sub-culture becomes insulated from the wider culture of the institution and the outside world through the self-confirming nature of its academic ideology and the progressive retrenchment of certain ideas that all within the organization adhere to and take for granted, and which are not exposed to any bracing challenge from the outside.

Students also draw comparisons between experiences of different groups and between the learning milieu in different departments and these often serve to underline the prevailing folklore. There is evidence from research (Massy *et al*, 1994) that department cultures adopting many of the values and principles espoused in this book in relation to teamwork decision-making, evaluation, openness and tolerance of differences prove more effective in the teaching provision. It might not therefore be too big a leap of imagination to suggest, if we accept the concept of what systems theorists call 'parallel processes', that the effective operation of group structure and processes within a department or subject area will be reflected in the culture of group learning in and outside the classroom.

Bridging cultures

Action learning sets

One kind of group strategy that can function as part of the staff and the student culture alike is the action learning set. This organized form of peer group may operate as well within a course as outside it as a problem-solving forum for tutors and other members of staff. Action learning sets show that learning can be achieved, and practical problems solved, in modes other than discussion groups, agenda-based meetings and one-to-one counselling. This special approach has been designed and used to provide an opportunity, within a mutually agreed set of rules and procedures, for groups (known as sets) to deal with issues and problems of their members in a way that ensures a clear focus on the needs of each. In the sets, the focus is on the problems that individuals bring and the action that results from the structured attention and support given by the group. The set is less concerned with personal development and discovery than with learning and action. Put simply, it is about solving problems and getting things done.

McGill and Beaty (1992) define action learning thus:

> *Action learning is a continuous process of learning and reflection, supported by colleagues, with an intention of getting things done. Through action learning individuals learn with and from each other by working on real problems and reflecting on their own experiences. The process helps us to take an active stance towards life and helps to overcome the tendency (merely) to think, feel and be passive towards the pressures of life.*

There are no golden rules about what to bring to a set, although clearly a problem over which the presenting member had no influence or control, or one so trivial as to have no impact, would not be worthy of the set's attention. Most problems have an inner and an outer domain: the inner feelings and thoughts about an event or a decision, and the outer world of the environment in which it occurs.

Time is usually allocated evenly to each member within meetings of the set, though there may be occasions where the set may decide that one member with a special need should have more time at any one meeting and re-allocate time accordingly, but explicitly.

Time is a clear focus of attention in an action learning set; the responsibility of the timekeeping role is paramount and the meetings need to be kept free of interruptions. Three hours is the normally allocated time for a group of eight and this needs to be divided into a sequence of periods such that roughly equal time is given to each set member, plus the same amount for opening and closing.

As we have already observed, one of the paradoxes of groups is that, until everyone has a sense of their own separate identity, the group cannot cohere. In action learning sets this can be achieved by processes like group rounds at the start, but there should also be a recognition that the continuing effectiveness of the set will be enhanced if it can mirror the cycle of normal human contact. A useful cycle proposed by Beaty and McGill is:

- connecting – eg, saying hello, shaking hands, hugging, etc;
- nurturing – eg, having coffee ready, asking 'How are you?'
- energizing – eg, sharing latest events, short interesting game / story / joke;
- working – eg, individual time slots;
- rewarding – eg, thanking and offering support outside the set;
- leave taking – eg, checking on action points, next dates, saying 'Goodbye'.

Attention to these stages can make all the difference between a formal and purely functional meeting and one that conveys a sense of wholeness and enjoyment.

A *sine qua non* of action learning is that the set formulate its own ground rules at the beginning of the process and these last for the duration of the set, subject to agreed amendments and additions. There are usually ground rules about confidentiality but others concerning attendance, punctuality, communication and behaviour may emerge. Ground rules may be generated by brainstorming.

Rounds are usually a good way of starting a meeting. Each person in turn has, say, a minute to relate 'what's on top' (something that's occupying their minds at the moment) while the others listen silently. Another popular theme for a round is 'joys, trauma and trivia' in which each member in turn describes something joyful, something traumatic and something trivial that has happened to them recently. Other useful processes include buzz groups, circular interviewing and brainstorming.

Apart from action planning itself – the main goal of each meeting – it is important for the set to record and circulate the agreed actions and to review the meeting in order to improve the process for subsequent ones and to decide who is doing what.

A facilitator may sometimes be a valuable factor in the success of action learning sets, especially in the early stages when there can be a tendency to revert to unfocused discussion or conventional processes. The main task of the facilitator is to model many of the skills so that they can become integrated into the regular practice of the set. For this to work effectively the facilitator may find feedback from the set a valuable asset. A truly effective active learning set can thus serve as a model for a learning culture in the wider context of the organization.

Student management teams

'Cross-cultural' group dynamics can also operate in the sphere of course management. Nuhfer (1994) describes a scheme in which, mimicking industrial total-quality management philosophies, he set up student management teams – 'a partnership between students and professors that are formed for the improvement of the classroom community'. The team comprises about four students and a tutor who have a managerial role and take on part of the responsibility for the success of the course. The students meet each week to monitor progress and discuss possible improvements, and the tutor joins them every other week. All meetings are held in a 'neutral' area and a written log of suggestions and related progress is maintained. Students receive compensation for their time, a clear indication that their work and the improvement of teaching is institutionally approved. Nufher claims that the teams can improve the classroom learning environment by considering how the course may be improved – sequence of material presented, designating areas of students' difficulty, removing students' misconceptions, preventing absenteeism, dealing with irritating behaviour by consensus and preventing observed problems, and how the delivery of material might be improved (with the permission of the tutor in question).

Teams were also drafted for special purposes. An engineering professor wanted to know why engineering courses appeared unpopular with women and recruited an ad hoc team of female students to find out why. A foreign professor who had low evaluations because of his thick accent asked for help from the team with his communication; they helped him with his pronunciation, suggested more overhead transparencies and handouts with lecture outlines, as well as a glossary of terms that were difficult to understand. Another professor who was troubled by a hostile cluster of hecklers in a race and gender class was advised by the team to tell them to 'Shut up!', which worked for a time. When the hecklers resumed their activity the team turned on them, and eventually 80 per cent of the class confronted them with a concerted 'SHUT UP!'

Student management teams offer a less threatening scenario for the admission of shortcomings and the collaborative search for solutions than is likely in the more confrontational climate of student representatives and staff–student committees. The model defines students as colleagues and represents an astute use of group dynamics within an organizational system, which traditionally regards students as receivers rather than creators of courses.

The physical environment

Whatever the aims of a curriculum or the motives of individuals, the physical arrangement of teaching rooms, staff offices, corridors, social and domestic amenities and constraints of the timetable will be significant factors in determining the pattern of communication and relationships in an institution. To some extent powerful drives such as the need for personal affiliation can mitigate many of the physical barriers – distance for one. However, where the desire to learn is (as it often seems to be) a less than powerful drive, physical proximity and frequency of encounter may have a marked effect. The nearer one lives to somebody, the greater the likelihood that chance meetings will occur and even where they do not, their likelihood may itself exert a strong influence. Of course, the very fact of meeting does not ensure that effective communication will occur; nor does the lack of meeting mean that it will not. Festinger *et al* (1950) quoted in Smith (1973), reported in a study of friendship patterns in The Massachusetts Institute of Technology, that students whose rooms were relatively inaccessible had fewer friends, and those whose rooms were more accessible had more friends and they tended to be from nearby.

A similar situation exists where the proximity of a 'significant' person or object causes a person to attend to them more readily than another at a greater distance. People are always more alert to immediate demands. It is likely, therefore, that frequent casual encounters with tutors and group colleagues will serve as a regular reminder of agreed tasks and a spur for new ideas for the group. The frequency of group meetings will determine the extent to which the group ethos will prevail over other priorities.

To some extent the total size of the institution will also affect the sense of group identity because the likelihood of chance meetings is lessened both with physical distance and with a larger population. It would seem likely that the anonymity and the sense of alienation that may grow in bigger institutions would push people into small (and perhaps deviant) affinity groups and discourage participation in organized group activities. This hypothesis is supported to some extent by Barker (1968) who found that with the increasing size of a school, students tended to become audience rather than participant in many of the school activities.

In the same way, it is probable that the physical shape of the environment will influence the nature of casual interaction. A building designed as a set of rooms leading off long corridors limits encounters to hasty exchanges in the corridors or specially arranged meetings in designated places, neither of which promotes spontaneous communication. A conveniently situated open area or refreshment facility can offset this sort of environmental drawback to some extent, but there is no substitute for rooms arranged round a central area with refreshments immediately available.

The problems of communication and relationships in the environment appear to echo those experienced in the learning group. Size, physical layout, personal proximity and so forth all play their part. The style of interaction present in a learning group could also be influenced to a large extent by its general environment. The implication of these considerations is that whether one is thinking of the learning group or its environment, physical arrangements must be taken into consideration if the kind of educational and social relationships we desire are to occur.

Educational matters

The design of a course or curriculum involves many value judgements about styles and techniques of teaching and learning and the order in which they should occur. Ideally these judgements should be subsumed under a general educational style or philosophy agreed by the teachers and even the students. However, the limits imposed on educational procedures by logistics, such as disposition and availability of rooms and timetabling of other classes, frequently make the reality of curriculum development an untidy compromise. More often than not, educational ideals are decimated by timetables, which organize course programmes into a fragmented collection of learning experiences for the student and give a similar sense of disconnectedness to the teachers.

However, it would be unfair to place the blame for this kind of course entirely on timetabling committees. Teachers themselves are prone to equally myopic tendencies in at least two ways. One is connected with course content or subject matter, which is frequently regarded as a sort of academic territory to be established and defended against the encroachment of other warring tribes of academe. The second is the way in which the subject content is transmitted and the apparent need to control its dissemination and boundaries. It is normally the teacher who determines what is to be learnt, and how, and what counts for an acceptable standard of learning. However, beneath all this there may exist a hidden curriculum: one in which the teaching is geared to the interests and levels of achievement of only the brighter students to the neglect of the majority whose main, and perhaps only, concern is to qualify competently and get a job. What Stenhouse (1975) describes as, 'Official policies which tend to encourage those (school) teachers who turn away from the practical and vocational realities of their pupils and turn to higher things', has even more significance in tertiary education where the power of abstract reasoning, in which many otherwise able students are not proficient, is highly valued.

Tutors usually define what they regard as reality, and 'acceptable' knowledge, in discussion groups and can quickly and firmly establish norms about the kind and level of knowledge that may be discussed. Many of these norms are determined by the style of tutor intervention. Sometimes the style can be inhibiting; for example, where tutors open a seminar with a learned introduction or where their eloquence sets too high a standard for students who are still struggling to put their half-formed ideas together, never mind express them.

On the other hand, tutors can equally well set standards while still drawing students into the discussion. They can, for instance, pick out what they consider loose or 'incorrect' thinking and reflect it back either to the contributor or to the whole group using some of the interventions given in Chapter 7 and in Rudduck (1978).

In their capacity as both leaders and organizers of learning groups, tutors are involved in mediating the values, requirements and ultimately the authority of the institution which, willingly or not, they will be seen to represent. They also have the quasi-administrative role of passing on and collecting organizational information: small groups provide an effective means of ensuring that some of the more difficult administrative guidance is given and properly understood. How a tutor carries out the administrative/organizational function can be crucial to the relationship established with a group. However, there is one organizational role that can have a much more critical effect on the atmosphere of the group: that of assessor. Whether the concern is with setting exams, marking essays/lab work, or in appraising contributions to the discussion group, the tutor's authority can be seen by the students as all-pervading because of the typically unilateral nature of assessment.

It is a fact (an unfortunate one perhaps) of academic life that both tutors and students frequently collude in a sort of protocol or game, the rules of which may be expressed by: 'You may be too mature or free to be controlled by my asserted authority but I know you know I'm your assessor, even if I pretend that I'm not.' The anxieties surrounding assessment affect many seminar groups:

> *The seminar, ideally, is a place where people can take risks with ideas. Risk-taking is more likely to occur in a secure structure and the security of the seminar is sometimes threatened for students by uncertainty about assessment. Are they being assessed? And, if so, on what? The obvious conclusion, in the absence of any explanation of the assessment procedure, is that they are being assessed on their spoken contributions (frequency? length? or the elusive concept of quality?) (Rudduck, 1978)*

The tendency of some seminar tutors to maintain power by preserving the ambiguity of their assessment role can therefore create a group atmosphere that is both counter-educational and uncomfortable. As Rudduck explains: 'The shadow of assessment is likely to make the enquiry more teacher-oriented than it might if there were no assessment or if the rules of assessment were made clear to the students.'

There is, of course, an essential tension between the two roles of mentor/facilitator and that of assessor. This is particularly so where continuous assessment takes place or where students' seminar performance is appraised. In such cases as Richardson (1967) describes, the responsibility for assessment has to be recognized by teacher and student alike as part of the fabric of the personal relationship between them; there is no longer any way of externalizing it.

Richardson's approach to the problem when working with student teachers was to bring the subject of assessment out into the open and work through the anxieties that the duality of her role implied. It was apparent to her that student behaviour changed both when essay titles were given and when essays were due to be handed in. The complex of behaviours, developed in school, to handle the student–teacher's hopes and fears about assessment in classroom revealed itself in an uncharacteristic rivalry for the tutor's approval and a mutual sense of embarrassment and secretiveness about what they were learning in preparing their essays.

After the problems of assessment had been openly discussed within the group, the atmosphere changed dramatically to one of cheerfulness and buoyancy, and the group acquired a 'personal commitment and intellectual enjoyment not previously evident except in one-to-one sessions'. Yet again the value of self-disclosure as a trigger to having a more open climate of communication seems to have worked.

At the University of East Anglia, the 'assessment problem' has been tackled in one subject area (moral philosophy) by the drawing up of a learning contract in which the assessment function of the tutor is openly described. For example:

> *It is important to make explicit that nothing you do (or fail to do) in the small group meetings will be assessed for grading purposes. Grades for the course will be determined by two essays . . .*
>
> *Although grades will be determined by the above essays no grade will be given unless you keep a record of the work done for and in the small-group meetings. This record will consist of a loose-leaf folder containing:*
>
> *— accounts of your work in the sub-group;*
> *— accounts of the themes and arguments raised each week in the small group meetings;*
> *— three summaries of your own, developing views, to be written at the end of weeks 3, 6 and 9.*
>
> (Rudduck, 1978)

In this way, what happens in the groups becomes a necessary part of the assessment procedure yet is not itself assessed. How effective this procedure was at UEA is not reported.

This section would not be complete without some reflection on the pervasive influence of a more traditional assessment procedure: the three-hour unseen examination. The mounting anxiety that increasingly afflicts the group discussion as the 'exam season' approaches is familiar to most tutors, and there is often little they can do to offset it, except to recognize it and perhaps take 'time out' to discuss its nature and possible remedies. Like most anxieties, its effect is to cause regression among the student population to the point where many of the higher-level aims cannot be realized. Students become increasingly concerned with picking up bits of knowledge to tuck away under their belts and are unwilling to engage in the more open-ended and creative kind of discussion that may have prevailed before.

Where the tutor is also the examiner or, as is even more likely, has sight of the exam papers, students may take up various stratagems to reduce their anxiety. Miller and Parlett (1974) discerned three groups of students in their study of the effects of examinations at Edinburgh University: the *cue seekers*, who actively sought to pick up hints about exam questions and tried to make a good impression on tutors; the *cue conscious* who were equally aware but not active in their approach; and the *cue deaf* who believed that only hard work achieved success and that any impression they made on tutors would have no effect on their marks. (How these practices affect the quality of interaction in group discussion is not reported; one could make an inspired guess without much difficulty.) However, there was a clear indication that tutors became involved in an equivalent set of behaviours – hinters, tantalizers and non-hinters, depending on whether they were anxious about students not doing well in their subject, wanted to relieve unproductive student anxiety, or liked to play a one-sided power game. As in most interactions involving anxiety, a collusive pattern of behaviour between students and tutor can easily develop. All this activity can be seen as part of what Snyder (1971) calls the 'hidden curriculum' – strategies that students resort to in order to survive.

Groups in courses

Let us now look again at the legitimate framework of learning in which tutors and groups are engaged. As we have already noted, the amount of time and physical space available for discussion groups can have a profound effect on the kind of learning that takes place. There is a world of difference, for instance, between the small group of eight students working intensively with a tutor for three hours, with a 20-minute coffee break included, and a science 'tutorial' in which 20 students assemble for one hour in a room with fixed benches or large tables arranged in rows.

Small-group teaching must not be seen in isolation from the rest of the curriculum or its associated culture. In physical sciences, as indicated in Chapter 5, there has traditionally been a tendency to view small-group work as an added extra, a means of improving students' understanding of lecture material for instance, rather than as a coherent mode of learning in its own right. Part of the problem is the enormous load of information in the syllabus, which science and engineering lecturers believe must be transmitted (though how much is actually learnt is a different matter). Yet whatever view we may take of the students' role in learning, it is evident that knowledge, to be learnt effectively, must be processed, its meaning incorporated into the students' patterns of thinking, and ultimately communicated by the students in a coherent and acceptable form. If the syllabus is taught as an accumulating sequence where each stage of learning is dependent on the previous one, then it is essential that the students learn progressively and not terminally: they must integrate their understanding as they go along rather than through a 'flash in the pan' revision at examination time. Group discussion is an invaluable aid to this kind of continuous learning. If it is to be used, the course must be tailored to accommodate it as an integral feature.

Timetabling group discussion

Several frameworks are possible for the inclusion of group work in the formal timetable. Some of the groups are planned to occur within lecture periods, some between; yet others are linked to practical classes. Whether or not several groups can operate concurrently will depend upon the number of students, tutors and available facilities. For example, within a large hall with moveable furniture, any number of small groups could be formed before, during or after a lecture. In a terraced lecture theatre, however, any sustained small group discussion would probably have to be left till after the lecture. Some possible arrangements for the integration of group discussion are shown in Figures 8.1, 8.2 and 8.3.

In Figure 8.1 we can see how in teaching a large group we can introduce the kind of practices described in previous chapters while maintaining a sense of continuity and momentum. The session begins with the lecturer displaying on the OHP, while the students are still assembling, a set of headings that review the previous lecture(s), thus making effective use of what is normally 'dead' time.

The lecturer then goes on to address the outline on the OHP, thus pulling together ideas and topics dealt with in prior reading, seminars and lectures. No new material is

Time

Stage	1	Revision OHP displayed		10.00 am

10.05 am

Stage 2   Revision talk on last lectures   10.14 am

Stage 3   Task: discuss in pairs   10.19 am

Stage 4   Talk   10.26 am

Stage 5   Task: discuss in pairs   10.30 am

Stage 6   Lecturer summarizes student answers.
          10.33 starts lecturing again.   10.36 am

Stage 7   Task: specific questions on a map;
          discuss in pairs   10.42 am

Stage 8   Lecturer answers first two questions   10.43 am

Stage 9   Continued discussion in pairs   10.45 am

Stage 10 Talk: lecturer gives answers, and lectures
          (using OHPs)   10.48 am

Stage 11 30-second task: in pairs   10.48 am

Stage 12 Lecturer refers to handout not covered
          in lecture   10.54 am

Stage 13 Students summarize lecture for themselves   10.56 am

End

Total lecturer talk   : 31 mins _____
Total student work   : 25 mins _____
Longest lecturer talk   : 9 mins
Longest student task   : 6 mins
Number of 'segments' of lecture :   13

Source: Alan Jenkins, Oxford Brookes University

Figure 8.1 *Integrating group discussion into the lecture*

added at this stage. Note that this is the longest formal input in the session – only nine minutes!

For Stage 3, a new transparency poses a question that directs students to work in twos or threes in making an application of their previous work. The lecturer moves round the class listening, helping and clarifying where necessary.

Stage 4 comprises a further short lecture with explicitly new material: students add new points to their handouts. This is followed by students discussing these new points in pairs while the lecturer moves round to check for understanding. A review of the students' responses is given by the lecturer in Stage 6. In Stage 7 the lecturer poses more difficult questions to the pairs concerning interpretation; this stimulates a buzz of activity at a point when one would typically expect a trough in the level of attention.

The lecturer then answers part of the question in Stage 8 and leads students to more advanced issues. The pattern of lecturer–student interaction continues till the last few minutes when students are asked to write a brief summary of the lecture.

This style of presentation requires not merely a considerable amount of assertiveness on the part of the lecturer in making sure that events move on crisply, but also a sensibility of the time needed to carry out each activity. However, a central ingredient for success in this approach is a very clear and explicit statement to the students on why one is lecturing in this way.

The sort of structure suggested in Figure 8.1 for a lecture session requires both careful planning and firm but sensitive direction by the tutor, particularly in making decisions about when to change the learning activity.

A more extended version of the above scheme is shown in Figure 8.2. Figure 8.3 demonstrates a combination of group and individual work for practicals, which carries over the distilled learning from one session to the next.

This arrangement primes students for a collective encounter with the lecturer. It makes a clear contrast to the kind of lecture that ends in a throwaway comment like: 'Oh, next week we will be looking at the application of complex numbers to space frames', a type of ending not unknown in physical science, or a lengthy and unannotated book list in social science.

The permutations of these arrangements are considerable and each tutor would have to work out a plan according to the aims and logistics of the course. In some cases, alternation and linking of lecture and discussion can be tightly organized as a total strategy for the whole course. In others, given some leeway, it can be incorporated within an otherwise standard timetable.

In looking at ways in which sequences of group work may be organized within a fairly traditional curriculum, we should not forget that there are many courses or parts of courses where there may be much more freedom to experiment and to provide for varying degrees of self-direction in the groups. Some approaches of this kind are described in the second part of this chapter, but for the sake of contrast it is worth mentioning here three other approaches.

One is the kind of group project, already discussed on pages 146–48, which is scheduled so as to allow students to learn, as the project evolves, the knowledge and skills required for its successful completion. This they do by using the staff as individual consultants on certain topics, having lectures arranged in response to emerging interests, and attending training sessions in teamwork, creative thinking and report writing.

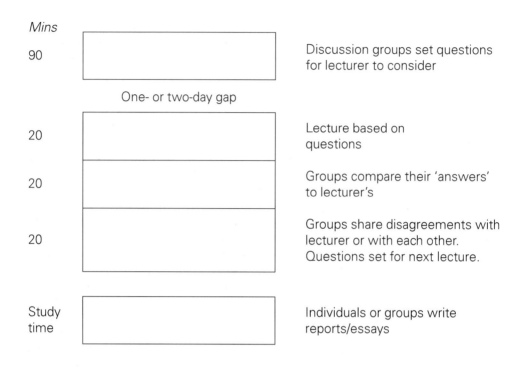

Figure 8.2 *Sequencing lectures and group discussion*

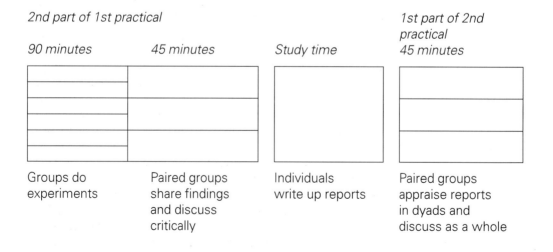

Figure 8.3 *Combining group and individual work in practicals*

Another approach is described by Fransson (1976) as 'group-centred instruction'. In this, though there is a curriculum to be followed, the organization of learning lies with the group who may determine how, within certain guidelines, they wish to use their tutors. The tutors in turn make certain demands of the groups, instances being the writing of diaries, assessment discussions and questions that demand cooperative work.

The third approach is the scheme in operation in the medical faculty at McMaster University and other places where the students learn clinical work in groups, frequently with simulated patients. Their formal assimilation of knowledge mostly takes the form of library study in response to the practical problems presented to the group. Group work is considered sufficiently important for each student to be presented with learning resources on group work – eg, 'The Small Group Tutorial', obtainable from the faculty of Medicine (see also Neufeld and Barrows, 1974).

Schemes like these make special demands of the students and tutors in overcoming the various constraints, habits and norms of the educational institution of which they are part. Any evaluation of success must therefore take into account the influences of the total learning milieu, which may include implacable opposition by colleagues and by some of the students for whom the dispersal of authority may be extremely unsettling. Nevertheless, more traditional schemes of teaching, it seems, are often followed purely because they fulfil mutual expectations – college is, after all, the place where eminent people are supposed to give lectures and demonstrate their expertise, and where students congregate to gain benefit from them. The problem is that teaching on the one hand, and learning on the other, are likely to follow two different rhythms. When one is active, the other is frequently passive, whether we take a short- or a long-term view. Accordingly, if we want to establish a curriculum that balances democratic learning principles with academic expertise we will need to take firm and continuing checks and measures to ensure balance and synchronicity.

A further consideration relates to the problem already touched on in Chapter 6 of coping with increasing class sizes to the point where the group becomes too large to comfortably achieve the aims prescribed for it. There is no reason, as we have already seen, why groups should not work independently on alternate weeks, provided rooms and appropriate tasks are organized. For example, when meeting without a tutor, students could prepare questions and reports, pool their reading, solve problems set by the tutor or act as a peer tutoring group by answering for each other the questions they might normally ask of the tutor. When they meet with the tutor they would present the work they had discussed, interact as usual with the tutor and receive further briefing. Some of the options for timetabling these meeting are shown in Figure 8.4 (Gibbs, 1992b).

Within any curriculum, some aims may have priority over others at different times, and an important but often neglected job of the course tutor is to organize and monitor the teaching and learning so that some sort of coherent experience may emerge. Alert group tutors can plan their own unfolding patterns with the group, but there may be wider considerations to be dealt with. One of these occurs on the modular or unit system of course design, where students can often experience a sense of 'bittiness' in their studies (Parlett *et al*, 1988). Some institutions have attempted to achieve a degree of integration across the modules by scheduling a 'synoptic study' session into the timetable. In the synoptic study students might discuss relationships between the elements, apply the separate knowledge to a particular focus (eg, science and society) or solve integrative

Model 1 Pre- and post-meetings

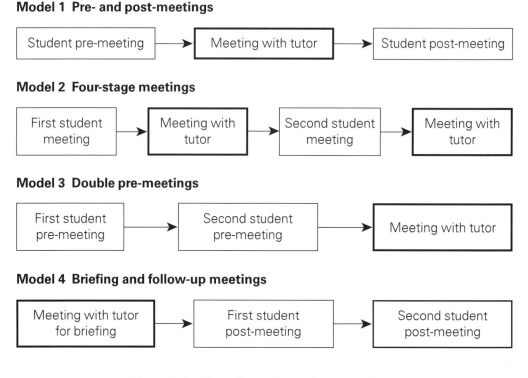

Model 2 Four-stage meetings

Model 3 Double pre-meetings

Model 4 Briefing and follow-up meetings

Figure 8.4 *Alternative patterns of group meetings*

problems. A somewhat less conventional but nevertheless valuable task would be to discuss the experience of learning in each module and to explore ways of enhancing it – though this might be politically risky without the full agreement of all the tutors teaching the modules.

Nevertheless, some sort of small-group experience would seem vital in the unit or modular system to give students the possibility of developing a sense of social identity and a feeling of belonging, and commitment to the intellectual life of the institution. Parlett and King (1971) report an attempt to overcome many of the fragmenting effects of an orthodox timetable in which students of physics worked on 'concentrated study' – the full-time study for a month of a single subject with no competing academic demands. This curricular innovation provided enormous scope and freedom for varied and spontaneous group work. At Worcester Polytechnic Institute in the USA (ASEE, 1976) students take part in a project-based unit of seven weeks' duration in which they work exclusively on their project.

One aspect of student experience of higher education that does not appear to have received much attention is that of multiple group membership, often coupled with a complex of tasks. What looks on paper a well-coordinated and reasonably demanding course can be experienced by the individual in a very different way. Unfortunately, the day-to-day experience (not to speak of the hour-to-hour experience) of the student is not often studied by course designers. The constant need in a traditional course programme for students to switch attention across specialisms, and align themselves to different groups of people, can be either an inspiring stimulus or a muddling burden, depending on the individual student's capacity to cope with a variety of demands or, in less fortunate cases, to defend against increasing bewilderment and anxiety by opting out and possibly failing.

Whatever kinds of group activity are formally organized, informal peer grouping will inevitably, and quite properly, occur. There are, as Newcomb (1967) says, diverse motivations for students in aligning themselves with peer groups: some, for example, have strong tendencies toward conformity, while some others seem to be compulsively deviant. Both can find support from like-minded groups. Some need to be dependent on authority whereas independence is essential to others. Although the latter may seem to be immune to peer-group influence, the fact seems to be that they need it as much as the others but tend to find it in smaller and more selective circles. For some, membership in high-prestige groups is the crucial thing. Positions of 'leadership' or dominance, or perhaps just prominence, are required by still others. Some students become group members because of the interests and attitudes for which the group seems to stand, while others appear quite willing to adopt the norms of any group that becomes important to them for other reasons. Many of these and other motives can be combined in the same person as he or she finds different kinds of satisfactions in multiple and doubtless partially overlapping groups. The effects of peer-group membership will vary with such motives and with the degree to which they find satisfaction through affiliation.

It is clearly not the task of tutors to become involved in maximizing or otherwise determining peer-group affiliation and influence; to do so would be intrusive and could deprive students of essential opportunities for change and development not available to them in the organized curriculum. It can, however, be enormously helpful for tutors to understand something of the nature of students' extracurricular concerns and their motives for such involvement. Information of this kind could be quite valuable in forming judgements about what the course may be failing to offer any student, particularly where most of his or her energies appear to be diverted from the educational programme. What is more, there is always the possibility, if there is no overlap between the values of peer groups and the learning group, that peer group norms entirely divorced from intellectual concerns will develop. For some students this may represent a necessary and welcome relief from the considerable demands of the legitimate educational culture. For others it could represent a disturbing influence, a constant doubting of the values of the learning group. It is probable that, as Newcomb suggests, this sort of isolation will occur where there is a feeling of anonymity within the learning groups either because of large numbers or a lack of concern for the students at a personal level. If this is so, it serves to underline the worth of aims in learning groups directed to personal development, self-esteem and a sense of belonging.

Case studies of group teaching and learning

In this section we shall see how various academic teachers in institutions both in the UK and abroad have incorporated principles of group learning into 'real-life' teaching schemes.

Self-development groups

A course at the Crewe and Alsager faculty of Manchester Metropolitan University was designed to promote awareness of reactions and responses within the group and interpersonal context by using content from Humanistic and Social Psychology. The unit content was divided into three main sections:

1. group structure and dynamics;
2. self-understanding and self-management;
3. interpersonal interaction and communication.

The first of these was of particular interest: specific topics included the nature of groups, norms, group cohesiveness, 'group think', deviance, group goals, cooperation and competition, management of conflict, and leadership.

Students were actively involved each week in an experiential exercise that aimed to illustrate some particular aspect of group dynamics. This exercise would have been a role play, a simulation or a problem-solving activity.

Discussion in the debriefing was promoted through two procedures: a post-exercise questionnaire, which encouraged students to focus on important aspects of the interaction, with observers often providing different perspectives on the process of the exercise during the debriefing; and the relevant literature being discussed in student-led groups – the expectation being that such discussion would provide a better opportunity for students to link academic content to their own experience than could be possible within any kind of lecture set-up.

The third feature concerns the provision of assessment that related to the aims of the unit in that it encouraged reflection on personal functioning within the group situation.

One of the most crucial parts of the overall assessment involved the students keeping a weekly journal, which encouraged them to reflect in writing on their own experience and reactions. Grading of this was on a pass/fail basis provided it fulfilled certain basic requirements. They were also encouraged to use their journal in producing an 'evaluative review of personal learning' in which they were expected to discuss analytically and reflectively what they had learnt about themselves, their own behaviour, feelings and interactional responses from their experience in the programme.

(Based on Cuthbert, 1994.)

Transferable skills

In 1989, University College London initiated a programme intended to equip under-graduates with a range of personal transferable skills, which could subsequently be useful to them both during their university studies and thereafter. The focus of the programme was on teamwork, leadership, communication and project management skills. The resulting personal development programme was designed to:

- be college-wide, to work in collaboration with employers; and
- act as a 'seed' activity from which experience could be gained and cascaded down the departmental structure in order to, eventually,
- embed these skills in the curriculum.

Group work skills were applied in a variety of situations designed to illuminate the dynamics of a group and the roles individuals take, including aspects such as problem-solving, planning, communication, the functions of leadership, and the organization of information material and people, in order to achieve specific tasks.

A set of core skills was identified, each of which was introduced and then developed through a series of activities that utilized all learning gained from earlier exercises and developed it further. The pilot course included:

- Introduction to teamwork – intended as an opportunity for participants to develop their understanding of group processes and the elements of leadership through a series of exercises and reviews.
- Teamwork and leadership – designed to develop further the understanding of group processes, planning and communication through a challenging series of practical, team-based exercises offering leadership opportunities to all participants, including reviews, reflection and action planning.
- Communication skills – intended to develop communications skills in a variety of situations, through video-recorded oral presentation skills training with group feedback and team-based role plays, in a variety of communication settings and including reviews and action planning.
- Project management – to develop an understanding of the processes of managing a project by means of a number of exercises, covering individual time management and project-management skills, concluding with a complex competitive team exercise involving all the preceding skills.

Assessment was formative and conducted by facilitated peer review during group review sessions. At the end of the course the facilitators wrote open references for each of the participants. This served a dual purpose: first, it formed a basis for discussion in a final course interview in which performance was reviewed; and second, it was available to the student to use in support of subsequent applications for employment or further education.

Participants reported an increase in their self-confidence, particularly with regard to oral presentations and in negotiations of various kinds. Some said that the programme had helped them to make decisions that they might not otherwise have made (course changes, career decisions and so on) and several said they had become more confident in making decisions than they otherwise would have been.

Because the personal development programme was based on group work and as it extended right across University College London, it proved to be a vital mechanism in demonstrating the practical benefits of, and encouraging department interest in, group-based learning activities. The departments of Chemical and Bio-chemical Engineering, Italian, Geology, Geography, and Anatomy and Developmental Biology have all begun to embed team-based experiential activities into their curricula.

(Based on Guzkowska and Kent, 1994.)

Assessment of group projects

The Diploma in Management Studies at the University of Teesside organized group projects using peer assessment. It was introduced because the previous system of personal interviews that had been held, among other things, to establish individual contributions, had become to be seen as ineffective, and a more reliable, formal system was sought. It involved group members in assessing the contribution of both themselves and each other on a variety of dimensions. There was no requirement for agreement on the final results: each person's assessment was made independently and in confidence. Peer assessment fed into the overall examination process, one of its main uses being as a mechanism to ensure equitable distribution of grades within a group.

The tool devised for this purpose examined the group processes under two headings: task management (behaviours that move the group towards the completion of its working goals) and process management (behaviours that determine the quality of the relationships between the group members). It also included consideration of project output (contribution to the task in terms of time and/or effort and/or quality) and an overall evaluation category.

Assessment of the group project fell into two main areas: first, the appraisal or a consultant-style report submitted on completion of the project, plus a video presentation of five to seven minutes duration; second, self- and peer assessment of learning from, and contribution to, the project activity.

Responsibility for final assessment rested with two members of staff, one of whom was the project tutor, who established the baseline of assessment and determined any variation in grade between individuals in the group. The latter relied on the tutor's knowledge of the individuals in the group, on factual evidence provided by the group or individual members, and on peer assessment. The peer and self-assessments both provided valuable input for the assessment process but were not the sole means of differentiation between individuals.

An analysis of the peer assessments provided some interesting revelations about student values:

- Equality. In some cases group members were so sure that they all contributed equally that they gave readings of 10 points for each and every area. It seemed that students were not willing to provide any information that might be detrimental to their fellows.
- Normal distribution. Group members in this case attributed a rating of between 5 and 15 on the dimensions. Although it seems unlikely that there was a genuine equality of input, group pressure and people's goodwill made this the most common alternative. It demonstrated a give-and-take within the group and a sensible distribution of workload and responsibility.
- The reluctant finger. Where there had been free-wheeling on the part of one member, the responses from other members showed a consistent level of under-contribution for that person and this might be mirrored by the individual's self-rating. It seemed that in most cases students would bend over backwards not to 'shop' their friends.
- Stitch them up. There was sometimes an apparent collusion between some of the group members. This was characterized by an over-similar pattern of assessment giving a clear indication of poor performance on the part of one individual; this

pattern was perhaps the most difficult to deal with as a tutor. If there was a systematic victimization of one individual, then there may have been a good reason to penalize the group as whole.

■ Out of kilter. From time to time there were cases where the pattern of responses varied considerably within the group. The simplest case was where someone thought that they had done considerably more than anyone else. In this case the average of marks for reports of others gave a more consistent assessment.

The hardest decision to arrive at was to fail one individual and pass the rest of the group. The projects was, after all, a group project, and if individuals did not contribute to the group then this undermined the entire ethos of the strategy.

The project evaluation (assessment) form is shown below.

DMS PROJECT PEER GROUP EVALUATION FORM

Your name _____

Member 2 _____

Member 3 _____

Member 4 _____

Member 5 _____

Member 6 _____

Peer Group Ratings –
Please rate the contribution of each group member on the dimensions below. The total on each row must equal the number of team members times ten; ie for four members the total score for all members must be 40.

Project Ouput	You	2	3	4	5	6
Ideas for the Project						
Background Reading						
Collecting Data						
Analysis and Interpretation						
Writing the Report						
Task Management						
Initiating						
Seeking Information and Opinions						
Giving Information or Opinions						
Clarifying and Elaborating						
Summarizing						
Consensus Testing						
Process Management						
Confronting Self and Others						
Gate Keeping						
Encouraging						
Standard Setting and Testing						
Overall Evaluation						

(Based on Mathews, 1994.)

The UPshot programme

First-year business and accounting degree students at the University of Plymouth took part in innovative business skills programme. It involved groups developing knowledge of the university campus and city. At an initial meeting in induction week, students were asked to divide into groups of six and to choose a leader. Each group member was given different tasks and they were then asked to meet the following day when they would take part in a time-constrained group work exercise. The groups had to gather information and equipment from a variety of points in the university. They had to collect and solve cryptic clues; obtain and use maps of the campus and city; collect and follow instructions; take 10 photographs of the campus and/or city using a Polaroid camera; and finally, select 3 of the 10 photographs to submit as the most effective and appropriate illustrations for insertion in the university prospectus.

Students were also expected to keep the team 'log', which was to include information such as the key decisions taken, and by whom, the problems encountered and interesting events. At the end of the exercise, students were required to complete individually a group behaviour questionnaire to help in analysing the effectiveness of individual and group performance. The students were also given reading material containing an overview of major theories relating to working in groups.

During the following three weeks, each group reconvened and planned a short video presentation summarizing the exercise. They were also asked to use the team log, group behaviour questionnaires and further reading material to help them draw conclusions as to how effectively the group worked. Groups then prepared and made the videos, which were intended to be as innovative and creative as possible. Debriefing sessions were held to review the programme and the learning gained. The photographs were judged by the dean of the business school and a representative of the university's marketing department, prizes were awarded to the winning groups, and some of the photographs were used in the next university prospectus.

All students involved in the UPshot programme subsequently took the organizational behaviour module, which builds on the group experience previously gained.

(Based on Garland, 1994.)

Teaching creativity through group work

At Leicester Business School the recognition that qualities like creativity, intuition and originality are rarely developed through common pedagogical processes led to the design of a business game in which groupwork, decision-making and creativity were developed in a non-deterministic fashion. In this, each tutorial group had to demonstrate application of basic marketing, personnel, managerial and accounting techniques to situations that developed as they introduced change into the company. Students were expected to work under sustained and increasing pressure of deadlines and organizational constraints. The accent was on decision-making, forcing students to experience both the process of, and solutions to, the business problems.

Students began by organizing themselves on company lines, electing their managing director and other senior staff from within their tutor group, with areas of responsibility given to individual managers and departments. Each group had responsibility for choosing the products and markets in which the firm operated, but the business had to be a manufacturing company and its span of operations broadly consistent with an inherited balance sheet. Successful groups selected, for example, paper cartons, industrial toasters and garden gnomes.

Information inputs of strategic marketing, finance and manufacturing were given through formal lectures and appropriate videos. Practice in skills development was achieved through workshop tutorials, some of which were voluntary, others compulsory. Each group had access to a tutor acting as facilitator through 'open' tutorials. Students were expected to use this input to find ways of achieving their mission by devising a strategic marketing plan, and introducing 'just-in-time' manufacturing methods and total quality management to the factory. These plans could be constructed using software such as PLANVIEW.

Students were thus exposed to crisis management techniques, short report writing and people management issues, putting into practice theory already learnt on their course. To give immediate relevance to the programme, each group visited a local manufacturing firm to get hands-on experience of production, engineering and capital investment, and their inherent advantages and problems. Creativity, innovation and communication of mission and objectives were all heavily weighted in the assessment.

There were no formal teaching inputs at the end of the game. Students were expected to finalize their plans, and a series of meetings were videoed. In these meetings, a strategic decision at board level was transformed into operational plans at department level – including negotiation with the workforce in the production department. A final meeting was necessitated by an unexpected emergency that required immediate action.

The programme required students to manage themselves and their peers effectively and to identify situations where their competence was insufficient to complete tasks to the required standard. Once these were identified by the students, remedial inputs were provided by the staff, or the students were directed to other sources. By designing the programme in this way it was intended that many skills had to be demonstrated by successful students. In particular, planning and organizing the time and activities of themselves and their peers was imperative, as was the efficient negotiation and delegation of areas of study and work within each tutorial group.

The prime aim of the assessment was to focus the group's mind on the decision-making processes rather than on the plan itself. It had three elements:

1. As each group finalized its plans the series of meetings were videoed. Credit was given to students able to show the ability to manage organizational change in a controlled fashion, demonstrate originality in their marketing ideas, and respond quickly and intelligently to the unexpected crisis described above. All students had to appear on and contribute to the video.
2. Five or six items of groupwork, including a presentation in which credit was given for intelligent application of techniques – minor errors in theory and financial accuracy were tolerated.

3. A short formal written examination, based on a seen case study, in which individuals proposed solutions to specific business problems similar to those experienced in the game itself.

(Based on McHardy and Henderson, 1994.)

Contracts and learning journals

Learning journals and group-based learning were part of a multi-disciplinary education programme for Health Visiting and Nursing at the University of East London. Nurses have traditionally been educated for roles in which there are seen as constantly attending the sick, under the direction of doctors and within a hospital setting. Thus the pattern of nursing curricula has, until recently, stressed preparation for efficient task-doers assisting at the doctor's orders. Nursing programmes have in the main been located in schools attached to hospitals, resulting in convergent thinking and instrumental training.

This initiative in curriculum development was designed to increase student-centred learning by developing skills of self-confidence and collaborative enterprise within the context of a shared multi-disciplinary learning in the fields of health education and primary prevention.

Learning contracts were introduced in order to increase the opportunity for students to negotiate their learning processes and resources within the constraints of the syllabus content and the overall curriculum. For the first cohort involved in the process, the idea of the learning contract was introduced in the second week of the course and the programme completed with tutor feedback on a written assignment towards the end of the year. After a classroom presentation on learning contracts, students were informed of the non-negotiable taught content and were given a timetable structure providing classroom space and tutor availability for negotiating encounters when experiential learning might occur. The cohort was organized into 12 small groups, each of which was allocated a topic to study from ' Social aspects of health and disease'; a tutor identified for each topic was to act as consultant.

During the groupwork training the students and a project tutor collaborated to negotiate the assessment criteria, which included a journal of their experiential learning encounters. At this stage, the assessment guidelines were also reviewed to include an appended copy of the journal. The groups were encouraged to have at least one meeting with the topic consultant and to negotiate further meetings according to their wishes.

The students appreciated the journal as a tool for self-evaluation, to focus learning on the skills of reflecting upon action in group work. The journal was also seen to form the basis of an individual student–student discussion in the group, or as a tutor–student discussion on self-awareness in the area of group dynamics. Once the group workshops and taught sessions on health promotion had taken place, a change came over most individuals towards a collective consciousness. Some attempted to forge group allegiances in order to negotiate a shared approach to the task. The presentations by each of the 12 groups were held separately, attended by the topic specialist and the students' practice teacher. Interestingly there was some sensitivity expressed about including any material from the journals in these presentations.

(Based on Talbot, 1994.)

Projects in aerospace design

As the culmination of three years of study towards the BEng in aerospace engineering, students at the University of Hertfordshire undertook a group aircraft design study. During the project students found that the problems of group dynamics rival the technical problems of aircraft design. The course aimed to simulate the situation that occurs in the industry during the early stages of a new aircraft design. At that time there are relatively few engineers involved but they will have a good deal of experience. Political and economic factors will invariably be present and will tend to produce obstacles only overcome by the most persistent design organization.

The task specified for the project was topical in that it was one of the most critical issues facing the aircraft industry at the time, namely the regional airliner. About 100 students operated in groups of five or six, their work being largely self-directed, with staff acting in a consultative or advisory role. The project represented one module of student work.

The work requirement for each student designer was individually defined. Each student was expected to work as a collaborative partner within his or her team, to face the technical issues together, and to share the decision-taking. The student team leader, responsible for organization and management, played a unique role in promoting the harmony of the team and had to be elected by the group with some care.

A member of staff was attached to each project group, on a five-week rota. Within this regime it was possible that a group wanting to do aerodynamics work would have a supervisor who was an expert on instructional design. It would then be important that the group made full use of the advice immediately available, while ensuring that some group members pursued aerodynamics by self-directed reading and research.

The design groups were expected to imagine that they represented an international consortium of manufacturers, with the necessary finance to launch a new aircraft. The project was timetabled to operate for three hours a week; there were 16 student groups tutored by eight academic staff organized in a rota so that each staff member handled eight groups in total. The programme was divided into four phases of supervision, the last week of which was for staff/peer assessment of each student's effort. The course concluded with submission of portfolios of work and group presentations.

Assessment marks came from four individual phase assessments of 12 per cent each, a group presentation representing 22 per cent and an individual portfolio of work which carried 30 per cent. The emphasis on team activity was thus reflected throughout the assessment.

(Based on Pressnell, 1994.)

Setting up independent first-year seminars in Italian

This case study involved the first year of an Italian course in which students had weekly seminars for the historical component. Throughout the year the students would take turns in giving seminar presentations. In the past the seminars had gone very badly, with little interest or preparation from anyone other than the seminar presenter, poor-quality presentations and a far from conducive atmosphere in the groups.

Seminar Group Training Session

Aims
- To introduce students to each other.
- To establish effective seminar groups.
- To develop effective seminar group working practices.
- To develop seminar presentation skills.
- To establish a method for giving feedback to seminars.
- Presenters to improve their presentations.

Programme

10.00   Introduction

10.10   Team formation
Establishment of seminar groups of eight and a team-building exercise in which students had 30 minutes in which to turn themselves from an anonymous cluster into a functioning team.

10.40   Doing it wrong
A negative brainstorm and discussion of how to make tutorials dreadful, helped by second- and third-year students, followed by a display of posters.

11.00   Coffee

11.20   Doing it right... Ground rules
Groups discuss the opposite of how to make seminars dreadful in order to establish the ground rules they wish to work to. Each group displays and signs their own set of ground rules on a poster.

12.00   Effective presentations and discussions
A very brief presentation based on a handout.

12.20   Preparation for seminars in the afternoon
Each pair in the seminar groups of eight will have the chance to give a 20-minute seminar: 10 minutes presentation and 10 minutes discussion, followed by 5 minutes feedback. The pairs have until 2.20 to prepare.

2.20   Practice seminars
2.20   1st seminar pair
2.45   2nd seminar pair
3.10   3rd seminar pair
3.35   4th seminar pair

4.00   Tea

4.20   Closing exercise
Each person in turn completes one of the following sentences:
'Something I'm going to do to make my seminar group work well is . . .'
'How I feel about being in my seminar group is . . .'
'Something we have learnt as a group is . . .'

4.30   Close

Eight parallel independent seminar groups of eight were set up for a class of 64 students. A training day was run during the students' induction week, to help the groups to form, discuss how they wanted to operate, and practise giving seminars. The programme for this day is reproduced below. It was run by one tutor who could easily have handled more parallel groups and more students. Second- and third-year students were invited to share their experience of dreadful seminars in the negative brainstorm exercise.

In the practice seminars students chose their own topics (such as 'Rock bands in the 70s') and prepared overhead transparencies, flipchart posters and handouts. They gave the seminars as pairs to reduce the stress involved and increase cooperation.

The handouts, 'Improving Seminar Presentations' and 'Involving Students in Discussion' (Gibbs, 1992b) were used in briefing students about how to run their seminars. The practice seminars all took place in one large room, and with no involvement whatsoever on the part of the tutor. The students' first experience of seminars in higher education was therefore of independent groups where the groups themselves had total responsibility for their own operation. The handout, 'Seminar Presentation Feedback Form', was used by the groups to give feedback to the seminar presenters.

The day ended with each student making a statement about what they had learnt about seminars or about what they would do to make their seminar groups more pleasant and effective. Each seminar group formulated plans for monitoring their own performance as a group.

Student forums without a tutor

Oxford Brookes University experimented with students running their own discussion sessions in English Studies as a supplement to the existing patterns of lecture, seminar and office hours. The experiment was marked by both glittering triumphs and 'howling disasters'. The basic pattern of teaching and learning adopted was in three parts as follows:

- a staff lecture introducing terms, techniques and theories relevant to a specific topic;
- a student forum (without tutor but with guidelines) which had the task of engaging in a preliminary discussion of this topic and framing a provisional critical agenda;
- a seminar (with tutor present) in which the preceding agenda was modified and put into practice, with the tutor supplying further guidance and information.

In practice, occasionally, this format worked wonderfully well. All three parts interlocked productively and the result was, in the words of the tutor, 'a genuinely empowered student group and a really energized and purposeful final seminar'. More often, however, students seemed confused or uncertain about their roles and responsibilities in the student forum, and did not contributed fully – or simply failed to turn up.

All this prompted some changes in the second run-through. The guidelines on how the sessions were to be organized were firmed up, with clearer advice on the appointment of a chairperson and secretary and a stronger insistence on the responsibility to produce a properly framed and reasoned agenda. A subsequent redrafting of the guidelines took place, with a member of staff attending at least the first student forum to help get it going, and who might even drop in periodically later to help sort out continuing organizational problems. The tutor was against the idea of a register to enforce attendance ('A session is either worth attending or it isn't'). He and his colleagues remained convinced that if 'student-centred' was to mean more than the usual 'blast of flatulent rhetoric', some such experiments in the transfer of responsibility and power were necessary.

No taste for accounting?

Imagination and excitement are not normally terms associated with subjects like Accountancy and Financial Management. But at Oxford Brookes University in the School of Hotel and Catering Management the introduction of role play coupled with present-ation helped to create seminars that stimulated enormous interest and controversy among the group. The combination of the two approaches kept the academic integrity of study and research while facilitating communication and interaction in a live scenario, to the benefit of both presenters and peer group.

Students in a class of up to 24 were asked to research an agreed topic in teams of two or three, submit their findings to the tutor in the form of a seminar paper, together with a one-page executive summary containing the key issues. Each team was then required to present a role play to the group, comprising one or more aspects of their findings and using a scenario of their own choice. The role players were expected to involve their peer group by encouraging members to question, challenge and engage in a discussion of the topic. The seminar paper was graded by the tutor while the role play presentation was peer assessed against predetermined criteria. The assessment form is reproduced in Figure 8.5.

An example of a topic would be: 'Is it possible to predict financial distress or failure of businesses in the hospitality industry?'. One scenario selected for the concomitant role play comprised an examination of multi-variate models through a client meeting in the office of a firm of consultants. Two consultants were confronted by an angry restaurateur who had recently become insolvent, despite prior reassurances on the reliability of the prediction models. In another session on company mergers and take-overs, two students took their idea from the film 'Romuald et Juliette' and posed (and dressed up, complete with mops and brushes) as two cleaners who had discovered, in clearing out office waste bins, some papers about a secret deal by a senior executive to leak information to a rival, predatory firm.

Even animals were not excluded from presentations: two 'pandas' at a zoo arrived on one occasion to engage in an animated discussion on the problems of labour turnover at their zoo.

Passports for seminars

Absenteeism and poor preparation can demoralize a seminar group. This double problem was dealt with in an unusual and imaginative way at the School of Business at Oxford Brookes University. Faced with 'increasingly decreasing' numbers – a 60 per cent attendance apparently being connected with inadequate preparation, low energy and a

Seminar – role play peer assessment form

Please complete this form by the end of the role play, ie circle one box for each of the criteria, add comments (or not), and enter total score at the bottom of the page. Hand in to **Peter Harris**.

STUDENT _____   ROLE PLAY GROUP _____

Criteria:

Introduction
Setting the scene,
Identifying the roles

Excellent   Poor

| 5 | 4 | 3 | 2 | 1 |

Comment:

Creativity
Innovative, imaginative,
surprising

| 5 | 4 | 3 | 2 | 1 |

Comment:

Convincing
Acting out the role,
maintaining the scenario

| 5 | 4 | 3 | 2 | 1 |

Comment:

Communication
Clear, well-presented

| 5 | 4 | 3 | 2 | 1 |

Comment:

Technical Content
Relevant to the topic,
use of theory

| 5 | 4 | 3 | 2 | 1 |

Comment:

Audience Management
Quality of discussion,
questions

| 5 | 4 | 3 | 2 | 1 |

Comment:

Total score [   ]   (Maximum 30 points)

Figure 8.5 *Peer assessment for a role play seminar*

poor quality of discussion – students started to 'vote with their feet'. When attendance dropped to 25 per cent and pleas had failed to make much difference, the tutor decided, paradoxically, to make it more difficult for students to attend rather than easier, by introducing a 'passport system'. He notified students that in future no one would be allowed into the seminars unless they presented a 10 cm by 12.5 cm card with both sides filled with notes from their reading of the recommended texts. He promised them he would collect these, listed under each name, and return them to the students when they were seated in their end-of-term exam. (There were no exam rules that banned the use of specified and scrutinized notes.) Proxy submission of the cards was not permitted.

Attendance shot up rapidly to 90–100 per cent, the discussion was energetic and well-informed and students evaluated the seminars positively and enthusiastically. Moreover, students with high anxiety about exams claimed that they felt more relaxed and were therefore able to perform better.

The interesting feature of this strategy was that, far from changing the overall system, it used it to advantage and gave the students the sort of connectedness between their discussion and assessment that is not easy to achieve within an otherwise fairly traditional course.

Grading contributions

Another method used asked students who participated in groups to make a note of what they said or wanted to say to the tutor at the end of the class. Then he graded the slips as soon as possible after a class, while the class content was still fresh in his mind. Grades were limited to three points per class session so as to discourage excessive participation. The slips were returned at the next class with feedback comments. Most slips contained valid material and thus received one credit per item.

A claimed benefit of this method is that the students tended to rethink and rewrite what they said and in so doing reinforced their learning. It was also very useful for shy or quieter students who were allowed to write down what they were thinking or would like to have asked, and thus not need to feel so excluded. Moreover the tutor had the opportunity to include many of these ideas in the subsequent class so as to give more confidence to such students that their ideas were valued.

A new way with debates

Students involved in an English degree at Anglia Polytechnic University on a 'Gender, sexuality and writing' module found themselves in groups of 20–24 dealing with a large amount of poetry and some prose. They also had to cope with some rather 'turgid and lengthy' prose fiction often in a highly opinionated form – ie, women's equality and 'the woman question' of the later 19th century. Initially the tutor feared that the students would not read the material – there were hundreds of pages of it – and would be unable to move away from mere opinion into using the material to really engage with arguments made at the time (rather than contemporary). The tutor could also envisage a class in which there was far more teacher talking than desired, and therefore had too much authoritative and authoritarian control of what went on. This would prevent students from 'owning' the material and the ideas within it. They also might not read what was essential for the course.

So the tutor divided the group into four units: two groups for equality for women and two against. For an hour one week they worked together, without the tutor being present, but with detailed instructions and the texts. Together they read through and processed the different prose essays for and against, and marshalled arguments, while at the same time ensuring that they could see what arguments, from the texts, could be put up by the 'other side' and how to counter them, again from the texts. They were told they must use the texts in all their points, quoting and referring, in order that opinion did not take over from the use of argument and reference.

The following week started with 20 minutes devoted to putting the two sets of groups together, making one group for and one against. Students had to handle this pulling of ideas and points together – this involved negotiation and explanation. They elected a speaker and seconder from each of the (now) two groups, and everyone else knew they must plan a question, with back-up evidence quoted and referenced, or plan a point to make, or one that could be made against a point raised by the other side. The rules were:

1. Roles and comments and positions are decided by teamwork.
2. The speaker and seconder must not dominate once the debate is under way.
3. Everyone must speak once the debate is under way and others must help to prompt and bring in their colleagues where appropriate.
4. The comments made, questions asked, etc, must always be backed up by textual references.
5. No mere opinion!

One person was elected as chair to help run it, and the tutor stayed on the sidelines.

One of the surprising results is that sometimes the group (largely female) 'won' the debate with a strong argument against women's equality, thus proving that they could argue even when they did not themselves believe in what they were arguing for (always an issue in debates). The dynamics and interaction were high, the use of text well handled, and everyone took part.

In the de-brief the group looked not only at the process and teamwork that led to it, but at the 'graduate skills' that they had demonstrated during the course of the debate and build-up to it. These included:

■   teamwork;
■   communication and interaction;
■   synthesis and engagement with knowledge and primary sources to develop their own learning and arguments;
■   oral presentation skills.

One of the other achievements of this session was that the tutor as teacher remained on the sidelines and did not enforce their readings or authority – the students ran it themselves, and clearly learned how to handle evidence and referencing in argument, and the skills of sharing out work, roles and points between them. It was not assessed directly, although each module carried 10 per cent of the marks for oral work of all sorts, and the students were aware that this would be counted towards their seminar oral assessments.

(Based on e-mail correspondence sent by Gina Wisker, Anglia Polytechnic University.)

Outdoor teambuilding in Law

The Law department at Exeter University recognized that the traditional concept of higher education did not fit well with employers' requirements for graduates with 'drive and commitment, teamwork skills and oral communication skills'. A model developed at the university encouraged the embedding of transferable skills into the traditional core of a subject in the hope that the false dichotomy between teachers of academic knowledge and trainers of skills could be reduced as students began to articulate their knowledge and understanding through the integration of skills.

First-year students were divided into groups invited to participate in a teamwork training programme sponsored by BP/Amoco with three specific aims:

1. To emphasize the benefits of effective teamwork.
2. To give students a framework and process for tackling group projects.
3. To help build an identity for each team.

Students in teams of eight were involved in a one- to two-day course, comprising a series of (mostly) outdoor exercises, emphasizing students' learning from experience and review, with the intention that such learning and specific insights gained from the course should be continued in the context of future experiences – whether academic study or within the world of work. The training course represented a great shift in emphasis for those many university teachers who maintain strong support for traditional academic skills and values. An ethos was created in which many students may have been enabled to value their strengths in new ways, to feel a personal commitment not just to the team, but to working at personal failings and weaknesses. The reviews and the process of reflecting on their performance provided the greatest benefit for the students by making learning strategies and techniques explicit. This was assumed to be of particular importance in relation to future progress since, 'the ability to review, reflect and develop meta-cognitive capacities is central to effective learning, whatever the content or context. It may also be the key to an ability to transfer and adapt learning in new contexts, whether in higher education or the workplace'.

As a follow-up to the team development day, each group was allocated one of five different tasks to be undertaken as a group, requiring research and analysis of a general legal theme. The aim was to determine whether the students could transfer the skills gained from the BP programme to a legal exercise. The tasks required preparation for short group presentations on given topics, including viability of the World Wide Web as a legal resource, a visit to and analysis of a case under way at the local courts, a consideration of how the media report on controversial legal topics, and an examination of how legal journals and periodicals could aid legal studies. Tutors commented on the enthusiasm, quantity and quality of information and the creative style of some of the presentations, as well as evidence of deliberate organization to make the best use of a team within its human and temporal resources. Peer tutoring was also apparent, especially in relation to the World Wide Web.

In order to extend the learning from the teambuilding further, students were asked to maintain a learning log and to discuss entries in their log books with their personal tutors in order to monitor success in meeting the aims for self-improvement they had noted at the end of the teambuilding course.

Because two of the central aims of the teambuilding course were the continuation of self-reflection and effective group work, there was a need to include tutors in the programme so that they could be more aware of team dynamics and peer tutoring in providing informed support for the students as they continued with their studies. Accordingly, several academics, many of whom would have been more accustomed to didactic teaching methods rather than facilitative, interactive and student-centred ways of working, were recruited to a two-day training event specifically for them so that they could act as tutors for teams in subsequent programmes as the course widened its constituency to other faculties.

(Based on Prince and Dunne, 1998.)

Handling change

The foregoing case studies include a cross-section of several different but interrelated elements: subject area, activities, organization, planning and evaluation – all within the context of various aims and purposes. There should be sufficient reference points for readers to recognize or identify with similar concerns in their own institution. The case studies are in the main not so much a description of problems but of their solutions. If any of them seem to fit your own concerns and inspire some sort of action, that is all to the good, but beware – colleagues might not share your analysis of the problem any more than your proposed solution. Your understanding and handling of a wider group process may be well and truly tested in your attempts to introduce even small changes to the system. So the best way forward is likely to be:

- start where you can;
- start small and simple;
- find allies;
- start planning longer-term change;
- produce documentation;
- collect evaluation evidence.

If you experiment and it doesn't work out, well, don't despair: it's part of the rich tapestry of teaching. The problem is that it is not a problem external to us: our own ego is on the line. But let me end, at the risk of mixing metaphors, with a quotation from Brookfield (1990) in which he describes teaching as the equivalent of white-water rafting:

Periods of calm are interspersed with sudden frenetic turbulence. Boredom alternates with excitement, reflection with action. As we successfully negotiate rapids fraught with danger, we feel a sense of self-confident exhilaration. As we start downstream after capsizing, our self-confidence is shaken and we are awash with self-doubt. All teachers sooner or later capsize, and all teachers worth their salt regularly ask themselves whether they are doing the right thing. Experiencing regular episodes of hesitation, self-doubt and ego-deflation is quite normal. Indeed the awareness of painful dilemmas in our practice, and the readiness to admit that we are hurting from experiencing these, is an important indicator that we are critically alert.

Discussion points

- What external influences are there on the work of groups you belong to? In what ways do they affect what happens?
- Discuss the differences between the ways members of your group relate to each other inside as opposed to outside the seminar/meeting. What seems to determine these differences?
- To what extent does the physical location and timing of various groups you belong to affect the liveliness and the level of participation in them?
- What principles of learning in groups seem to be evident in the various case studies? Draw up a classification chart.

9 | Assessing and evaluating with groups

There are three versions of an experience; the one you planned, the one you had, and what you learned from the difference between the two.

(Peter Honey)

By the end of this chapter you can expect to be able to make informed choices in the assessment and evaluation of groups and to feel reasonably confident in using them as part of a 'constructively aligned' strategy.

The linking of assessment of students and evaluation of groups in the same chapter may seem unusual, but is intentional because of their close relationship where group learning is concerned. The performance and contribution of individuals will to a large extent determine the overall success of the group. The contribution of a tutor (where there is one) will of course be an additional factor when it comes to evaluation, but in a group that is working collaboratively it could be argued that there is little or no distinction.

One hears many arguments against the assessment of students in groups, some ethical and some practical. Some say that it is not the job of tutors to make judgements of personal qualities and skills, let alone develop them (though perhaps that is fear of the unfamiliar); others might claim that it is impossible to do so in a valid and reliable way, or that students would merely engage in 'faking good' – a false performance of the requisite behaviours in order to gain marks. Yet these issues are, to a greater or lesser degree, relevant to all areas of assessment. What makes assessment in group work so valuable and exciting is that in tackling the above as problems it can open students and staff to a more shared and democratic level of awareness about what is going on, what is being learnt and what skills are needed to achieve that learning.

Biggs (1999) has drawn attention to what he calls the need for 'constructive alignment' of outcomes processes and assessment. He quotes Shuell (1986): 'If the students are to learn desired outcomes in a reasonably effective manner, then the teacher's fundamental task is to get the students engaged in learning activities that are likely to result in their achieving those outcomes.' Given the strong motivation that derives from assessment as attested by several contributors in Brown *et al* (1998), the need to assess students' contributions to groups appears quite compelling.

Yet the problems of fairness and the ability to make valid judgements are often used to reject the idea that one can do anything but assess individuals and then only on activities that are observable and capable of being judged by a teacher. In this chapter we shall look at methods that are capable not only of encouraging learning about subject knowledge but the development of skills and a disposition to group and teamwork, which can be of lifelong value. In some cases they may also relieve the teacher, through the unaccustomed practice of delegation, of a considerable amount of work in marking and giving feedback.

Assessment at a tacit level is going on in groups all the time, tutor of student, student of student, student of tutor, and (as we have seen on pages 71–72) each of these can affect others in terms of what they think the others are making of them. Better then, many would argue, to make the activity of assessment more explicit and beneficial by opening it to informed scrutiny and participation.

The idea of group assessment raises questions not normally considered, which are all the more important for that.

- Are we assessing learning, contribution of ideas, or contribution to group process, and how does the fact of assessment affect the natural flow of discussion?
- In what ways can the assessment aid the learning process?
- What method or process should be used?
- At what stage does the assessment take place?
- Who actually does the assessment and of whom?
- Who decides on the criteria?
- Does the method require skills that need practice for both tutor and students?
- How is feedback given: written or spoken, written and spoken, positive before negative, openly, anonymously?
- Are the rules of feedback (see pages 66–67) respected; can feedback be regarded by the receiver as a 'gift'?
- Is feedback in itself all that is needed?
- What triangulation (self–peer–tutor) can be achieved, bearing in mind the feedback rules on checking with a third party?
- What is the impact of assessment on relationships in the group?
- Are the necessary time and resources available to do it effectively?

What assessment is for

Assessment has many purposes, some of them not always made explicit. It provides encouragement to achieve, to diagnose strengths and weaknesses, to provide a profile of what students have learnt, to give feedback to the student and the teacher, to remind students about what is important, to predict success for future work and to accredit this. It is, or can also be, about gaining a profile about what each member of a group has learnt or contributed. But, when used to assess work in progress, it can also serve to clarify key concepts, criteria and standards, and the extent to which the overall aims are being achieved.

The Wingspread Principles of Good Practice for Assessing Student Learning (Chickering and Gamson, 1989) provide substantial support for the use of assessment of group work as an integral part of students' learning experience but also as a contribution to the personal and professional development of students.

Principles of good practice for assessing student learning

- The assessment of student learning begins with educational values.
- Assessment is not an end in itself but a vehicle for educational improvement. Its effective practice, then, begins with and enacts a vision of the kind of learning we most value for students and strive to help them achieve. Educational values should drive not only what we choose to assess but how. Where questions about educational mission and values are skipped over, assessment threatens to be an exercise in measuring what's easy, rather than a process of improving what we really care about.
- Assessment is most effective when it reflects an understanding of learning as multidimensional, integrated, and revealed in performance over time.
- Learning is a complex process. It entails not only what students know but what they can do with what they know; it involves not only knowledge and abilities but values, attitudes and habits of mind that affect both academic success and performance beyond the classroom. Assessment should reflect these understandings by employing a diverse array of methods including those that call for actual performance, using them over time so as to reveal change, growth and increasing degrees of integration. Such an approach aims for a more complete and accurate picture of learning and therefore firmer bases for improving our students' educational performance.
- Assessment works best when the programmes it seeks to improve have clear, explicitly stated purposes.
- Assessment is a goal-oriented process. It entails comparing educational performance with educational purposes and expectations – these derived from the institution's mission, from faculty intentions in programme and course design, and from knowledge of students' own goals. Where programme purposes lack specificity or agreement, assessment as a process pushes a campus towards clarity about where to aim and what standards to apply; assessment also prompts attention to where and how programme goals will be taught and learnt. Clear, shared goals that are capable of implementation are the cornerstone for assessment that is focused and useful.
- Assessment requires attention to outcomes but also and equally to the experiences that lead to those outcomes.
- Information about outcomes is of high importance; where students end up matters greatly. But to improve outcomes, we need to know about student experience along the way – about the curricula, teaching, and kind of student effort that lead to particular outcomes. Assessment can help us understand

which students learn best under what conditions; with such knowledge comes the capacity to improve the whole of their learning.

■ Assessment works best when it is ongoing, not episodic.

■ Assessment is a process whose power is cumulative. Though isolated, 'one-shot' assessment can be better than none, improvement is best fostered when assessment entails a linked series of activities taken over time. This may mean tracking the progress of individual students, or of cohorts of students; it may mean collecting the same examples of student performance or using the same instrument semester after semester. The point is to monitor progress towards intended goals in a spirit of intended improvement. Along the way, the assessment process itself should be evaluated and refined in the light of emerging insights.

The important difference with assessment in groups is that the process, in contrast to most other areas of assessment, enters the public arena – it is visible to others. We are looking at a degree of openness in the sharing of data whether it is about written work or personal behaviour. But more importantly, it raises questions and more open debate on what education is all about and more specifically what the learning outcomes of a course are; how explicit they are; what encouragement and support the students get in attaining them; and how responsibility may be shared for their assessment.

Assessment in groups brings with it a fundamental question: who is qualified to make that assessment? The word 'qualified' here has two dimensions, one to do with being a valid observer and the other with being properly trained in the assessment role. Clearly a tutor when leading a discussion is in a position to make some evaluation of students' contributions. But what can he or she say about students involved in any of the structured activities or group projects discussed in Chapter 6, where they do not have access to the process of each group? Then there is the question of reliability. If a tutor is part of the group, is his or her judgement alone adequate? Does what the tutor observes tally with what is noticed by the rest of the group? A student who constantly confirms the tutor's position or is always ready to give an academically sound response may restrict the contributions from the rest of the group. The argument for including the students in their own assessment is therefore a compelling one.

There are probably three major areas in which groups can be engaged in assessment: where they are used for assessment of written or spoken presentations; for functions or behavioural skills that help group discussion; and for contributions to project teams.

Groups used for assessment

Grant (1996) describes a form of viva voce, or oral assessment, for an in-service diploma course for teachers in which the group served as a context in which individual assessment took place. Students had already been given the option of being assessed by written examination or in a small group of four or five. The idea of using a group in this way was based on the view that teaching is a cooperative activity.

Prior to the assessment, students were given planning sheets with the learning outcomes of each unit of the course and a set of questions to help them focus on the sort of questions they might be asked. The structure of the assessment process was made clear beforehand as a way of reducing anxiety, and every effort was made to create a physical environment that was as relaxing as possible. Before they started their assessment, students were reminded of the ground rules: they had to speak from their own experience, making 'I' statements, as the assessors were mostly interested in what they actually did in their own teaching. They were also encouraged to interact with each other in the group and add to each other's contributions: *the event was intended to be a learning experience as well as an assessment.* The two assessors made notes on the achievements of each student against the prepared criteria and whenever they were satisfied that these had been met for any one unit, they moved on to the next, the choice of this sometimes being given to the students. The students knew in advance the areas in which they would be assessed. Once the assessors felt they had enough evidence from any particular student on which to make their decision, the student was invited to give a brief oral self-assessment of his or her performance before being given feedback on how well he or she had performed. The assessors discussed their assessment openly in front of the other students.

The assessors asked challenging questions and had to exercise considerable group skills to ensure coverage of any learning outcome and to judge when to move on to another. A reasonable degree of objectivity was achieved by having one of the two assessors take notes, which could be used as documentary evidence.

On some occasions the students were allowed to choose those of their colleagues with whom they would be assessed, but that was not always convenient and there was also a risk that a particular mix of group members might not be conducive to the task.

Groups can also be used to develop a deeper appreciation of criteria and standards in written work. Here is one example from my own practice. Students are asked, 'What are we looking for in a "good" essay/report/review' or other written work and, using a cumulative method like the snowball or pyramid, generate a set of criteria, one in turn from each of the final sub-groups. These can be compared with, and moderated by, those of the tutor before the students go away to write their assignment. The submitted work, brought to a subsequent group meeting, must have attached a self-assessment based on the criteria. The assignments are then handed to the group or sub-groups for circulation, each person giving the writer a grade and at least 50 words of feedback. The tutor then takes the assignments in and marks them with feedback, not only to the writer but to the peer assessors. While this may seem to create a lot of extra work, it can pay enormous dividends in getting the students to internalize criteria and standards, thus relying less on retrospective feedback from the tutor. It can also serve to prepare the students for self- and peer assessment of future written work.

The main principle in using groups for this kind of assessment is that, by comparing themselves with others and by identifying with peers in familiar and similar situations, students are opening themselves to a wider range of possible skills and behaviours. This is particularly so when seminar presentations are assessed. As we have already noted, seminar presentations are often poorly executed by anxious students to a group of peers who are likely to be equivalently anxious on their behalf. There are ways to reduce this anxiety, such as the role play described on pages 205–06, but there is still the problem of how students can learn to present more effectively. Here again a 'front-end investment' of a brief training session can be of great benefit. The back-to-back exercise on pages 72–74, requiring only 30 minutes to run, will give students enjoyable practice and a set of criteria with which to prepare their presentations. A more specific tool such as the seminar peer assessment form or the seminar presentation mark and feedback sheet (Figures 9.1 and 9.2) may then be used for an assessment. Note that both of these include items concerned with skill of handling group discussion.

Assessing group skills

The skills required for effective participation in groups are, of course, complex and inter-relating, but as we have seen in Chapter 2 there are some very clear 'functions' that can be identified and thus promoted. Much interest in the past 10 years in the UK has centred on the development of transferable or key skills. Whether skills are in reality 'transferable' or not is discussed thoroughly by Neath (1998), who concludes that they are transferable only in the sense that people who have well-developed problem-solving skills are able to interpret a new situation and find the necessary means to match it.

The need for skills in group work to be embedded in the curriculum is portrayed in the TDMA model in Figure 9.3. If a skill is to be effectively developed the students must first receive some training in it – they cannot all be expected to possess it to the required degree – and it seems unfair to allow the experience of a group or project team to suffer as a result. If they are to apply what they have learnt from the training, the students will need to practise the skill and in the competing priorities of student life; there must therefore be a demand for its use and for appropriate learning time to be allocated to tasks in which the skills are employed. The acquisition of skills is, as we already know, an uncertain process in which other factors like anxiety and surprise can have a profound effect; and it does not take place as an immediate consequence of a training exercise. Skills continue to develop over a period of time until they become embedded in the subconscious, but that development needs monitoring through rehearsal, feedback and review. Self-assessment can, in the context of group feedback, be especially valuable here, and it is assessment that provides the final element in successful skill development.

However, whether we describe items as skills, behaviours or functions, they cannot operate without a recognition of concomitant dispositions and values. Someone who is a brilliant initiator or clarifier in terms of the content may be so arrogant or dismissive of colleagues' contributions that discussion is uneasy and tense.

At Alverno College, Milwaukee, students are trained and assessed according to a task-oriented group model, the purpose of which is to provide students with an exterior view of their behaviour in a group, and an exercise/assessment to help them determine which behaviours of the model they will 'work on to improve or to acquire' during their subsequent classes/courses at Alverno. In task-oriented groups it is assumed that 'efficient and effective group process is possible when group members collaborate through a series of interdependent behaviours to accomplish the task in hand'. Students are assessed on their group skills using a checklist which includes the following four stages:

1. **Orientation**:
   Leading (initiating, keeping on the right track);

Seminar peer assessment form

During the course you are expected to run two seminar sessions. Each will contribute 10% towards assessment for the course. You are responsible for informing your group of the topic, date, time and place of your seminar, and strongly advised to provide guidance for them to prepare. The following criteria will be used:

STUDENT ....   **SEMINAR PRESENTER** ....

		Excellent	Good	Adequate	Poor	None
1	**Quality of preparation** Handouts, advanced reading, briefing, support and advice	2	1½	1	½	0
	Comment					
2	**Quality of explanation** Clear grasp of topic, clear answers to questions	2	1½	1	½	0
	Comment					
3	**Quality of sources** Wide range of relevant sources. References provided for reading	2	1½	1	½	0
	Comment					
4	**Quality of presentation** Good use of AV aids, handouts, pace, lively	2	1½	1	½	0
	Comment					
5	**Quality of discussion** Interesting and effective group methods used, all took active part	2	1½	1	½	0
	Comment					

Total ☐ (Maximum 10 marks)

Overall comment:

Figure 9.1 *Seminar peer assessment*

Seminar presentation mark and feedback sheet

20% of course marks are awarded for each of two seminar presentations. The following criteria will be used. Descriptions of these criteria and advice on seminar presentations can be found in the course guide.

Criterion	Mark						Comments

Content:
    clarity of argument,
    understanding,
    overview, conclusion
	0%	1%	2%	3%	4%	5%	

Sources:
    breadth and relevance
    acknowledgement
    references
	0%	1%	2%	3%	4%	5%	

Presentation:
    voice, use of AV aids,
    pace, variety, notes
	0%	1%	2%	3%	4%	5%	

Group skills:
    structuring, engaging
    questioning, answering
	0%	1%	2%	3%	4%	5%	

Total (maximum 20%)

Your best skills

Your weakest skills

How you might improve your performance

Tutor ....

Date ....

Figure 9.2 *Seminar presentation marks and feedback*

Learning how to work in groups

Tutors can help students learn new skills and use them effectively by ensuring that their courses provide **Training** for the skills, **Demand** for them, **Monitoring** and **Assessment** of them.

Training

Assume students have the skills and knowledge about how to work in groups	*Provide training courses that help students work effectively in groups*

Demand

Teach the course in such a way that students are only expected to work individually	*Structure the course so that working in groups is an integral part of class sessions and required in out-of-class work*

Monitoring

Leave students to themselves	*Ensure that you check on how groups are progressing: get groups to monitor their own progress*

Assessment

Assess solely what individuals produce. Do not draw on any work that has contributed or behaviour demonstrated	*Make the students' work in groups; how well they take part, an integral part of the assessment*

Figure 9.3 *The TDMA model for developing group skills (traditional practice in plain type; preferred practice in italics)*

Information/opinion seeking (establishing a broad range of opinions);
Information/opinion giving (offering information on accomplishment of task);
Reinforcing (supporting opinions of others, showing openness and acceptance of others' ideas).

2. **Examination**:
Advocating (defending a position, offering evidence, persuading);
Challenging (confronting, asking for justification/supporting evidence);
Mediating (helping to analyse differences, trying to reconcile, being willing to compromise).

3. **Synthesis**:
Summarizing (restating major ideas, identifying contributions made);
Evaluating (commenting on group process, assessing whether group solution meets criteria);
Leading (assigning members to task, achieving consensus and drawing attention to consequences of decisions).

4. **Termination**:
Closure (reaching consensus on completion, making plans for further action);
Reinforcing (giving recognition and support to others).

In addition to these positive behaviours, Alverno includes a set of blocking behaviours – *attacking, dominating, interfering, withdrawing,* and *being defensive* – that undermine group effectiveness.

The assessment is done by self, peer and a member of the local community called the 'off-campus assessor'. All three parties are given training in assessment processes. The actual event, which Alverno has been pleased to demonstrate at their Summer Workshop, has each group in turn seated at a round table with the task of reaching consensus on a given problem. External assessors for each student are also present. As soon as the task is completed, or the allocated time is up, the external assessors leave the room while the self- and peer assessment take place. In another room the external assessors meanwhile come to a consensus about the students' effectiveness or less productive behaviours, and agree on the main areas to discuss with each of the two students they have observed. Each assessor then provides feedback privately to their students. The succession of events is: discussion, self-assessment, peer assessment and external assessment, each done independently and revealed in that order. The students' self-assessment of the group interaction and the external assessor's feedback are entered into the students' digital diagnostic portfolio, and as the students progress through their programme of studies, they enter selected performances and their self-assessments of them. Faculty and external assessors also continue to enter selected feedback into the digital portfolio. The students can look at their self-assessments or feedback over many performances and see how they are developing, so that they can compare how they interacted in a group assessment in the first semester with an assessment in the third semester, and so on.

In formal discussion groups where there may be more emphasis on academic discourse, a slightly different set of criteria may be more relevant. The following list (for which credit to an anonymous author), a favourite of mine, describes 'the important things students do for which they should be given credit':

General	Discussing this list with peers
	Attendance and attending
To do with the content	Preparing for the session by thinking and/or reading
	Asking questions: clear questions; open questions; creative questions
	Clear explanations, definitions of terms
	Making logical connections
	Keeping to the topic
	Condensation (being succinct)
To do with the process	Intellectual risk-taking
	Not dominating or oppressing by speaking too loudly, too long or too oppressively in any way
	Expressing appropriate emotions
	Thoughtful, comfortable silence
	Altruism, sharing
	Bringing others in by verbal and non-verbal means
	Awareness of group dynamics for self and others
Personal matters	Willing to speak personally and bring personal experience as well as cognitive stuff into the discussion
	Acceptance of all group members
	Equal rights for self and others
	Finding and using own voice
Other comments	

Whatever the complications of organizing the assessment with such a rich array of criteria, it is hard to believe that what the students learn in discussing and agreeing them would not make a substantial contribution to an effective learning process in the group. Such is the power of openness and sharing responsibility.

The skills of assessment

As we have already noted (Chapter 3), self- and peer assessment are very influential in the promotion of meta-cognition. To assess oneself and a peer, and to draw comparisons between the two, causes a level of thinking in which one goes 'beyond' and 'without' the problem identified. In other words one is thinking at more than one level in both time and space. Students can perform a variety of assessment tasks in ways that both save the tutor's time and bring educational benefits. They need to develop their ability to make this kind of judgement and to give constructive feedback, and this takes time and practice. They need to be convinced of the value, and validity, of self-assessment. For this reason it is safer to start with self- and peer assessment for the purpose of feedback rather than to get involved straight away with marking that counts towards a final qualification. It is important that students have a chance to test and refine their judgements and marks against those of the tutor before their own marks are taken into account. It also makes sense for tutors to provide their own criteria when trying out self-assessment for the first time before allowing students to use their own criteria.

There are many possible stages and choices in this self- and peer assessment, each of which involves some form of delegation or relinquishing of control to the students; and they can be mutually exclusive. For example, students can be offered a choice of assessment tasks or invited to set and conduct the assessment. They may be invited to discuss prepared assessment criteria or to set them. They can give feedback to themselves or their peers with or without giving marks. They can assign marks, suggest marks for the tutor to moderate, or negotiate them with the tutor. Self-, peer and tutor assessment can be 'triangulated' between the three parties.

All of these practices can be part of a process for the students in which they learn more about group skills and the task of giving a fair assessment based on them. Boud (1991) describes research which indicated that two of the most important skills for professional work (which are two of the most under-emphasized in higher education) are teamwork and the ability to assess one's own work.

The evident fact that to engage in self- and peer assessment, to some of the degrees suggested above, can be very complex and time-consuming if done properly has to be seen in the light of the learning benefits that can nevertheless accrue. In their handbook 'Student Assessment as Learning', the Alverno College Faculty promote the view of assessment as a 'multidimensional process, integral to learning, that involves observing performances of an individual learner in action and judging them on the basics of public developmental criteria, with resulting feedback to that learner'. They ask fundamental questions like:

■   How do we know a given performance is representative?
■   Is the student having an unusually bad day?
■   Can he or she exhibit the same abilities under different circumstances?
■   How varied need the samples be to suggest the complexity of an ability?

And they pose the further questions:

■   Are the abilities being assessed integrated (with values, attitudes, behaviours)?
■   Are they developmental (can they be extended, inferences made)?
■   Are they transferable – preparing students for new and different roles and settings?

The Alverno assessment process is so central to the learning strategy of the college that all concerned are given rigorous training in the designing of learning outcomes, criteria, modes of assessment, assessment and feedback strategies.

Self- and peer assessment can be used in at least two other ways that promote meta-cognitive learning: assessment of the written work of each of their fellow members and one group conducting the assessment of another – a 'fishbowl' assessment.

A full, fair and rigorous assessment is never a straightforward task. One reason for the traditional system of essays, reports and exams is that it has been thoroughly tried out and has stood the test of time, at least in the sense that all involved appear to be familiar with its processes and procedures. Another reason may be to do with the fear of losing control by using unfamiliar and more visible methods: to involve students intimately in the process is to lose some of that control and with it some of the arcane aspects of the relationship between tutor and student. That aside, it is apparent that participatory assessment can be a complex process and that the justification for it must be in the learning value of it and the greater sense of student commitment (Creme, 1995), democracy and fairness that can or should accompany it. This is certainly true for the assessment of group projects, which we will look at now.

Assessing group projects

The kinds of behaviour valued in project work differ from those in discussion and therefore require different criteria. Projects are of necessity more task-oriented, using a wider range of skills such as problem-solving, organizing, chairing and editing. They are not subject to a regular timetable, nor are they accessible to regular observation by the tutor. Their autonomous nature means not only that the groups themselves are often (but not always) the best judges of how effectively they have worked, but the tutor may have to rely principally on what the group reports rather than on live interactions.

Assessing the contribution of individuals within a group

Where group projects are undertaken the work is often assessed as the single product of the group and each individual within the group gets the group mark regardless of the value of his or her individual contribution. In terms of the values already expressed in this chapter, an appropriate assessment would be one that would retain the value placed on group cooperation and the submission of a single group product for assessment, but also add a dimension of individual assessment which:

- provides a sense of fairness to individuals such that good students don't have to 'carry' or get dragged down by poor or lazy students;
- takes into account the different levels and qualities of contribution that individuals can make to their group;
- serves as guide to the students on the behaviour, skills, attitudes and work styles likely to lead to the successful completion of the project.

The methods described all assume that the group still submits a group project report of some kind. The group mark is then added to or modified by one or more of these methods: shared group grade, peer assessment of contribution to the group, peer feedback on contribution to the group, project exam and oral assessment.

Shared group grade

A major difficulty in assessing the contribution of individuals within a group is that the tutor may not have much idea about which individual students have done what. However, the students themselves are in a very good position to make such judgements. Though the tutor can only award a mark to the group, the members of that group can be left to distribute the mark between themselves in a way that they think reflects the relative contributions of individuals. For example, if a group of five students were to be awarded 60 per cent for a group report, they would be given 5 x 60 = 300 marks to distribute among themselves. There are three ways in which groups tend to react in this situation:

1. Some groups will agree at the start of the project that all marks will be shared equally at the end, in order to avoid unpleasantness. Such groups must face the prospect of individual group members doing little work, safe in the knowledge that they will get the same mark as the rest of the group.
2. Other groups will not discuss assessment at all until it comes to dividing up the marks. They then find that they disagree about the basis upon which the marks should be divided. Some will value creativity, some will value workload, some will value leadership, some will value the ability to communicate the project outcomes, and so on. Without prior agreement about criteria there are likely to be arguments about who should get what marks for which contributions.
3. Some groups will sit down at the start and decide what criteria they will use in allocating marks, and will keep to these criteria. Everyone will be clear about what their contribution ought to be, and will be more likely to accept the final allocation of marks.

This third way of dealing with shared group grades is clearly the most satisfactory and the tutor can help students by organizing discussion and negotiation of criteria at the start of the project. If time doesn't permit this, the tutor can impose his or her own criteria, which the students then use to allocate the marks. It is crucial, however, that the criteria are made clear and accepted at the start of the project, and not pulled out of thin air at the end. There are two rather different ways in which criteria can be used. First, students may naturally adopt different working roles within the group, or the project may even specify such roles. For example, one student may become the chairperson, one the note-taker, one the data-analyser, one the report writer, one the 'ideas person' and so on. In this case assessment criteria can focus on how well each student performed his or her different role. Second, every student may be expected to contribute equally to all aspects of the project (for example, each writing one section of a group report). In this case each criterion should be applied equally to each student.

Peer assessment of contribution to group

One technique, illustrated in Figure 9.4, is where the tutor marks the group project and then group members rate every other member of the group in terms of several key aspects of their contribution to the group's work. The criteria used here are for illustration only: other criteria concerning creativity, supportiveness in the group, or ability to keep to deadlines could equally be used. The average rating for each individual is then added or deducted from the group mark and allocated to that individual as his or her mark. In this case a student who made an above average contribution to the group's work in every respect would have a rating of 10 and receive the group grade plus 10 per cent. A student who made a below average contribution to the group's work in all of these respects would receive the group grade minus 10 per cent.

Student .... has contributed to the group's work in the following ways:

	Above average Contribution	Average Contribution	Below average Contribution
1. Leadership and direction	+1	0	−4
2. Organization and management	+1	0	−2
3. Ideas and suggestions	+1	0	−1
4. Data collection	+2	0	−2
5. Data analysis	+2	0	−2
6. Report writing	+3	0	−3
Total penalty or bonus			

Figure 9.4 *Peer assessment of contribution to group*

More or less severe penalties can be devised either by varying the number of criteria used, or by varying the penalties associated with criteria. The relative importance of criteria can be reflected in different penalties, as in the example here. The criteria and size of penalties can be negotiated with the students, or even determined by them, at the start of the project so that they are aware of how they will be assessed, and have a commitment to the criteria. Groups can be required to make sure that the average group members' total scores come out at exactly the same as the group score ie, that they do not all rate each other as above average!

Figures 9.5 (page 228) and 9.6 (page 234) are more explicit and perhaps more 'user-friendly' pro forma for assessing individual contributions to the process and report respectively.

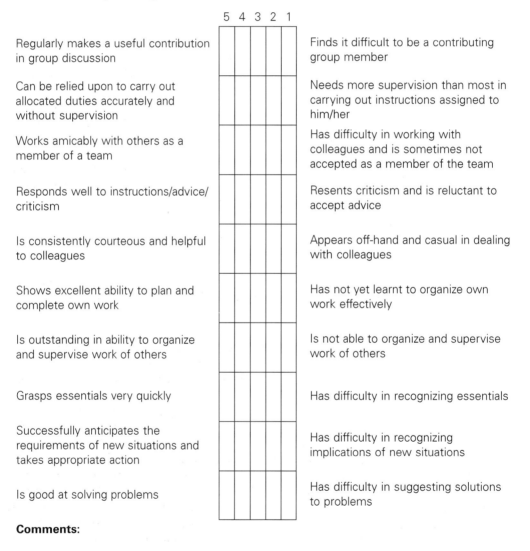

ROBERT GORDON UNIVERSITY   **CONFIDENTIAL**
School of Computer and Mathematical Sciences   **PEER GROUP ASSESSMENT FORM**

BSc in Mathematical Sciences with Computing – Mathematical Models and Methods

Please assess your colleague by giving a mark of 1–5 (by ticking the appropriate box) in each of the following 10 categories.

NB This form will be treated in strict confidence

Name (of colleague being assessed):

5 4 3 2 1

Regularly makes a useful contribution in group discussion — Finds it difficult to be a contributing group member

Can be relied upon to carry out allocated duties accurately and without supervision — Needs more supervision than most in carrying out instructions assigned to him/her

Works amicably with others as a member of a team — Has difficulty in working with colleagues and is sometimes not accepted as a member of the team

Responds well to instructions/advice/criticism — Resents criticism and is reluctant to accept advice

Is consistently courteous and helpful to colleagues — Appears off-hand and casual in dealing with colleagues

Shows excellent ability to plan and complete own work — Has not yet learnt to organize own work effectively

Is outstanding in ability to organize and supervise work of others — Is not able to organize and supervise work of others

Grasps essentials very quickly — Has difficulty in recognizing essentials

Successfully anticipates the requirements of new situations and takes appropriate action — Has difficulty in recognizing implications of new situations

Is good at solving problems — Has difficulty in suggesting solutions to problems

Comments:

Your Name: **Date:**

Figure 9.5 *Peer assessment of group activity pro forma*

Peer feedback

As with all assessment, the process can and should include feedback. In those cases where there are problems in giving responsibility to students for grading each other, peer feedback can still be used, with clear learning benefits, when done properly, to the giver and the recipient.

Project exam

One way to test individuals' knowledge when group work has been assessed is to set an exam. However, conventional exams, with their tendency to emphasize memorizing and regurgitation of factual information, are quite unsuitable for a project-based course. They can completely distort the aims of the course by distracting students from their project work because they know that they are not going to be tested on it in the exam. However, there are forms of exam that avoid these problems by asking students questions directly related to their project work.

For example, on an Estate Management course, students undertook a substantial case study involving the simulated purchase of a building site and its subsequent commercial development. This they wrote up in a report consisting of a log of their calculations, decisions, problems, etc. The examination questions took the form:

> Q. If there was a three-month national building strike starting on week 3 of the simulation, how would this affect your handling of the case?

> Q. If outline planning consent were granted for a competing major shopping precinct at the north end of the High Street on week 14 of the simulation (see details below), how would you advise your client?

Students had their log books and other case material to hand and were expected to use these in answering the questions. Such questions cannot be answered from memory, or even directly from this information, but only from students' experience and understanding of the case study.

In this first example, all students undertook the same project work individually. In the second example, below, students had been working in separate groups and individuals had been awarded a group grade. The exam in this case was designed to test individuals' understanding and to produce a mark for each individual student. The context was a Catering Management course in which groups of eight students tackled a simulated management problem. Within the groups students performed different roles (for example secretary, report writer) and so they almost certainly learnt different things. The course was designed to apply management principles to a specific and complex situation. An exam was used to test individuals' ability to apply these principles to the work of their own groups.

Exam questions took the form:

Q. How can pricing and marketing policies influence other management decisions concerning catering outlets? Give specific examples from the simulation to illustrate your points.

The first part of this question is general, in that it is based on management principles learnt at an earlier stage in the course. It is the second part that tests students' ability to apply these principles to their project work. This type of exam has the added advantage that if students know at the outset that they will be expected to answer questions of this form, they are more likely to be reflective about theory and general principles during the simulation than to get overwhelmed with practical details and forget the purpose of the exercise.

Oral assessment of projects

This serves the same function as a project exam: it allows individuals to be questioned about their understanding of the group's final report. This can be done quickly and flexibly in an interview. An interviewer can ask about:

- the content of the report;
- the group processes involved in creating it;
- problems encountered and how these were overcome;
- the particular elements of the group's work for which the individual was responsible (and not responsible).

The interviewer would have the marked group report to hand in order to ask specific questions, possibly using the same model as described on pages 216–17. Marking could be undertaken in one of two ways. Either the group report is marked out of 80 and the project viva out of 20 (or some other balance such as 60/40). The individual student gets the group mark plus his or her project viva mark. Alternatively, the group report is marked out of 100 and the individual mark is arrived at by modifying this up or down 10 per cent according to how well the student performs in the viva.

Assessment procedures focussing on process

A major aim of some projects is to develop the students' cooperative group work skills and an accompanying awareness of how groups operate effectively. If students are going to take this aim seriously, then the group process, rather than only the product of the group's work, needs to be assessed in some way. If process issues are to be assessed, then some mid-project feedback to groups is probably necessary to guide them in the right direction.

Assessing process is often trickier than assessing an end product, partly because process is more transitory, partly because both lecturers and students lack experience in the assessment of process, and partly because it is not so readily accessible to a second opinion. Whatever methods are tried, they are likely to suffer from unexpected problems to some extent. The choice and operation of assessment methods will need to be kept under review. The crucial measure of the success of the introduction of the assessment of process will be evidence of students' increased awareness of, and attention to, process issues in the ways they run their groups, and a corresponding improvement in group performance. Assessment methods need not be particularly reliable or valid to achieve this. The following options may be used for assessing group process.

Observation of process

The tutor sits in on each group once and assesses the way they conduct and plan their business. The group are not warned when this will be, but receive explicit criteria in advance. One of the checklists on group process in this chapter, for example, could be used, modified as below in order to grade the group on each rating scale. This would give a total score out of 35.

Assessment interview on process

Each group could be interviewed about how they had operated as a group and carried out the project. It should become clear whether a competent leader is 'faking good' to cover up the failings of weaker group members. Such an assessment interview could be undertaken by one of the other groups, given appropriate briefing.

Presentations on process

Groups could be asked to each give a 20-minute presentation about the way they operated, the problems they encountered working together, how they tackled these problems and what they have learnt. These presentations could be assessed by the tutors or peer assessed by the other groups. Each group could discuss the presentation for 5 minutes and give a group grade. The group giving the presentation would get the total of these grades (4 and 2 are simply intermediate positions):

> 5 = Group showed great awareness of group processes, tackled process problems with vigour, sensitivity, imagination and demonstrable success.
> 4 =
> 3 = Group showed moderate awareness of group processes, tackled some problems with some signs of sensitivity, but with limited vigour and imagination and with limited proof of success.
> 2 =

1 = Group showed little awareness of group processes, appeared not to tackle problems, or tackled them half-heartedly and/or insensitively and with no sign of success.

With five groups of eight, each group would be graded by four groups, giving a maximum score of 20.

This presentation and peer assessment could be undertaken (without contributing to the final mark) midway through the year in order to tune the groups into process issues and demonstrate effective and ineffective ways for groups to pay attention to process issues.

Process review

The groups could have a review of their group processes with a tutor prior to any of the other assessment processes (eg, prior to presentations on process). This would not itself be assessed, but act as a tutorial for groups so that they can prepare themselves for the assessment of process more effectively.

Essay on process

Groups could be asked to submit an essay, at the end of the year, based on the diaries of individuals in the group, on the process issues that have arisen and been addressed by the group through the year. A brief essay or report could be written by each group and shared between groups halfway through the year. This would not be for marking, but in order to tune the groups in to process issues and demonstrate effective and ineffective ways for groups to pay attention to process issues.

Final report: section on process

One section of the final group project report could be on process issues. The number of marks allocated to the discussion of process issues out of the total allocated to the report could be specified (eg, 20 per cent).

Use of diaries or logs

The diaries themselves could be assessed in terms of the awareness and analysis of process issues of individuals as revealed by entries throughout the year. Some of the other assessment processes described here (eg, interview on process) could contribute to diaries and the diaries be assessed rather than the contributing events. There is a danger with assessing individuals' reports of group processes that they might invent, idealize and blame others in ways that a whole group would not.

Assessment criteria

Whatever assessment process is used (exam, essay, report, presentation) criteria should be specified explicitly and include those concerned with awareness and analysis of process issues. The criteria may be predetermined, negotiated with all the groups or negotiated with each group, while including a core of common criteria. The process of proposing and negotiating criteria can be of great help in the students' awareness and ownership of group process. Typical criteria for group assessment (Heathfield, in Brown and Glasner, 1999) might be:

- regular attendance at group preparing material for the task;
- contribution of ideas for the task;
- researching, analysing and preparing material for the task;
- contributing to cooperative group process;
- supporting and encouraging group members;
- practical contribution to end product;
- competitive cooperation (op. cit.).

Figure 9.6, a pro forma used in assessing group activity, is illustrative of both factors that contribute to successful teamwork and the wider range of behaviours that can be used in peer assessment than can ever be observable by a tutor.

Profiles

A list of specified desired group behaviours could be drawn up and groups assessed by writing up a profile rather than by awarding a grade. This might involve one of the checklists on pages 227–28. A description of the strengths and weaknesses of the group as a working group might be more valuable to the group than a mark. Each student could also have a profile drawn up to compare with that of the group as a whole.

So the assessment of groups, far from being an optional extra, has an important and integral role to play in the all-round education of students. It raises their awareness of their own responsibility for making the process work and, if we include self- and peer assessment and feedback, to learn about two salient professional skills – teamwork and the ability to judge the work of self and others. By focusing on collective outcomes, the students can achieve more in comparing and contrasting themselves than they would as individuals working alone. What is perhaps even more important is that they are likely to give any assessment of their group skills and their contribution to the work of the group much more notice, to the extent that they feel some ownership of the process and identification with each other in it. And we should not forget the benefits to the tutor too: it can (indeed should) lead to a raised sense of autonomy and improved quality of group work as students continue on the course; and the tutor will have less marking to do with a consequent reduction in the demand on resources.

ROBERT GORDON UNIVERSITY   **CONFIDENTIAL**
School of Computer and Mathematical Sciences   **PEER GROUP ASSESSMENT FORM**
                                                WRITTEN REPORT

BSc in Mathematical Sciences with Computing – Mathematical Models and Methods

Please assess your colleague by giving a mark of 1–5 (by ticking the appropriate box) in each of the following five categories.

NB This form will be treated in strict confidence

Name (of colleague being assessed):

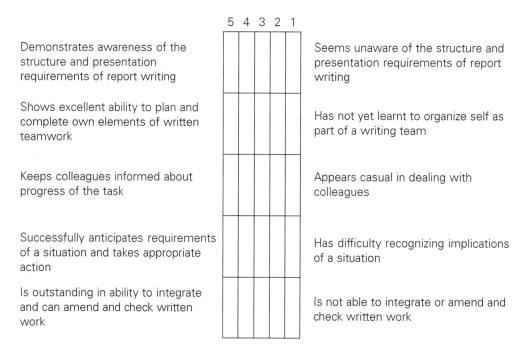

Demonstrates awareness of the structure and presentation requirements of report writing — Seems unaware of the structure and presentation requirements of report writing

Shows excellent ability to plan and complete own elements of written teamwork — Has not yet learnt to organize self as part of a writing team

Keeps colleagues informed about progress of the task — Appears casual in dealing with colleagues

Successfully anticipates requirements of a situation and takes appropriate action — Has difficulty recognizing implications of a situation

Is outstanding in ability to integrate and can amend and check written work — Is not able to integrate or amend and check written work

Comments:

Your Name: **Date:**

Figure 9.6 *Peer assessment of group report writing pro forma*

Evaluating groups

Whenever two or more people interact they are in some sense evaluating one another. Teachers do it of students, students of teachers, each of their own colleagues. Though as teachers it is our job to make judgements about students, we may not feel so happy about students openly reciprocating the process and judging something we feel responsible for. Something much more precious and sensitive seems to be at stake: our self-esteem. There are, too, understandable doubts among teachers about any evaluation that attempts to judge complex phenomena in simplistic terms. Teachers, as Miller (1975) remarks, are sceptical that the intricate network of their experience, which contributes to their concept of themselves as a teacher, can be encompassed in some kind of measurement that is either meaningful or helpful. Yet even if a suitable kind of measurement were available, the probability is that most teachers would find 20 good academic reasons why their self-image should not come under scrutiny.

The major part of this problem is possibly that a sense of being judged is likely to create a defensive reaction. In the view of Gibb (1961), a defensive climate results from the sort of communication that displays evaluation, control, strategy, neutrality, superiority, or certainty. Supportive or cooperative climates, on the other hand, have the following qualities: description, problem orientation, spontaneity, empathy, equality and provisionalism. Each of these corresponds to its equivalent defensive quality taken in the same area. Thus it is more supportive to say, *'Just then, it seemed as if you were having difficulty with students who wanted to go their own way in the discussion'* (provisionalism) rather than, *'You can't control discussions!'* (certainty).

The way in which evaluation is handled is clearly of great importance if the results are to be accepted and acted on positively. A lot of the threat can be taken out of an evaluation if as much initiative and responsibility as possible rests with the person being evaluated, as may be seen in the approach for a tutor with a group in Figure 9.7. This process need not be just for the tutor. It could be used for any student or the whole group.

The value of this approach is that, in first requiring a description of events, it is less threatening to the person being evaluated and should develop a greater awareness among all concerned of process as it occurs. Then, in commenting first, that person can anticipate the potentially hurtful things others might say or might feel inhibited about saying. Last, in having negative points converted into problems, a constructive future-oriented view is encouraged.

The timing of evaluation is important too. We do not like to hear something critical of ourselves, either when we feel vulnerable (eg, when something has just gone wrong and there is an audience watching) or when it is too late to do much about it (eg, at the end of a course). A 'formative' evaluation – that is, one done in order to achieve useful changes for those involved – is generally less threatening and of greater learning value than a 'summative' one, completed at the very end of a course.

Who initiates the evaluation? Who conducts it? Who processes the results and how? Where is it done? Who else is doing it in parallel? All these questions may also be of consequence in determining how efficiently an evaluation is carried out and, more importantly, how conscientiously its results are implemented. More significantly, where evaluation is seen as more of a regular process in which all group members view

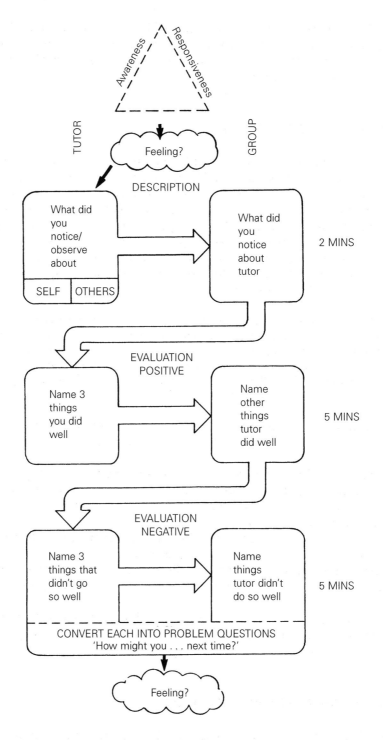

Figure 9.7 *Evaluation procedure for a tutor with a group*

themselves as contributors and take responsibility for outcomes, there is more chance of change through cooperation. Five minutes set aside at the end of each meeting to review how things went, are therefore likely to be of greater benefit to all concerned than any formal, externally applied, procedure.

Evaluation as learning

It is a perhaps fair (if trite) to say that if you haven't got problems in your group then something is wrong. As Johnson and Johnson (1987) observe, 'a productive group is one that realizes that there will be process problems and is willing to evaluate its progress in managing these problems effectively'. Evaluation presents an opportunity not merely to gauge the quality of group work but to give individuals the chance to reflect on their own behaviour in groups even, and especially, when their is no assessment of this. In this sense they comprise a creative source of learning, one that informs both individuals and the group as a whole about their part in its work and suggests ways in which they can contribute to the needs of the group.

> *Significant developments in the evaluation of teaching will not come from staff thinking about their own courses, or from students as consumers expressing their judgements about the courses which are provided for them, but by an integration of evaluation into the learning process so that an important part of the students' learning is in fact coming to understand their own strengths, weaknesses, inhibitions, and styles of thinking and working in relation to the varieties of constraints and opportunities presented by the course. (Cox, 1978)*

Evaluation, whether it be of individual students, the group, the tutor or all of these, is likely to enhance the prospects of training and improvement:

- if it enhances the experience of teaching by creating a climate of openness and honesty where there might otherwise be a sense of secretiveness and mistrust;
- if it is organized as a cooperative act in which both teacher and students articulate their experience and learn from it;
- when there is no question of its being used for promotion or other public purposes, except where this has been clearly opted for;
- where it is organized at stages in the life of a group rather than at its conclusion, and all concerned can have the opportunity to develop and change for mutual benefit.

As Miles (1981) comments, group members feel better about evaluation when they see the specific methods as clear and sensible, and that it is an integral part of the training programme and feeds directly into improvements.

Evaluation methods for groups

The method or technique that one chooses to evaluate group work must, of course, be established and agreed within the context of the group and the overall climate of the learning situation. The consequences of unacceptable evaluation can be disastrous. Before evaluating, questions like 'Who is it for?', 'How is it to be used?' and, 'How honest can we be?' have to be faced and answered.

Observation

Though the observations of an evaluator external to the group may to a certain extent be invalid and superficial, a collection of such views, provided they are to do with the group as a whole and do not refer to the behaviour of individuals, can form a useful basis for appraisal of the groups' success. The fishbowl technique can therefore be a useful device. In this, one group arranges itself concentrically round the other and the outer group acts as observer, and evaluates. This relationship is reversed to allow the second group to be observed.

Diaries

Whenever the life of a group extends over a period of time, members can derive great benefit from keeping diaries in which they can record what ideas, concepts, principles and information they learnt; what they learnt about their own ability to discuss, agree and express ideas, as well as their own contribution to the group process; how they saw the group as a whole.

Rainer (1980) offers a host of ideas on diary writing. If these diary comments can be shared in the group, even on a selective basis, many helpful insights can be gained by students and tutors alike.

Reporting back

At the beginning of each group meeting, 5 to 10 minutes may be allocated to one or two members who report back on what happened in, and what they gained from, the previous meeting. For this to work the reporters for the following week must be selected at the beginning of each session so that they are alerted to the task in good time. As with most forms of open evaluation, there is an incidental spin-off: a sense of continuity between one meeting and the next.

Paired appraisal

This process lies somewhere between assessment and evaluation in that its primary focus is on individual needs, though it can be expanded to include the whole group. For paired appraisal, students work with an appropriately chosen partner (perhaps the 'learning partner' described in Chapter 6). Each of them prepares a set of written answers to questions such as:

■   How is the group working out for you?
■   What about your own part in it?
■   Is there anything about the way you are in the group that you'd like to change?

- What kind of things are you learning about groups?
- Is there anything about the group that you'd like to change? How might you do that?
- How effectively are you learning?
- What seems to be getting in the way and how could you deal with that?
- Putting all this together, what do you plan to do, by when, and how? If you want, can I be of help to you in this?

It is not the job of the appraiser to comment or advise.

The process is then reciprocated. Each appraiser can report back on any generic issues that came up, so that the group can become more aware of how it is seen by its members and what they want of it. Paired appraisal can take place at different times through a course.

Checklists

Any group is, of course, free to determine its own criteria and marking system for evaluation of its performance. On pages 242–47 are five schedules for use in groups and workshops. They are valuable as triggers for discussion as much as for a thorough evaluation. They may be used by the group itself or by another group in a 'fishbowl' arrangement.

'Do-it-yourself' checklist

Using the 'snowball' technique (see pages 114–15), individuals are asked to write down a maximum of three statements worth making about the group/class/course, and these are successively pooled and refined in sharing them with a progressively larger number of colleagues. Finally, the whole group is asked to draw up a list of statements (which must be shorter than the aggregate number produced if any real discussion is to occur). These are written on a board or newsprint on public view. Each statement is then given a three- or five-point scale from 'strongly agree' to 'strongly disagree' and everyone marks their rating for each statement with a blob to make the weighting or preferences more visually apparent (see Figure 9.8).

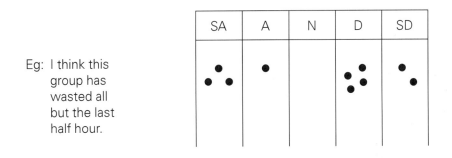

Figure 9.8 *Statement ratings for group evaluation*

The great virtue of this technique is that everyone contributes and the results are immediately visible. The group can thus quickly discuss some of the salient features of the ratings, particularly those where close agreement is apparent and those where there appears to be a fairly equal balance between opposing views.

Temperature reading

This comprises a set of special heading under which members may contribute:

- Appreciations. An expression of what each person has valued about the group and any of its members.
- New information. Anything anyone would like to share with others, any information they would like to have.
- Puzzles. Anything they still can't work out or would like to know before they leave.
- Complaints with recommendations. Expressions of what was not so valuable, enjoyable, helpful, *but* it must be accompanied by a recommendation. The ground rule is 'No complaint without a recommendation'.
- Wishes, hopes, dreams.
- Visions for the person contributing or for the group as a whole.

Temperature reading can occur as a group round for each category in turn or with all five categories for each person in turn.

Interviews

While one-to-one interviews for all students are hard to justify in terms of time and energy spent they can be of unpredictable benefit, both in what they can reveal of the less-than-conscious experience of students and tutors, and in the way they help students to integrate their learning; interviews require participants to reflect intensively and comprehensively. One-to-two interviews are more economical but not so confidential, while one-to-group interactions can reveal to the interviewer a lot about how effectively the group operates. Who conducts the interviews is of course a problem; given an open and trusting relationship between tutors, however, there is no reason why one should not interview members of another's group. It is not our purpose here to learn interview techniques, but it might be helpful to indicate to budding interviewers some of the sorts of questions that might stimulate revealing answers (though they may not all be suitable for every situation):

- How did the group go for you?
- What did you like best about it?
- What did you like least about it?
- What sort of things, apart from content, do you believe you learnt from it?
- How would you describe the climate of the group?
- How would you describe this group, as distinct from any other you've experienced?

- Any suggestions on how the tutor might improve the handling/the work of the group next time round?
- Anything you would like to have said to the tutor at the time but preferred not to?
- What else stood out for you?

Questions of this kind are usually sufficient to provoke a wealth of comment on group experience. With the additional use of 'eliciting' questions there should be little problem in getting a comprehensive picture of what went on.

Pass-round questionnaire

Each student is asked to divide a sheet of paper into three areas to cover:

- Things you found most valuable, and why.
- Things you found least valuable, and why.
- Ideas for improvements.

The students are then asked to write responses to each. Once completed, each sheet is passed round the group and read quietly in succession by the other students. When the sheets have circulated to the last person before returning to their author, students are invited to read out or recall any comments they agreed or disagreed with, or which stood out in any other respect. Finally, the authors receive their sheets back and add any further comments before they are collected for processing.

Self-made evaluation

More sophisticated groups may be asked to split into two or more sub-groups, each of which has to devise a technique of evaluation that it will use on the other sub-group(s), and then to administer it. It could choose from one of the above techniques or create an original one. Whether the self-made evaluation is set up as a regular monitoring task throughout the life of the group or is organized only at the end is a matter of choice, but it does have the enormous virtue of being good fun and thus raising spirits at the end of a course when they are typically at a low ebb.

Video playback

Provided the group can be recorded in its natural setting, video recording and playback can serve to alert everyone in the group to behaviours and events that they may have failed to notice at the time they were recorded. A consultant from outside the group can be brought in to start and stop the playback at the behest of the group and to ask facilitating questions about the interaction, such as:

- What was going on there?
- What were you thinking/feeling at the time?
- What effect did that have?

- What did you fear might happen?
- What was your strategy?
- What do you think he expected of you?

Alternatively, the playback could be sprinkled with questions such as in the checklist on page 247.

Managing the evaluation

It is easy for an evaluation of group work to resolve itself into a critique of the tutor rather than of the whole group. Certainly, the tutor will in most cases feel responsible if things go 'wrong' but, recognizing the mutual nature of human interaction for what it is, we must avoid the temptation of judging the success of a group in terms of the tutor's skills alone. This notion becomes more compelling when we understand the value of the students themselves learning about their own group skills through the process of evaluation.

Evaluation works best if it is seen as a continuous process engaged in by all those who contribute to setting up and participating in the group. Many of the evaluation methods or instruments included in this chapter can be used equally well for training purposes. The choice of which one to use may depend on the preferences of the group, the style of its operation or the kind of problem that seems to beset it. The group may choose to develop new instruments and methods more responsive to their immediate situation. Whichever approach we use, we must be aware of the sorts of bias to which evaluation may be subjected, particularly the wish to please (or displease). For this to be revealed for what it is, the 'results' of the evaluation must be processed through discussion in an open climate where a balance of support and challenge can create the possibility of change (see Smith, 1980). The way in which results are presented is therefore of the utmost importance; this may be another matter to be determined by consensus in the group.

There follows a series of checklists for use in evaluating groups, from UTMU, 1978:

Observation of discussion:
- Objectives. What was the purpose of the discussion? Was it clear to the participants? Did they accept it?
- Is the teaching method appropriate for these objectives?
- Setting. The room itself – what associations does it have? Does it encourage intimacy and relaxation?
- Seating – are the chairs comfortable? All the same? Draw a plan of their arrangement. Note empty chairs, distances between participants, prominence of any one group member, including the tutor.

Role of the tutor:
- What role seemed most dominant – facilitator, chairman, instructor, etc? (See pages 164–66 on the role of the tutor.)
- Was it clear, accepted, appropriate?

- What kind of questions were asked – open, factual, personal reactions, critical, appropriate to the level of the students, loaded . . .?
- For what proportion of the time did the tutor talk?
- What techniques were used to involve group members? What use was made of praise and encouragement?
- Were students discouraged from participating? How and why was this done?

Roles of individual students:

- What interpretations (if any) can be made about individual students' characteristic behaviour? What observable effects do they have on relations within the group (including the tutor)?
- What role does each student have (eg, leader, playboy, passive observer, clarifier, consensus-taker, reconciler, etc)? Are these roles temporary, changing or permanent? Are they sought, accepted or thrust upon them?

Dynamics:

- Length and frequency of each member's contributions.
- What status does each group member have? (NB – the tutor is a group member.)
- Is the group harmonious or competitive? How were conflicts dealt with? Denial, avoidance, repression or made explicit and worked through?
- What emotions or motives are aroused? (eg, do questions produce fear, curiosity, laughter . . .?)
- What are the goals of group members? Do they coincide with the tutor's objectives? How much commitment?
- Did the group stay formally as one or did it split up for different phases? What effects were produced by the changes or lack of change?
- What rules appeared to prevail? What behaviour is appropriate in the group? (eg, order of speaking, not disagreeing with tutor, avoiding specifics?)

Teaching small groups – checklist for self-evaluation

Read the list of statements in Figure 9.9 and tick the box that describes your own teaching best. Add four statements of your own.

Read the following list of statements and tick the box which described your own teaching best. Add four statements of your own.

1. I find it easy to learn students' names	☐ ☐ ☐ ☐ ☐	I find it hard to learn students' names
2. My sessions start working slowly	☐ ☐ ☐ ☐ ☐	My sessions start working quickly
3. It is easy to get students to contribute	☐ ☐ ☐ ☐ ☐	I find it difficult to get students to contribute
4. Most students prepare well	☐ ☐ ☐ ☐ ☐	Most students prepare poorly
5. I find it easy to keep discussion to the point	☐ ☐ ☐ ☐ ☐	I find it difficult to keep discussion to the point
6. I find it easy to keep discussion going	☐ ☐ ☐ ☐ ☐	I find it difficult to keep discussion going
7. I speak more than I would like	☐ ☐ ☐ ☐ ☐	I speak less than I would like
8. I find myself talking to one or two students	☐ ☐ ☐ ☐ ☐	I find myself talking to the whole group
9. My sessions lack structure	☐ ☐ ☐ ☐ ☐	My sessions are well structured
10. My students seldom express their own views	☐ ☐ ☐ ☐ ☐	My students freely express their own views

11. ....
12. ....
13. ....
14. ....

Now write a statement of what you intend to do to deal with problems implied by this checklist.

Figure 9.9 *Evaluating your own teaching*

Statements for evaluation of group function

	Always				Never
1. Members of the group have agreed upon and understand the specific goals for the group					
2. Members of the group have agreed upon and understand the ground rules for the group activity					
3. The group has responded to the feelings or moods expressed by its members					
4. The group has listened to and responded to members' ideas and comments and expressed recognition of contributions					
5. All members of the group are involved and have participated in the discussion					
6. The atmosphere of the group has been friendly and open, encouraging members to express criticisms or ask questions which expose themselves					
7. The group leader encouraged discussion by group members before presenting ideas to the group					
8. The group leader has synthesized related ideas and summarized concepts that the group has been discussing					
9. The group leader has determined if all group members have reached agreement about a particular point or are ready to move on to something else					
10. The group has confronted a member who was hindering the group in achieving its task such as undue arguing, going off topic, etc					
11. The group has been able to discuss areas of differences between members such that it does not cause conflict or allow the discussion to become destructive					
12. The group leader did not dominate nor did the group defer unduly to the leader's recognition of contributions					
13. The group has evaluated its progress toward its goals during and at the close of the session					
14. At the end of the session the group has decided on its specific task and work required to be done for the next session					

COMMENTS

Figure 9.10 *Evaluation of the group function*

Source: 1972, *The Small Group Tutorial*, McMaster University Educ. Monograph 3

Analysing group activity

Please rate each aspect in terms of the description at each end of the scale by circling the most appropriate number.

1. *Degree of mutual trust*
    High suspicion   3 2 1 0 1 2 3   High trust

2. *Degree of mutual support*
    Genuine support for   Everyone for
    each other   3 2 1 0 1 2 3   themselves

3. *Communications*
    Guarded, cautious   3 2 1 0 1 2 3   Open, authentic

4. *Group objectives*
    Not understood by group   3 2 1 0 1 2 3   Clearly understood by
                                                               group
    Group is committed to   3 2 1 0 1 2 3   Group is negative
    objectives   toward objectives
    Low attainment of   3 2 1 0 1 2 3   High attainment of
    objectives   objectives

5. *Handling conflicts within group*
    We deny, avoid or   We bring out conflicts
    suppress conflicts   3 2 1 0 1 2 3   and work through them

6. *Utilization of member resources*
    My ideas, abilities,   My ideas, abilities,
    knowledge and experience   knowledge and experience
    were properly drawn out   were *not* properly drawn
    and properly used   3 2 1 0 1 2 3   out and not properly used

7. *Suitability of group method*
    Group method suitable   Group methods
    for the objectives   3 2 1 0 1 2 3   unsuitable for the
                                                               objectives

GENERAL COMMENT

Figure 9.11 *Rating the group activity*

Checklist for group-based learning

Does the tutor:

Ensure the venue is suitable in terms of seating, heating, lighting, etc?
Establish a congenial atmosphere in which students' viewpoints are valued?

1. Venue and climate

Ensure that students understand the aims of the session(s)?
And how these relate to other parts of their course?
And what they can expect to achieve from the session(s)?

2. Aims and purposes

Make sure the students know what is expected of them by way of preparation?
That they understand when it is appropriate to contribute, to raise a question or to challenge points made by others?
Make explicit what the tutor's role is?

3. Ground rules

Select tasks appropriate to the aims of the session?
Do the tasks offer the students a variety of learning experiences (eg, the chance to draw on their own resources and experiences, but also share with and learn from others)?

4. Planning tasks

Ensure tasks early in the session(s) enable all to be involved?
Make sure the outcomes from one task lead to another?
Give clear and succinct instructions?
Set and keep to realistic time allocations for tasks?

5. Structuring and sequencing tasks

Give positive attention to what students say?
Reflect readiness to listen in verbal responses and in body language?

6. Listening

7. Questioning

Use a variety of questioning strategies in a sensitive and flexible manner?

8. Explaining and clarifying

Allow students space to attempt tasks and think about questions before giving own explanations? Build students' ideas into own explanations?

9. Encouraging participation

Encourage all students in the group to contribute, to talk to each other (as well as the tutor)?
Avoid dominating the proceedings?
Intervene appropriately (eg, to restrain the vociferous, to encourage the silent, to defuse unhelpful conflict)?

10. Responding to students as individuals

Act sensitively to students as individuals (ie, taking into account their backgrounds and prior knowledge)?

11. Monitoring

Provide opportunities for the group to take stock and to review its effectiveness as a learning group?

12. Closing

Make provisions for summing up what has been achieved?
Establish what is necessary to follow up the session and consolidate what has been learnt?

Exercises

1. Principles of good practice for assessing student learning

Take each of the principles of good practice for assessing student learning on pages 215–16 and write a brief account (20–30 words) on a single sheet of paper under each of the headings about how you would see this reflected in an assessment of group work, either in a discussion or a project format.

   Pass the sheet round the group, inviting other members to write any comments before they pass it on. When you receive your own sheet back, study it again before taking part in a group 'round' completing the sentence, 'What I've learnt about assessment in groups is . . . and what I would like to see happen (or do) is . . .'.

2. Dealing with difficult incidents in groups

This is an exercise that works at two levels: solving group problems and experiencing self- and peer assessment. It will take between an hour and one and a half hours.

1.   Each member of the group reflects silently on their experiences in groups and writes down as many problems as they can recall that have occurred in relation to the following:
   – preparation for the group;
   – during the group meeting, for yourself;
   – during the group meeting, for the group as a whole.
2.   In groups of four or five, reveal the problems through a 'top-slicing' process – a group 'round' in which each person in turn describes the top item on their list – and the process is repeated around the group until all items are exhausted. Do not discuss the problems at this stage.
3.   In your groups choose one problem each, a different one for each person, which you would like to solve with the group's help.
4.   Each person has 5 minutes as a 'client' to briefly describe their chosen problem and enlist the help of another member of the group in solving it. The person on the client's right should be the 'timekeeper', the person opposite, a 'consultant' and any remaining members acting as 'observers'.
   – The task of the consultant is to help the client find their own solution to their problem. They do this by exercising the skills of listening, exploratory questioning, clarifying, checking for understanding, giving full attention to the client and offering advice only at the end, having checked first that it is welcome.
   – The timekeeper must signal, preferably in a clear, non-verbal manner, 30 seconds before the allocated time is up as well as the completion.
   – The task of the observers is to make an assessment of the consultant's effectiveness and skills using the assessment chart below, and to communicate this at the end of the 5 minutes.

5.   The roles are agreed for the first of as many successive rounds as are necessary for everyone to have a turn. The 5-minute consultancy now takes place.
6.   Once the first consultancy is complete the consultant fills in his or her assessment sheet while the observer(s) show their peer assessment to the client and timekeeper for confirmation and addition (5 minutes maximum checked by the timekeeper).
7.   When the consultant is ready the assessment sheets are exchanged and any problems of understanding clarified (5 minutes maximum checked by the timekeeper).
8.   The exercise from 5 to 7 is repeated for each group member.
9.   A final plenary discussion may now be held to review the process and the effects of assessment on what happened.
10.   An additional activity before the plenary, if time permits, is to use the 'crossover' method described in Chapter 6, such that new groups comprising one person from each original group are formed to share their assessments and what they have learnt from them.

Observer' sheet

Peer assessment of consultancy skills
Consultant's name:
What the consultant did well:

What the consultant could improve on:

Any other feedback comments:

Rating:
Listening skills	1	2	3	4	5
Questioning skills	1	2	3	4	5
Overall as a consultant	1	2	3	4	5

Observer/Assessor's name:

Consultant – self-assessment
Please complete this as soon as possible after you have done your consultancy session.

What I think I did well:

What I think I could improve on:

Any other feedback comments:

Rating:
My listening skills	1	2	3	4	5
My questioning skills	1	2	3	4	5
Overall as a consultant	1	2	3	4	5

Comments:

3. Deciding how to evaluate the group

Take two of the evaluation checklists to compare and contrast in the group.

1. Each group member studies the two checklists with a view to their suitability for use in evaluating the way the group has worked.
2. In a group 'round', each person briefly presents their view of the relative merits of the two checklists and how they might be used and processed in the group.
3. The whole group then has to decide which checklist to use to evaluate the work of the group over the period of its existence and how it should be processed.
4. The checklist is completed and processed in the group.
5. If there is sufficient energy, the group may then use the other checklist to evaluate its work in (2) and possibly (3).

Discussion points

- What are the principal risks in evaluation for a) the evaluator and b) the person(s) being evaluated? What happens to these risks when these two are the same person?
- Choose one or more of the evaluation measures to review the work of your group(s). What makes the one(s) you choose more useful or valid than any other? How might you administer it? How did it work out? In what ways could (or did) the evaluation serve to integrate learning in your group?
- How would you describe the principle differences in the group dynamics of discussion groups and project groups? How does that affect the way they are assessed and evaluated?

10 | Training and development

Any experience which fails to confound expectations is not worthy of the name 'experience'.

(Hegel)

By the end of this chapter you can expect to have a useful collection of practical ideas for training others in group work and leadership, and a range of opportunities for the training and development of both teachers and students in groups.

The natural offspring of evaluation is learning and change. Without these consequences the task of evaluation would be sterile. The primary concern of this chapter is to consider ways in which improvement in group behaviour can be effected. Three possible approaches suggest themselves:

1. *The learning group:* seminars, tutorials, etc, in which the focus for learning about group process (and its assessment) is the tutor/student group itself.
2. *The task group:* for example, a staff working party or conference planning team who may, apart from their primary task, wish to learn how to work more effectively as a team.
3. *The training group:* in which a small number of people (tutors and possibly students) come together to study group process either in a workshop or a regular series of meetings within a risk-free environment whose boundaries are sacrosanct; and the training activity, usually in the form of a workshop led by someone with a training role.

Each of these has its own special features; each could complement the others as part of an integrated programme; and starting with one might well lead to the development of others.

Learning groups

Most of the exercises at the ends of the previous chapters are intended for use with learning/teaching groups, although most of them are, of course, multi-purpose. The opportunity for risk-free experimentation is much less in a normal tutorial or seminar group. It's not easy to stand aside from the tutoring task (though opportunities for role play of a different kind might arise) and we might risk undermining our credibility if we were to expose our failings (and feelings) to general scrutiny. Nevertheless, if assessment and evaluation can be viewed as a learning, as opposed to a judgmental, procedure, then the possibilities are boundless. Any of the techniques described in the previous chapter could be used, provided always that it is as a basis for developing more effective behaviours and processes in the group, and that it is conducted as a whole-group task rather than as one polarized between tutor and students.

Whether this work is done on a planned basis, or activated by critical incidents and crises as they arise, will depend on the kind of course being followed and the relationship between the tutor and the students.

Task groups

Both tutors and students are frequently called upon to work on specific tasks with a view to developing some kind of end product. Staff working parties and student project groups are examples of these, and there are close parallels between them. Yet rarely do either tutors or students reflect on their teamwork skills in their work together, or seek substantial improvement in their skills as the work progresses. This is understandable when we consider how unusual the demand for cooperative behaviour in a general climate of rivalry and competition must appear to members of a task group. Increasingly, however, the need for improvements in this basic management skill is being appreciated in negotiating problems in teamwork.

Here are two successful approaches to learning teamwork studies 'in the saddle'. Give team members a short induction in which they practise various training exercises (those on pages 260–87 for instance), in anticipation of problems to come. This could be followed by a shorter session in the middle of the project or task as a checking and topping-up exercise. In the second approach, encourage the group to use simple evaluative measures, checklists, or diaries, and to meet at prescribed times to discuss teamwork problems and make explicit what they are learning from their handling of them.

Eitington (1996) contains a range of ideas for the preparation and training of teams.

Training groups

Readers will by now be well aware that group processes embody a complex web of attitudes, understandings and behaviours. Some of us learn to function effectively within this web quite early in life but for most of us, it appears there is a great deal of unlearning to do: shedding some of the expectations and stock responses we have developed over years of parenting and schooling, and acquiring new ways of listening, perceiving and acting in groups. Such changes involve considerable personal adjustment and many might argue that this is too much to expect of adults, especially those in a teaching role. Yet, as Miles (1981) has pointed out, if the group itself is used as the learning medium, more change is possible than many of us are inclined to think. The various exercises included in this chapter are all based on small-group activity. They assume that the small cohesive group is the most effective medium for personal understanding and growth in group skills, whether it results from a regular meeting of committed tutors or as one of several sub-groups in a large-scale workshop.

The exercises are based on one further assumption: that participants are committed to improving learning in the groups of which they are part. This does not mean there is no value in one or two antipathetic members taking part. Far from it: one or two cynics may contribute hugely to the creation of a realistic group process and may also cause their colleagues to take less for granted. Yet if, for whatever reason, their purpose is persistently negative, their presence can destroy the fabric of the group and, more importantly, the spontaneity to learn.

Whereas academic discussion in seminars often deals with content divorced in time and space from what is occurring within the group process, training groups have to focus much more on the 'here and now' experience of their members. Just as there is no way in which one can comprehend group dynamics without seeing it in action, so it is virtually impossible to become aware of one's own effect on a group, or to acquire new skills, without participating in the dynamics of a group committed to these tasks.

In order to develop more effective group behaviours, the learner must have the chance to learn from doing, exploring, trying out and getting feedback on what he or she does. For this to happen, there has to be a climate with a degree of mutual trust and tolerance and where participants feel free to take risks in admitting failings and anxieties and in experimenting with newly learnt behaviours. As feelings of safety and trust grow in a training group, it becomes increasingly possible for members to reveal their own observations about themselves and each other. Though this trust may grow quite naturally in a well-run group, there are helpful exercises in developing it, one of the most powerful of which is the Johari Window (page 66). Nevertheless, an atmosphere of trust does not develop easily and it is often safer at first to employ distancing mechanisms (for instance video tape or role play), in which people can talk about their image or enactment. It is less threatening to learn about one's own group behaviour by watching and identifying with others in an enactment whether those others are: a) the group members themselves detached in time through the playback of interaction on video recorded shortly before; or b) involved in a role play or enactment in which members may (semi-legitimately) claim they were not being themselves.

Such activities, though always to be valued, become less and less necessary as the degree of trust develops, excepting always that a particular problem may generally or individually pose too great a threat for live confrontation, or that it is the only way of bringing an external scenario like a laboratory within the scope of the training group's immediate experience.

The central concern in training groups is to examine social rather than personal behaviour. The interpersonal has precedence over the intrapersonal (though the latter is of definite consequence). The training group is 'usually less concerned with the inner reasons for why someone does something and is more concerned with how they do it, what the impact is on others and how they can improve what they do to become more skilful' (Miles, 1981). A person may, in the course of such a group, gain vivid insights into some inner problems, especially in the way they may hinder his or her effectiveness in relating to others, but this is incidental to the primary concern of the group.

Planning

Once a training group has been launched – or even before – someone will have the responsibility of preparing and planning, whether that person is a designated or a self-appointed leader. There are various concerns he or she will have to address, each of which may affect the quality of learning in the training group. Among these are:

- assessing one's own motives;
- making judgements about the institutional context:
    - what attitudes and interests in group learning exist
    - what priority participants are likely to give it;
- deciding:
    - who should plan
    - who should participate
    - timing and physical arrangements
    - roles of leader(s)
    - evaluation strategy;
- organizing the content (a sequence based on psychological rather than logical criteria is usually more effective);
- choosing ways of maintaining continuity between activities or separate meetings.

Above all, the programme for a training group should be amenable to change in response to members' developing needs and interests. Ideally, it should be planned and monitored by them in the way described as a 'peer learning community' (Heron, 1974).

Leading

The role of leader in a training group (if of course it is relevant at all) need not be unlike that of the facilitator described in Chapter 7, but with a ready repertoire of techniques and skills to demonstrate, in response to issues that arise in the group. As leaders we must also be prepared to face considerably greater challenges to our position than academic tutors, with their legitimated authority, might expect. We should not be put off our stroke by this, but rather see it as an opportunity for further 'here and now' discussion of the way a tutor might handle critical incidents. For instance, if an incident arose in a training group the leader might ask, *'How would you handle this if you were in my position?'*.

As training group leaders we may expect to be confronted with the following sorts of problems:

- initial attack or challenge to our authority, or worse still, withdrawal;
- being 'trapped' by anxiously dependent members – 'Tell us what the tricks of the trade are; how would you do it?';
- conflict over expectations and aims, especially where there are involuntary members;
- resistance to change – 'This is irrelevant, it doesn't apply to us', 'What's the theoretical justification of all this?' or long abstract discussions;
- frustration – people feel they are not getting what they want from the group;
- revolt, where a group wants to go its own separate way (fight);
- cosiness – 'Aren't we a lovely group?' – which probably means that the conflict and pain necessary to learning and change are being avoided (flight);
- low points – where spirits are flagging – can occur at any time but almost always at the end when members are likely to be somewhat depressed that the life of the group is at an end, or merely that it's after lunch.

In tackling these problems the leader will have to draw on a range of skills, techniques and strategies, be alive to the need to maintain continuity and momentum, and be flexible in allowing reasonable changes of direction and alternative courses of action. Bramley (1979) gives several practical hints on handling these kind of problems, as does Tiberius (1999) in his troubleshooting guide to leading small groups.

Deciding on group sizes

You can usually choose what size of group participants may be invited to work in. The choice will depend as much on the purpose of a particular exercise as on such principles as sequences in learning and variety of stimulus.

Small groups (2–5) can be used for:

- intimacy and trust;
- warming up;
- feeling safe;
- taking risks;
- privacy in feedback;
- agreeing quickly;
- leaderless discussion;
- getting everyone involved;
- delegating facilitator 'control';
- comparing details.

Large groups (8–40) can be used for:

- variety of ideas;
- getting a wide perspective;
- keeping control;
- making things public;
- processing what has happened;
- meeting, greeting and parting;
- experiencing a more complex dynamic;
- communicating with the whole membership.

Inter-group processes can be used for:

- developing separate plans;
- producing a sense of competition;
- mixing cohesiveness with openness;
- building a sense of the whole group quickly.

Examples of group structures:

Small	Large	Inter-group
Pairs	A full circle	Fishbowl
Buzz group	Plenary	Pyramid
5 minutes each way	Line-up	Milling
Back-to-back	Brainstorm	Syndicates
Tutoring pairs	Circular questioning	Crossovers

Changing group membership:

It is sometimes beneficial to change the membership of small groups so as to:

- energize people by discouraging 'cosiness';
- provide opportunities for people to meet new faces and ideas;
- break up dysfunctional groups.

Handling problems in larger groups

As I provocatively stated earlier in the book, if you haven't got problems in your group then something is wrong. Problems, in other words, are to be expected and it is how we deal with them that determines the degree of success. There are three main strategies for dealing with problems characteristic of large groups (Gibbs, 1992b).

1. *Don't start from here.* This refers to problems that occur because appropriate steps were not taken at an earlier stage. For example, the students may not have been introduced to each other, the purpose of the seminar may not have been made clear, the preparation that was required may have been unclear or impossible, or the ground rules of the session may not have been established appropriately. Until these are sorted out you may repeatedly find yourself troubleshooting throughout the meeting and the incident will keep recurring.

2. *Use structures.* Unstructured large group discussions take a lot of skilful handling. Many incidents are an inevitable consequence of lack of structure. Both the process and the content need to be structured. Suggestions can be found in Chapter 6.

3. *Make leadership interventions.* These are the really skilful things experienced tutors learn to say and do that subtly redirect groups, defuse situations, bring in quiet students and so on. In larger groups you may need to be less subtle and more emphatic in your interventions, and skills you have developed in small groups may not be as effective. You may need to be a great deal more explicit about what you are doing and what behaviour you are expecting, and you may need the cooperation of the group to tackle any problems.

1. Don't start from here
Consider all these before the group starts:

- group composition;
- group size;
- room shape;
- furniture;
- preparation by you;
- preparation by students;
- learning tasks;
- expectations;
- check assumptions;
- draw up ground rules;
- agree contracts;
- use icebreaker / warm-up exercise.

2. Use structures

- buzz groups;
- pyramids;
- rounds;
- milling;
- circular questioning;
- fishbowl;
- line-ups;
- rounds;
- pyramids;
- crossovers;

- 5 minutes each way;
- role allocations (individuals or sub-groups taking different perspectives);
- role plays, including 5-minute theatre (see pages 116–17);
- brainstorming;
- games.

3. *Make interventions*

- *Use exploratory questions* (for example, 'Does anyone have any experience of . . .?').
- *Look around the group* (to pick up signals and to avoid being visually locked in one-to-one exchanges).
- *Open questions* to the whole group (for example, 'What do the rest of you think about that?').
- *Bounce questions back* to the questioner (for example, 'Well, what do *you* think?').
- *Resist answering questions.*
- *Echo* (for example, 'Made no sense of the theory').
- *Accept silence* (silently count to 10, 20 or even 30).
- *Bring in* (using hand gesture and, for example, 'What did you want to say, Mo?').
- *Shut out* (using hand gesture and, for example, 'Hang on a minute Les, let's hear some other ideas first and we'll come back to you later').
- *Check for understanding* (for example, 'So what you are saying is . . .').
- *Describe individual behaviour* (for example, 'You nodded then, Chris').
- *Describe group process* (for example, 'I notice that a lot of people haven't spoken so far today').
- *Support, value, encourage* (for example, 'Thank you Jo, that's very helpful').
- *Self-disclose* (for example, 'I'm finding it difficult to hear everyone in this room today – are you finding it the same?').

Training activities

The following examples of training activities are not in any sense a cookbook for improving group skills. Leaders or tutors will need to adapt them to meet the immediate requirement in the light of their own abilities and the situation in hand. It would probably not be wise, therefore, to use the activities without reference to the rest of this book. Readers will no doubt develop their own variations and create new exercises that make more sense in their particular setting.

The activities are designed for work with groups or sub-groups of no more than eight members, possibly in a workshop format. The aggregate number of sub-groups should not exceed four or five. In selecting any particular activity a tutor or leader might check that:

- it is appropriate to the interests and mood of members at the given time;
- it has relevance to their teaching / task needs;

- learning occurs at different levels;
- learning can readily be transferred or carried beyond the confines of the learning environment;
- the skills required for running them lie within the tutor's competence.

What may be acceptable, relevant and feasible by the end of a series of activities may be less so at the beginning. The beginning in fact requires special attention and it is usually sensible to start with some warm-up or introductory activities. The first two exercises described below are of this kind.

Paired introductions

Commonly in groups, individuals are invited to introduce themselves as a way of getting started. It is thus hoped that everyone will become more open and friendly towards each other and that defences will be somewhat lowered. Yet frequently people are either reluctant to say much about themselves or ramble on at an inconsiderate length about their own background and interests. Interpersonal boundaries often remain untouched. A procedure that appears to be much more successful in breaking the ice socially is as follows:

1. Individuals interview their immediate neighbour in the group for two or three minutes about their background, interests and what they hope to get from the group or workshop, with a view to introducing them in such a way that the rest of the group can get to know them as a person. They are in turn interviewed by the same neighbour. They are told that they will have one minute in which to introduce their partner to the group and that they must do so in such a way that the group will remember them (*finding out something unusual is a useful device*).
2. Each person then introduces their partner to the group (in no particular sequence) preferably 'as the spirit takes them'. A time limit of one minute is imposed on each contribution.
3. Any person who feels that something important about them was left out by their partner may repair the omission at the end.
4. Everyone may be asked to reflect on the experience and to consider whether they might use it with their own teaching groups.

This complete procedure should be explained to everyone before they embark on it.

Walking interviews

With a larger group it is often desirable to encourage a level of mixing that seated positions do not allow. Walking interviews encourage people to mill and ask questions of each other that they might not otherwise consider. The procedure is:

1. Members are invited to write down one (or two) questions that they would like to ask every other member of the group.
2. They then mill around, locate a partner to put their question to and themselves answer questions from. (There is an explicit proviso that anyone may refuse to answer any particular question without any consequence.)
3   When a reasonable degree of mixing has been achieved, the group may be reassembled and asked whether any general patterns of information emerged, and what specific items of interest people picked up.

Card exchange: a starting exercise

This is adapted from 'Game Game' by Thiagarajan (1978).

> *Aims:* to help a large group of students get to know each other; to share values about given issues; to form teams.
> *Class size:* 10 to 40.
> *Time required:* one to one and a half hours.
> *Materials:* five times as many index cards as the number of participants.
> *Physical setting:* an open-plan room.

1. Before the class starts, prepare several index cards by writing on them comments on the subject of the course or the topic under discussion. Make some positive, some negative and some neutral, eg: 'I think . . . has no future', 'A knowledge of . . . is essential to any well-run organization'. Prepare about twice as many cards as there are students and hold these in reserve.
2. In class, hand out four blank cards to each student and ask them to write comments like those above – one on each card. Encourage them to be witty, cynical, encouraging, political, philosophical or whatever. (Allow 5 minutes.)
3. Collect the cards from the students and shuffle them well with your prepared cards. Then hand back to each student an arbitrary selection of five cards. Tell them that they will find they now have cards they would or would not wish to be associated with. Their task is to walk round the room exchanging cards until they have a set they are happy with. It is important to emphasize that exchanges should be done on a one-to-one basis with cards unseen and that the wish to give or receive a card of a type should be justified, eg: 'I want to swap a card which cocks a snook at . . . because I don't like . . .', 'Have you got anything more positive?'. Scatter the spare cards on a table with the comment that these may be freely swapped with any cards. (Allow 15 minutes and encourage everyone to circulate.)
4. Having checked that everyone is reasonably happy with their hand of cards, ask them to form teams, each of whose task it is to select one of their pooled cards to represent their outlook or to devise a new statement with the same object. There are two ways these teams may be formed and you as organizer should decide which to choose beforehand:

- participants freely team up with any number of colleagues according to shared values as represented by the cards;
- they form preordained groups of a fixed size (this is particularly useful when work is to continue in these teams thereafter).

5. Once they have chosen a team statement, ask each team quickly to choose a name by which it should be known. Invite the teams to announce publicly their choice of statement and title with a short justification for each.

String circle – an opening exercise

Material: A ball of string or wool (make sure it's heavy and long enough to be thrown across the group as it unwinds as many times as there are participants).
Procedure: The first person, A (could be the trainer), holds the ball and tells the group:

- his or her name;
- something interesting or unusual about him- or herself;
- his or her reasons for coming to the workshop.

He or she then throws the ball to any other person whom they would like to find out about, *but* they must hold on to the free end of the string so that when the ball flies to the next person, they are still holding the end.

The next person, B, thanks the first person and repeats what he or she heard them say, before giving three similar bits of information about themselves. They then throw the ball to the next person of their choice, *but* hold on to the string at the loose end as they throw it to the next person, C, and so on. Each time the person receiving the ball repeats the information from the previous person before saying their own piece.

When everyone has received the ball and spoken about themselves, if there is time, the process can be reversed as the ball is wound up again. This time each person throws it either to the person who threw it to them or to anyone, *but* has to remember and tell the group what that person said about him- or herself.

NB. It is important to set a norm at the start of, say, 30 seconds each, and possibly to remind the group if later on they seem to be taking too long.

Becoming a group

When running a training event the problem of forming groups, both in the sense of choosing membership and becoming a working team, is one that has to be addressed. If people are left to choose their own partners, several problems may occur: all those who already know and like each other get together to the exclusion of the others; some avoid choosing partners whom they would really like to work with because they don't want to be seen to be choosing them; or some may wait to be chosen and end up feeling like a group of 'leftovers'. One way round these problems is to carefully designate group membership so as to break up cliques and ensure as heterogeneous a mix as possible. Another is to form a line-up (pages 122–23) and to number off from one end – 1, 2, 3, 4; 1, 2, 3, 4, etc.

One method that combines randomness with purpose is as follows:

1. Invite all participants to mill around the room greeting or acknowledging each other non-verbally and to keep moving.
2. After two to three minutes, ask everyone to stop, to look around them and form clusters of whatever size you need for the event, again non-verbally.
3. Now in the groups, they may talk. Their task is: 'To become a group (or team) and to report after 30 minutes how you did this and how successful it was'.
4. The reporting takes place and can, of course, be part of the evidence of how successful the group was.

If there is a risk of the groups having problems 'gelling', you can give them a list of *what to avoid*, for example:

■ theorizing;
■ not listening to each other;
■ not trying to understand each other;
■ not taking risks;
■ chatting aimlessly;
■ avoiding the expression of feelings;
■ not finding out special things about each other;
■ keeping things to yourself;
■ withdrawing from participation.

You could possibly give them a list of *what to do*:

■ find out about each other;
■ do something physical;
■ find out how you came to choose each other;
■ take some risks together;
■ change places in the group;
■ try something out;
■ identify what skills each member has;
■ build something together.

While the higher-risk strategy of withholding these lists and letting the teams experience the 'labour pains' of creating a group on their own may generate more learning about groups, the introduction of the above lists, at some stage even if not at the start, may reduce the risk of frustration.

Workshop activities

Prepared video

A tape or film of an unfamiliar learning group is ideal for this activity. One procedure is to play it with the leader in control of the stop/start switch but with everyone permitted to signal when they want it stopped. In the ensuing step-by-step discussion (see page 109) the leader asks questions about the group on the screen such as:

- What sort of atmosphere has been created – and how?
- What expectations does the tutor appear to have?
- What expectations do the students appear to have?
- How would you describe the manner of the tutor? What effect do you think it has?
- Have you any comments on the physical layout, numbers, apparent statuses? How do these affect interaction?
- How would you describe the tutor's relationship with the group?

The most suitable points at which to ask these questions, and others that will certainly arise, will be evident in the screened action as it evolves. The timing is a matter of judgement, bearing in mind what is to come. The workshop leader must therefore view the tape beforehand.

   At certain critical points on the tape, such as when the tutor asks the group a question or a student aims one at the tutor, more specific questions may be asked: 'What do you anticipate will happen?', 'How would you respond if you were the tutor/a student?'. At this point participants could be asked to role play in pairs what they might do. Then, after the tape has been played forward to reveal what eventually did happen, you can, for instance, ask:

- What did you think of that?
- What other ways could the tutor have gone about it?
- What would be going on in your mind if you were the tutor?
- How do you see the discussion developing now?

At other times it may feel right to ask questions that search for the emotional underlay of the discussion: 'How do you think the students/tutor feel?', 'What is going on?' or, for the intellectual life of the group: 'What do you think the students are learning?'. And, whatever answers are forthcoming: 'Anything else?', in order to press for less obvious issues.

Consultants and assessors game

This game provides a framework in which a variety of problems can be examined and solutions proposed. The class is split into two or three teams who take the role of consultants or experts working in parallel with one another, with the task of providing a solution to a relevant problem. Their solution or proposal is presented to an assessors' panel composed of one or two representatives who are themselves elected from each group; the assessors' job, in addition to making the final adjudication, is to set criteria for the acceptability of the proposals or solutions. The whole exercise should last one and a half to two and a half hours.

Though no mention of competition or authority is made, a sense of intense rivalry between the teams and respect for or resentment of the power of the assessors can develop. The format of the game, originally proposed as an exercise in inter-group relations by Kolb *et al* (1984), provides a dynamic that can give poetic life to otherwise prosaic tasks. I find it amusing to speculate how many committee hours could have been saved over the years had their members, when confronted with a knotty problem, split into teams to work concurrently for an hour, rather than farming it out to a working party for two years.

Here is the game in detail.

> *Aims:*
> – to experience working as a team on an agreed task within a limited time span;
> – to produce proposals or solutions on a given problem and to subject them to critical scrutiny;
> – to study some of the interpersonal behaviour and reactions arising from inter-group competition and perceptions.
>
> *Number of participants:* a minimum of 10 and a maximum of 25. All should have a reasonable level of experience in the field covered in the task (see the organizer's instructions, paragraphs 2 and 3).
>
> *Time required:* a minimum of one hour, but preferably two and a half hours (the smaller the total number participating, the less the amount of time needed).
>
> *Materials:* whatever the teams require for the presentation of their proposals. Flipchart paper or OHP transparencies with pens will probably suffice.
>
> *Physical setting:* a room large enough to accommodate the teams and the assessors panel without undue mutual sound interference, otherwise separate rooms for each team; also a room (possibly one of the above) in which the formal presentations of the teams' proposals can be made.

Here is what the tutor does:

1. Explain the aims of the exercise and describe its structure by using the diagram shown in Figure 10.1.
2. Either announce a selected problem or task to be worked on by the teams, or invite everyone present to suggest and agree one. The task should be one that the participants are competent to work on and which allows for a variety of solutions (for

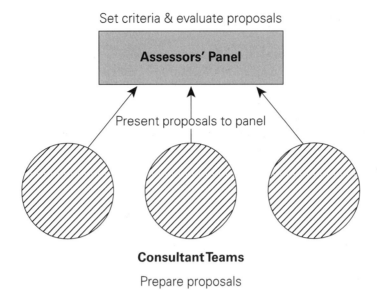

Set criteria & evaluate proposals

Assessors' Panel

Present proposals to panel

Consultant Teams

Prepare proposals

Figure 10.1 *Consultants and assessors game*

example, the design of a bridge or a study skills course, the formulation of a new law or a research submission). Agree with participants on sufficient background information to define the context of the problem. Remember that definition of too much detail is time-consuming, can stifle a lot of creative thinking and can detract from the central task.

For example, if the task is to design a study skills course the teams will doubtless need to know how many students there are in the institution, what subject areas are studied and possibly how much money the team has. Other questions such as how long the course should be, how many tutors are available, whether any members of the team are to be the actual tutors, when the course should be held and so on may be left to the teams to decide within the ambit of their proposals. Having negotiated the task, form two or three teams (not more than eight in each) and set them up in separate working areas.

3. Now distribute the consultant teams' instruction sheet (see below).
4. After about 20 minutes, remind each team to elect two members who will jointly form the assessors' panel. They will not represent the views of their original team so much as take them into account in determining criteria.
5. Once the assessors' panel is composed, find them a suitable place to meet. Give them the assessors' panel instruction sheet (see below).
6. Announce a timetable and make it clear to all that it will be strictly adhered to. (For certain problems a longer work time – and hence total time – may be needed if proposals of sufficient quality are to be achieved.) The timetable must allow at least 30 minutes in total for the presentation and discussion of all the proposals. For example, if the overall length of the session is one and a half hours, the following timetable might apply for three teams:

–	Introduction and negotiation	10 minutes
–	Teams work on proposals	45 minutes
–	Presentation and discussion	35 minutes

7. Act as referee to ensure that the instructions are clear and being followed. You may need to make interpretations and variations from time to time. These should be within the context of the game and, unless there is good reason for not doing so, should be announced to all.
8. You may also act as a neutral resource person in any way appropriate to the content of the exercise.
9. The teams will invariably be oblivious to the passage of time. They will therefore need reminding of approaching deadlines and of any other responsibilities.
10. Keep a check on any other decisions implied in the two instruction sheets.
11. Debrief (at least 30 minutes). There are several ways in which the review session can be conducted. A lot will depend on whether the game was run primarily as an exercise in group and inter-group dynamics or as a way of producing a rich variety of ideas and plans on the problem under consideration; whether the emphasis was on process or product. The main thing is to give some recognition to things that will have gone on both within and between groups and the fact that the experience will have been an intellectual and an emotional one for most participants.

Before embarking on any discussion of process or product you may find there are a few feelings floating around that may need to be defused. You might do well to ask, 'How is everyone feeling – anyone want to get anything out of their system?', or something similar, but then, as soon as the immediate response to the question has been given, quickly pass on to the process discussion.

After this you might adopt the following pattern:

- Ask the teams separately to discuss and report back, in plenary, questions about:
    - leadership and the distribution of tasks;
    - how conflicts were resolved and decisions made;
    - the effects of time pressure;
    - the criteria by which assessors were elected;
    - how the assessors felt during the presentation phase;
    - how the consultant teams felt about the assessors.
- In plenary, draw out the answers to the above questions and try to build up a more generalized picture of the events in the game and then the implications with questions about:
    - how easy participants would find it to join one of the other teams to implement the winning, or any other, proposal and what that implies;
    - what parallels there were with 'back-home' experiences, structures, relationships;
    - how they might use the format of the game in their own work;
    - what they learnt from the game generally and about themselves;
    - what things they might wish to do or change as a result.
- Then there are questions about the product:
    - What did they think of the quality of the proposals?
    - How did the proposals compare with equivalent ones 'back home'?

– What improvements could they make to the proposals?
– How might they use the ideas in their own work?

Of course the opportunity to ask questions at preordained times rarely arises. You will probably have to be fairly selective and pragmatic in the ordering of the above questions.

CONSULTANT TEAMS' INSTRUCTION SHEET

Your main task is to prepare a proposal for solving the agreed problem and to present it to a panel of assessors at the appointed time.

After you have discussed the task for about 20 minutes you should elect two of your members to join others similarly elected on the assessors' panel. You will have five minutes (10 if time allows – check with the tutor) to present your proposals to the assessors' panel, who have the task of determining criteria for judging the merits of the proposals submitted. After your proposals have been heard there will be a question-and-answer session with the assessors' panel, and they will then evaluate the separate proposals.

You should also decide how you are going to present your proposal, bearing in mind the strict time limit. The assessors' panel has full responsibility for the conduct of the presentation session.

ASSESSORS' PANEL INSTRUCTION SHEET

You are independent assessors and in no way represent the teams from which you were elected. Your task, while the teams are preparing their proposals, is to establish criteria for their evaluation. In addition you should agree a procedure for the adjudication.

Each of the teams will decide for themselves how they are going to present their proposal. They will each give a five-minute presentation followed by five minutes of questions and answers with you (times may be extended by the organizer). All the presentations should be completed before the question-and-answer session starts.

You should set up the room for the presentation roughly in the pattern shown by the organizer at the start and establish a reasonably formal atmosphere.

Once the presentations and questions are complete you will naturally wish to discuss your impressions and make the necessary decisions. This discussion should last no more than five minutes and should be conducted openly so that all the teams can hear.

The adjudication may take two forms. One is to announce one of the teams as the winner. The other is to discuss openly the relative merits of the proposals. In either case you should make public the reasons for your assessment and reveal the process of arriving at it.

You are responsible for the conduct of the presentation session.

Variations on the consultants and assessors game

The consultants and assessors game is capable of many elaborations. You can, for instance, make it more relevant to particular needs in the following ways.

Increase competition

Every participant puts 10p in a kitty and the winning team picks up the kitty. The final presentation can be assessed (peer assessed, by the panel using your criteria, or by you). Keep teams stable across a number of games and keep a league table on the wall.

Adding simulation components

Start the game with a comprehensive scenario and roles for the groups and / or separate players with plenty of background information and typical real-life briefs. For instance, the assessors' panel could be an institutional committee or a public inquiry board.

Focus on simulation

Sometimes you may wish to focus on the various processes that form part of the game, such as planning, problem solving, decision-making, teamwork, competition and the presentation of proposals. By drawing attention to these both in the preparation and the debriefing, and providing materials such as checklists to encourage reflection, you can develop a lively form of learning about these processes and more particularly the players' part in them. The game could even become a kind of test bed for the demonstration of skills previously rehearsed through other means.

I have used the consultants and assessors game in many contexts: management training, language teaching, staff development, study skills and problem-solving consultations, to name but a few, and with various purposes in mind:

- demonstrating what a game looks like;
- looking at group and inter-group relations;
- trying to get imaginative solutions to real problems;
- testing the likely response of a parliamentary committee;
- designing a simulation for a test run.

NASA exercise: seeking consensus

Aims: to compare the process of individual decision-making with group decisio
To develop an awareness of teamwork skills.
Class size: any number – several groups may be directed simultaneously.
Time required: approximately an hour and a half.
Materials: pencils; individual task and work sheets; group instructions; and answer sheets
containing rationale for scoring. You will also need the list of 15 items (see Figure 10.2).
Physical setting: An open room where participants can sit in face-to-face groups, preferably
in circles.

1. Give each participant a copy of the task sheet (see below) and tell them that they
    have five minutes to complete step I of the exercise.
2. Give each team a group instruction sheet and tell them: a) individuals are not to
    change any answers on their individual sheets as a result of group discussion; b) the
    teams will have 30 minutes in which to complete step II on the task sheet.
3. When the teams have completed their rankings, then either hand out or read out the
    NASA 'answer' sheet. Do not get drawn into arguments about the correctness of the
    answers. They have been made by a 'NASA expert': you are merely passing them
    on.
4. Ask them to complete steps IV and V and invite each team to call out a) its group
    score; b) its average individual score; and c) the highest and lowest individual scores
    in the team.
5. Draw up a chart such as the following (I have added sample numbers to illustrate)
    and write explanations of the differences, especially Team B: 'What went wrong?'
    and Team C: 'Was there not enough difference of opinion?'.

Group	Score/average individual	Range	Consensus
A	55	27–71	20
B	36	20–53	57
C	41	36–45	40
D	50	30–67	26

6. Draw comparisons between the NASA ratings (see below) and those of the part-
    icipants.
7. Invite open discussion on issues like: a) whether teams had any agreed procedures
    for making decisions and if these worked; b) what sort of arguments seemed most
    convincing; and c) what leadership roles emerged and what function they served.
8. If time permits, hand out the 'teamwork' checklist (see below) and ask each individual
    to fill it in separately with their rating of their team. Then ask them to compare ratings
    and discuss any discrepancies.
9. Finally, invite comments on what everyone has learnt about teamwork and what
    they, personally, might do about it in the future.

TASK SHEET

a space crew originally scheduled to rendezvous
ed surface of the moon. Because of mechanical
was forced to land at a spot some 200 miles from

of the equipment aboard was damaged and, since
the mother ship, the most critical items available
ile trip.

e Figure 10.2) are listed the 15 items left intact and
r task is to rank them in order of their importance for
o reach the rendezvous point. Place the number 1 by
the most imp   by the second most important, and so on, through to
number 15, the least impoi ant.

Step I: you have five minutes to complete this ranking exercise by yourself. Please
do not confer with anyone while deciding on your rank order.
Step II: now rank the items as a team. Once discussion begins, do not change
your individual ranking. Follow the group instructions on the separate sheet.
Step III: fill in the expert's ranking.
Step IV: compute the difference between Step I and Step III (all differences positive).
Step V: compute the difference between Step II and Step III (all differences positive).
Total the differences in both the above steps. Compute the average, for your team,
of the total individual differences in Step IV and compare these with the team total
(Step V).

NASA EXERCISE: GROUP INSTRUCTIONS

This is an exercise in group decision-making. Your group is to employ the method
of group consensus in reaching its decision. This means that the prediction for
each of the 15 survival items must be agreed upon by each group member before
it becomes part of the group decision. Consensus is difficult to reach. Therefore,
not every ranking will meet with everyone's approval. Try, as a group, to make each
ranking one with which all group members can at least partially agree.

Here are some guidelines to use in reaching consensus:

- Avoid arguing for your own individual judgements. Approach the task on the
basis of logic.
- Avoid changing your mind only in order reach agreement or to avoid conflict.
- Support only solutions with which you are able to agree somewhat, at least.
- Avoid 'conflict-reducing' techniques such as majority vote, averaging, or trading,
in reaching your decision.
- View differences of opinion as helpful rather than as a hindrance in decision-
making.

Items	Step I Your individual ranking	Step II The team's ranking	Step III Expert's Ranking	Step IV Difference steps I and III	Step V Difference steps II and III
Box of matches					
Food concentrate					
50 feet of nylon rope					
Parachute silk					
Portable heating unit					
Two .45 calibre pistols					
One case dehydrated milk					
Two 100 lb tanks of oxygen					
Stellar map (of the moon's constellation)					
Life raft					
Magnetic compass					
5 gallons of water					
Signal flares					
First-aid kit containing injection needles					
Solar-powered FM receiver-transmitter					
TOTALS					

Figure 10.2 NASA *work sheet*

NASA EXERCISE: NASA'S ANSWERS TO DECISION TASK

1. Two hundred-pound tanks of oxygen. Oxygen was seen as the most pressing need. Because the gravitational pull of the moon is only one-sixth of what it is here on earth, these tanks would weigh only about 30 pounds.
2. Five gallons of water. You get into 200°F temperatures on the moon's lighted surface. There would be a pressing need for water to replenish fluid loss.
3. Stellar map. NASA saw this as the most important single means of navigation.
4. Food concentrate. This would be very nutritious, and food would be one of your concerns.
5. Solar-powered radio. This could be used as a distress signal transmitter and for possible communication with the mother ship.
6. Fifty feet of nylon rope. It has a number of uses – tying people together, climbing small mountains, tying all the equipment together and pulling it.
7. First-aid kit containing pills and injection needles. The pills or injection medicine might be valuable.
8. Parachute silk. This would be ideal protection from the sun's rays. One thing the task requires you to figure out is that you are on the lighted side of the moon.
9. Life raft. This has a variety of uses. Inflated it gives protection from the sun, a means of carrying injured or equipment. NASA favoured using CO_2 bottles on the raft for propulsion across chasms, etc.
10. Signal flares. Possibly useful if you could get close enough to the ship for them to be seen.
11. Two .45-calibre pistols. NASA says that self-propulsion devices could be made from these.
12. One case of dehydrated milk. This could be useful as food mixed with water for drinking but less so if you already have food concentrate.
13. Portable heating unit. This would be useful only if you landed on the dark side of the moon.
14. Magnetic compass. If there is a magnetic field on the moon, it doesn't seem to be polarized. The needle would probably spin and angle and be of little use.
15. Box of matches. Since there is no oxygen on the moon, the matches wouldn't burn, so they would have little or no use.

NASA ratings:

0–20	Excellent
20–30	Good
30–40	Average
40–50	Fair
Over 50	Poor

TEAMWORK CHECKLIST

The following faults frequently impede the progress of discussion and decision-making. Please rate each item 5, 4, 3, 2, 1, or 0 on the following scale:

    5 = the error, weakness or failure is evident most of the time;
    1 = the error, weakness or failure hardly occurs at all;
    0 = the fault is irrelevant in this instance.

In column A give your rating of how typical, in your experience, each particular item is for teams/groups/committees. In column B give your personal rating according to how you saw the problems in your team/group.

		A	B
1.	Failure to listen to what other members are saying	___	___
2.	Constantly reiterating arguments	___	___
3.	Constantly interrupting	___	___
4.	Trying to put others down	___	___
5.	Failure to participate	___	___
6.	Silent members not drawn in	___	___
7.	Dominant members allowed to dominate	___	___
8.	Everyone pushing own views, not clarifying, developing, encouraging	___	___
9.	Unwillingness to make accommodations/compromises to others' views or needs	___	___
10.	Raising irrelevant or unhelpful points	___	___
11.	Not recognizing how members are feeling about the discussion	___	___
12.	Concentrating on making impressions rather than getting the task completed	___	___
13.	Failure to be aware of the effect of one's contributions on other members	___	___
14.	Disturbing the overall process with private conversations	___	___
15.	Failure to clarify the task or objective	___	___
16.	Failure to follow agreed directions and procedures	___	___
17.	Not checking on progress	___	___
18.	Failure to keep an eye on time	___	___
19.	Not being clear about what has been decided	___	___
20.	Lack of agreement on who is to take action on decisions	___	___

Planning a course

Below are three cases that represent problems to do with the choice and organization of teaching and learning methods. You are asked in your group to draw on your knowledge of different methods and their particular virtues in proposing a solution to each problem.

> *Aims:* to learn how to apply group techniques and principles in the context of a curriculum and evaluations.
> *Class size:* any.
> *Time required:* one hour.

This activity is best carried out by dividing the group into three teams, inviting them all to read the three case studies but to focus on solving only one, different for each team. You can then hold an inter-group plenary discussion in which each team presents its solution and the others can make informed observations.

Testing your hypothesis

A class of 20 first-year students is studying Statistics. There are five other separate subjects to be studied concurrently. In past years the lectures have been poorly attended – only overseas students seemed interested in attending. An essay and a sheet of problem examples are set, but they are rarely done except by overseas students. In the examination in the subject, most people scrape through, revealing only a bare knowledge of the subject.

You have been asked to take this course for a study entitled 'Statistical Significance and the Testing of Hypotheses'. You have a three-week period with six one-hour periods allocated to this topic. What learning/teaching methods might you use and how would you sequence them?

Worldwide projects

In the second year of their course in Environmental Studies, the students study six separately organized course units. During the second term they also undertake integrated projects. Partly, the idea is that they should thus become better acquainted with each course unit in order to make a more informed choice of two of them as third-year option, and partly that they should have a chance to integrate their understanding of the separate elements. The theme of the project is to be 'For the Greater Benefit of the Planet'.

In previous years the number of students in the second year never exceeded 30 and projects were pursued individually with regular one-to-one supervision by teaching staff. This year there are 50 students and it is proposed to try out the idea of group projects, dividing the students into 10 groups of five, each group undertaking a separate project. There are 10 members of teaching staff potentially available and there is a period of three weeks during which the students are freed of all class commitments. This block of free time must occur simultaneously for all the students, but its timing has yet to be fixed.

How would you suggest the learning experiences within the project be organized?

'And what seems to be the problem?'

There are troubles in the first year of clinical training. Among a string of complaints about the style of their education, the students have cited the learning of interviewing skills. In the last few years they have been taught how to conduct interviews through three lectures by a research psychologist from the College of General Practitioners and by subsequently sitting in with consultants on diagnostic interviews with real patients. The students do not think this procedure is thorough enough for what they feel will be a pivotal activity in their future profession.

How would you organize the learning activities of the students?

The clapping game

Aims:
– to provide experience of various issues to do with assessment and its effects on student performance;
– to focus on the concerns of students as they experience different assessment processes;
– to raise awareness of the way feelings and dispositions (on both sides) can affect the outcomes of assessment;
– to recognize what happens when the students are involved in some of the decisions in assessment.

Materials: none, except possibly a 'Clapping certificate' (an example is given below).

Three to five volunteers are asked to become an assessment panel. Four volunteers are asked to be students who are to be assessed. The rest of the group are to act as observers.

The four volunteers are asked to leave the room and told they will each be invited in when the assessors are ready.

The assessment panel sit behind a table with an empty chair placed in front for each student in succession to sit on. They are told that they must assess each candidate on their clapping ability: each will have one minute to demonstrate this.

Candidate 1. Before the first candidate is invited in, the panel are given clear instruction that they are to tell the candidate that this is an assessment in clapping and that they have one minute in which to demonstrate their ability. The panel time the activity and then ask the candidate to sit at the back of the room while they confer. The panel then issue a certificate of pass or fail without further discussion.

Candidate 2. The same as for candidate 1 except that each member of the panel awards a mark out of 10 and the panel convert these into an average mark.

Candidate 3. The panel again tell the candidate that this is an assessment in clapping and that they have one minute in which to demonstrate their ability, but this candidate is first presented with a list of criteria by which they will be assessed: volume, creativity and rhythm. At the end of the minute of clapping, the panel award a grade.

Candidate 4. The panel again tell the candidate that this is an assessment in clapping and that they have one minute in which to demonstrate their ability, but this candidate is first asked to negotiate the criteria for such an assessment with the panel. When the panel and candidate are happy with the result of the negotiation (a time limit of, say, 5 minutes may need to be set) the candidate performs the activity. The panel and the candidate then negotiate the assessment grade to be awarded. (The question of who goes first in revealing the grades – candidate or panel – can be part of the exercise.)

Each of the above stages should be revealed in turn to the panel once the previous one is complete.

Debrief

This can be done either with a whole group, starting with the observers and checking their observations with the experiences of the 'actors', or by starting with sub-groups each containing at least one observer, one assessor and one candidate.

The discussion can focus on each of the four aims above, how it relates to their own experiences and work situation and the implications for their own assessment practices.

Variation

The candidates can arrive in groups of two or three and conduct a peer assessment on the lines of some of the checklists in Chapter 9.

The following certificate can be awarded to candidates.

National Institute for Clapping

This is to certify that the following candidate, having been duly assessed according to the Charter of the Institute, has been awarded the following grade:

Candidate:

Examining Officers:

Numbers game

A simple yet powerful game, this has numbers and algebraic symbols for the content.

Aims: to study the group process, and in particular the relationship between individual and team work, when group members are faced with a simple yet ambiguous task.
Materials: a set of cards for each group – one for each member – on which is written one of a set of consistent simultaneous equations, for example:

$$A + 3D + C = 13$$
$$B + 2C + 4E = -9,$$
$$D - C = 3$$
$$A + C - E = 6$$
$$C - D - 2E = 3$$

Teams of five are established and each team is given, face down, their set of five cards. The teams are told, 'You are to determine the value of the letter D, and you will be timed.' (The wording is quite important as we shall see.)

The participants are puzzled. 'Do we cooperate in our team?', 'Have the other teams got the same equations?', 'Are we in competition with them?', 'What are we supposed to do?'. The uncertainties are momentarily crippling.

As organizer you can ignore these questions: the best you can do is to show no interest and look casually out the window, refusing to answer, while the teams learn to accept the ambiguity of the situation and get down to the task. When the first team shouts out the answer there is often agitation among the members of the other teams as they check their answers: they assume each team has been given the same set of equations.

Debriefing

This centres on how the players engaged in the task, what they thought the problem actually was, what assumptions they made about communication in and between groups, and how leadership, if any, was exercised.

Commentary

The numbers game is about the assumptions that people make in common social settings, particularly in the educational classroom, for example:

- competition is valued above cooperation;
- there is a single right answer to every question;
- authority will always guide you if you are uncertain about where to go.

But it also exposes assumptions to do with teamwork and leadership:

- each group has a leader;
- teams function best when everyone is discussing the problem in hand;
- the set problem or task is the only one that needs to be solved.

If there is any discussion of the equations problem as such, it quickly becomes submerged in revelations about what went on in the teams. The content is so basic that participants soon come to realize that what happened was a result of their own interpretation and actions. They cannot blame the numbers for their own behaviour.

Do-it-yourself

This is an exercise in group teaching methods for tutorless groups.

Materials: a copy of *53 Interesting Things to do in Your Seminars and Tutorials* by Gibbs *et al*, 1989 – see the bibliography) for each group. Handouts for participants as shown below (each handout on a separate sheet).
Time needed: 60 minutes for groups of six; 90 minutes for groups of eight.
Preparation: for each participant make a copy of the handout and the contents page of Habeshaw *et al*. For each group make one copy of the instructions for the announcer and the instructions for the timekeeper.
Before the event: get a copy of Habeshaw *et al*, or as many copies as you need to ensure that each group has a copy. Physically pull the book(s) to pieces and lay out the 53 items on tables, or on the floor, for each group. On a side table lay out one copy of each of the instructions for the announcer and instructions for the timekeeper.
At the event: divide the participants into groups of six to eight. Make sure that each participant has a copy of the handout for participants and the contents page of the book.

HANDOUT FOR PARTICIPANTS

Glance quickly through these notes:

1. This is a 'do-it-yourself' exercise. All the necessary instructions are provided. First, please introduce yourself to the others or remind them of your name.
2. The person whose name comes **first** alphabetically should take the **Instructions for the announcer**.
3. The person whose name comes **last** alphabetically should take the **Instructions for the timekeeper**.
4. Everyone, including the announcer and the timekeeper, takes part in the exercise as an equal participant.
5. Enjoy yourself.

INSTRUCTIONS FOR THE ANNOUNCER 1

Glance quickly through these instructions.

1. When names have been exchanged get everyone's attention and read out the following message:

    I am the announcer and I have to announce things to you. The authors of the book we will be using have sent this message to you:

    This session is about making your seminars and tutorials go better. We believe that 'experts' are not always useful during such discussions and we are confident that you can have a productive and enjoyable session by yourselves.

    There are no other instructions than these I am reading now. If you are confused, don't ask ME, just use your common sense.

    You have copies of the contents list of the book **53 Interesting Things to do in Your Seminars and Tutorials**. *On the surrounding tables are spread copies of the 53 items. Your task is to select an item that you'd like to find out about, find it and read it. I'll join in too. The timekeeper will tell us when we've had 8 minutes, at which point we will come and sit in the circle of chairs. We are asked . . .*

    – *to* **explain** *the item we've read;*
    – *to* **say what we like about it** *in the light of our experience of seminars and tutorials;*
    – *to* **describe how we would use it** *and to open up the issues involved with the others in the group, asking for their comments, and chairing any discussion that follows.*

    OK. You have the list of contents so off we go.

    REMEMBER TO PARTICIPATE YOURSELF.

2. After the timekeeper has announced '*You have had eight minutes, please come and sit down*', and everyone has sat down, please read the following:

    I have an announcement. Just to remind you, when it's your turn, you should:
    – *explain the item you've just read; then*
    – *comment on the item in the light of your experience of running seminars and tutorials; then*
    – *ask 'Does anyone else use a method like this?' 'Could we use it more?', 'What problems can arise as a result of this method?' and 'What do others think?' Then chair the discussion that follows.*

    The timekeeper will keep track of each five minutes of time. We'll go round in a clockwise direction, starting with the person who is nearest the door.

3. When the timekeeper announces it's time to move on to the last stage of the session, read out:

I have an announcement. To draw our personal conclusions from this session, the authors suggest that each of us in turn makes a personal statement starting with the phrase:

'One thing I intend to do in my seminars (or tutorials) in future is . . .'

Please take three minutes to think about your personal statement.

4.   After the timekeeper has announced '*You have had three minutes*', say: '*We'll go round anti-clockwise, starting with the tallest person here.*'
5.   At the end of the round of personal statements say:
    The authors would like to point out nine techniques, all detailed in the book, which were used in this session:
    a   *To start off, a very brief version of 2 –* **Learning names**.
    b   *30 –* **Distribute group roles** *for the announcer and the timekeeper and the rotating chair for discussion.*
    c   *35 –* **No-tutor group**
    d   *31 –* **Working alone** *to read items and prepare your presentation.*
    e   *14 –* **Break up the task**, *dividing the material between all participants and dividing reporting into three stages.*
    f   *22 –* **Rounds** *to get everyone involved in the discussion, and in making personal statements at the end.*
    g   *19 – Furniture to create a circle for discussion.*
    h   *47 –* **Open book tutorials** *since materials were available to everyone during the discussion.*
    i   *51 –* **Self-disclosure** *in making the personal statements.*

Thank you for participating. That is the end of the session.

INSTRUCTIONS FOR THE TIMEKEEPER

Glance quickly through these instructions.
   It is your job to inform others when the time allocated for a task has elapsed. Otherwise you should participate like everyone else.

STAGE 1

People have eight minutes to read before coming back to discuss what they have read. Let them know when eight minutes has elapsed by saying:

You have had your eight minutes. Please come and sit down.

STAGE 2

Each person has five minutes for their item. When each person has had five minutes say:

We have now spent more than five minutes on this item. Do you want to carry on with this discussion or move to the next item?

It is very important that you are strict about timing these five-minute periods if everyone in the group is to have a turn.

STAGE 3

If the group decides to read a second item each, you will have to time them again for a further period of eight minutes and then repeat Stage 2.

STAGE 4

When all members of the group have had their five minutes or when there are 25 minutes left before the end of the session, whichever occurs earlier, say:

It's time to move to the last stage of the session.

When the announcer says, '*Please take three minutes to think about your personal statement*', time each statement and then say:

You have had your three minutes.

Styles of teaching and learning (using Gardner's eight intelligences)

Aim: to look at ways in which we approach a simple teaching task and the limits we set ourselves in defining the task of teaching and learning.
Materials: 10 index cards per group with one word on each (see below) or a set of 10 random objects (some unusual). The multiple intelligences sheet (see pages 55–56. Observer's instructions.
Time required: one and a half hours.
Class size: any number.

1. Read the above aim and explain to participants that they will shortly be given a teaching task in which they can use some of the multiple intelligences activities as they choose. Invite two people to be teachers; three to six, students; the remainder to observe.

    Hand out the 'teachers' cards or objects with the following verbal instruction: 'Your task is to teach these. You have 20 minutes to plan your teaching and 20 minutes to do it! The task is clearly stated and there should be no discussion about its interpretation.' Hand the observers their checklist.

Possible words for the teachers' cards are:

> metal
> groups
> faculty
> poetry
> experiment
> hegemony
> subculture
> machine
> molecule
> relationship
> cavity

Possible objects: any, but one of the best places to find them is the office stationery cupboard.

2. While the 'teachers' are planning their teaching, ask the 'students' to consider their thoughts and feelings about their impending class.
3. After the 40 minutes precisely has elapsed, call a halt to the teaching and ask the observers to use the questions on their checklist as a basis for discussion with the 'teachers' and 'students'. This should take another 20 minutes.

Note: the 'teachers' will want to ask questions like, 'Can they have longer?', 'What is expected of them?', 'What can they use apart from the objects or words?' Tell them the time is fixed but they have to decide on the other issues.

Debriefing

Ask the teachers:

- What did you think the task was?
- What teaching strategy did you use?
- In what way did you involve the students?
- What was your impression of the students?
- How did your perception of the task and the students influence your behaviour?

- What limits to the task did you assume and why?
- How did you feel about the teaching?
- How well did you operate as a team?
- Which of the multiple intelligences did you find best matched the students' needs? Which did you find easiest and most difficult to use?

Ask the students:

- What did you think or talk about in anticipation of the teaching session?
- How was the learning task presented to you?
- How did you perceive the task: meaningful, useless . . .?
- What was your impression of the 'teachers'?
- How did your perception of the 'teacher' and the task influence your behaviour?
- What limits did you assume in your learning and why?
- How did you feel as learner?
- Which of the approaches to learning did you find worked best for you?

Leadership exercise

The behaviours described in Chapter 2, while simple in principle, are not so easy to put into practice, especially in a familiar and habitual context. They all require attention to the group process as well as the content, and judgements as to their appropriateness may not at first be easy to make. This exercise is designed to help not only in practising the interventions but also in deciding when and how to use them through feedback from observers and the group.

> *Aims:* To give practical experience of group leadership interventions and feedback on how appropriate and well timed they are.
> *Materials:* see Figure 10.3.
> *Time required:* 1 hour.

One member of the group is invited to generate a participatory discussion involving the *whole* group and in so doing consciously practise some or all of the behaviours listed below. The topic should be either one that is topical for the group, or preferably one that is well known to the person leading the group but less familiar to the rest of the group.

The group members can be advised that the learning may be maximized if they can responsibly simulate some of the common characteristics of the kind of groups relevant to the leader and the context of the training.

Observers, who can be the participating members of the group if numbers require this, put a tick in the relevant box against the items listed below, each time a particular behaviour is demonstrated.

Behaviour	Comments
Uses exploratory questions	
Looks around group	
Opens questions to the whole group	
Bounces questions back to the questioner	
Resists answering questions	
Echoes	
Accepts silence	
Brings in	
Shuts out	
Checks for understanding	
Describes individual behaviour	
Describes group process	
Supports, values, encourages	
Self-discloses	

Figure 10.3 *Leadership exercise*

Debrief

1. Invite the 'leader' to do a self-assessment referring to the checklist:
   - What I think I did and how well it worked.
   - What I found difficult.
   - Opportunities I missed and what I would like to do next time.
2. Invite the observers (if outside the group) to comment on what the leader did effectively, followed by opportunities he or she seemed to have missed.
3. Repeat 2 with the group members and add, 'And how it felt to me' to each of the above statements.

Powerful ideas in teaching

How to get workshop people engaged in processing written text is always a bit of a challenge in training events, especially when they would rather do something more active. This exercise (a kind of role play) is based on Gibbs *et al* (1992).

> *Aims:* to encourage deeper assimilation of a set of principles on teaching and learning; to demonstrate how reading can be integrated into a group activity; to illustrate the use of role differentiation and play in giving a sharper focus to learning. *Materials:* copies of the *11 Powerful Ideas* from Gibbs *et al*, edited as necessary and copied onto cards, enough for each person to have a copy of at least one of the 'ideas'.

1. Each person picks up a card and silently reads their chosen copy in order to answer questions on it. If more than one person has the same 'idea', they can discuss it for 5 minutes with those holding the same card.
2. The reading done, the first card holder to volunteer gives the rest of the group a 30-second summary (not read) of their 'idea'.
3. The task of the rest of the group is to act as students who are potentially interested in the course but have suffered from the inadequacies that the 'idea' is designed to remedy. The exercise continues with the rest of the 'ideas' taken in a random order.
4. On completion, hold a discussion on which of the 'ideas' the whole exercise exemplified and how, as a model, it could be varied and improved.

Workshop outline

Leading group discussion

Here is a suggested programme for a workshop on this topic:

0930   Introductions and checking of assumptions.
1000   Problems with groups 1: video with step-by step discussion.
1030   Problems with groups 2: checklist (see page 178) completed individually then compared in pairs.
1045   Coffee.
1100   Problems with groups 3: consultancy groups of four or five people, with self-assessment (Chapter 9, pages 249–51).
1230   Trident: a three-pronged strategy: presentation of handling problems in larger groups (pages 258–60).
1300   Lunch.
1400   Structures for large groups: practice with circular questioning and fishbowl methods using a topic chosen by the group and led by the facilitator.
1445   Interventions with large groups: demonstration and practice using the leadership exercise (pages 285–86).

1530   Tea.

1545   Assessment with groups: (video of case study from page 265) and sample checklists.

1615   Evaluating group work: two evaluation checklists from Chapter 9 or in shorter form by doing only the first three parts of the exercise.

1700   Action plans: 'What I intend to do as a result of this workshop, who can help me, what could get in the way, and what I might do about that.' Individuals complete and are checked and supportively challenged by a partner in pairs.

1730   Adjourn.

Learning outcomes

By the end of this workshop participants should:

- feel more confident in the use of a wider range of group techniques;
- be more resourceful in finding suitable solutions to problems that may arise with larger groups;
- have a wider repertoire of interactive skills;
- have clearer plans for assessing and evaluating students in groups.

Learning through groups

The activities described in this chapter represent but a sample of the many that are available to interested readers. Christopher and Smith (1991), Eitington (1996), Johnson and Johnson (1987, 1990), Miles (1981) and Napier and Gershenfeld (1985) all include further samples of well-tested training activities. Yet whatever games, exercises or methods we may use, there are certain assumptions and principles that perhaps need to be underlined:

- The accent is on 'whole person' learning: learning that involves thinking, feeling and behaviour.
- Behaviour and skills must be practised – practice that is informed by guided experience and constructive feedback (see pages 66–67).
- There should be a strong focus on the 'here and now'. The 'there and then' is of great use with a video playback (Kagan, 1982) but while it makes discussion of behaviour safer, it may also make it less immediate. The 'here and now' approach helps in the learning and monitoring of skills.
- There should be general acceptance that everyone has unique styles of personal behaviour, different needs and their own way of seeing the world.
- The emphasis should be on the 'social self' rather than on the 'inner world' of participants.

- Personal change is best achieved where there is a judicious blend of support and challenge (Smith, 1980).
- The primary orientation should be towards the development of skills, but these should be seen within a wider framework of attitudes and values (Miles, 1981).

Discussion points

- What principles of learning seem to be incorporated in the various activities included in this chapter?
- Draw up a contract for the work of your group.
- You have been asked to design and run a one-day workshop on group teaching. What are you going to include? How will you sequence and thread together all the activities?

Concluding remarks

The whole of this chapter, and indeed this book, is based on the supposition that participants, whether they be college students or practising teachers, are willing not just to learn, but to learn how to learn, and to integrate this into their future development. Learning is a cyclical process and includes the taking of risks, willingness to share, acceptance of feelings and the ability to monitor one's own experience and progress.

The exercises in this chapter may not vary noticeably from many of the post-chapter exercises earlier in the book; this should be no surprise, given the versatility of most group exercises. But workshop exercises are but one technique in academic staff development and there is some evidence that taken by themselves they are limited in their effect. Their integration into a culture of exchanging ideas and sharing good practice is essential, as is the added support that comes from consultancy and resources devoted to the generation of new forms and structures. The title *Learning in Groups* applies as much to the academic teacher as to the student. Both can learn so much through an awareness of themselves, and the effects they have, whatever the focus and purpose of the group may be. The principles of practice for 'good teaching and learning', proposed by Prosser and Trigwell (1999), add a further dimension to this thesis. Teachers, they say, must:

1. Become more aware of the way they conceive of learning and teaching within the subjects they are teaching.
2. Examine carefully the context in which they are teaching and become aware of how that context relates to or affects the way they teach.
3. Be more aware of and seek to understand the way their students perceive the teaching and learning situation.
4. Be continually revising, adjusting and developing their teaching in the light of this developing awareness.

It could be said that these principles apply equally to academic staff developers in their pursuit of change through training activities.

In many ways, the ability to talk and work effectively in groups is an essential part of everything we do. It demands the exercise of so many of the skills required in professional work, in which category, because of the increased focus on quality and accountability in higher education, we must now include the academic world. No longer can we assume the supremacy of the individualistic model of either the learner or the academic teacher in higher education. The Dearing Report on higher education in the UK (HMSO, 1997) drew attention to the need for greater emphasis on academic staff widening their repertoire of teaching methods, placing students at the centre of the learning process, reflecting more on their teaching and being more ready to embrace change.

The importance of teamwork in this process is in ensuring that full discussion and informed debate take place so that responses to policy developments (and the improvement of learning and teaching in particular) reflect a 'deep' rather than a 'surface' approach. It may also mean raising the status of learning modalities other than the linguistic and the logical/numerical in the hierarchy of academic values. Effective teamwork brings people together not merely to compare and contrast ideas and experiences but to gain a sense of shared purpose alongside a recognition and valuing of differences.

Groups permeate all levels of institutional life and insofar as we regard any institution as a social system, effective groupwork in one area is likely to be mirrored in others. The culture of collaboration is infectious and a very necessary support in the change process, whether we are talking about academics and better teaching, or students and improved learning strategies. Change has to be a collaborative activity. And in terms of 'parallel processes', the skill of networking in order to learn and gain support is a further form of group work, often underestimated, but always rewarding and economical. A further need is therefore for support from leadership and management by:

- establishing the same climate of inquiry about the art of teaching applied to research in other academic areas – the scholarship of teaching should be encouraged, valued and discussed;
- providing (tutors) with clear and consistent communications about expectations regarding teaching;
- encouraging alternative (learning and teaching) strategies to meet the needs of students' different learning styles – their diversity enhances different styles of teaching;
- creating a nurturing atmosphere that supports risk.

(Adapted from Bonwell and Eison, 1991, p74.)

Courses and their assessment must promote the kind of learning that exemplifies and is consistent with our value systems. In the case of group work, that means encouraging and rewarding collaborative learning activities not only in the design of courses but in the social and physical infrastructure in which they are planned to occur. The commitment of leadership and management will further need to be underpinned by appointment and promotion policies that reward effective teaching, and research into what happens in the special interactions that lead to effective learning.

The group as a social unit constitutes an ideal locus for change, whether its purpose is learning, training or the completion of a task. The learning group, where it involves both teacher and learners and is run in the spirit of collaboration, offers many of the best opportunities for the kind of cross-cultural change that is, in reality, what training and development are all about.

Appendix

Possible solutions to group problems

Knowing what the problem is in a group does not necessarily mean that we have the resources to solve it. The following list of incidents and possible ways of handling them may give some clues:

Incident	Intervention
Group silent/unresponsive	Use buzz groups Ask 'What's going on?'. Do round of 'snapshots' on 'What I find tricky/want from this group.
Individual(s) silent	'I'd like to give Chris some space to express her ideas.' 'Anything on your mind, Chris?' 'I'm aware that some people haven't said anything yet.' Use open/exploratory questions.
Students not listening to each other/not building/point scoring	Use listening exercise. Introduce rule. Describe what you observe, eg, 'There seems to be a hidden agenda.'
Sense of group secret/private joke/clique	Break them up. Confront, eg, 'What's going on?'. Self-disclose, eg, 'I find it impossible to lead a group where . . .'.
Sub-groups form/pair starts conversation	Confront, eg, 'We seem to have two separate groups.' Invite them to share with the whole group.
One or two students dominate	Use hand signals. Support/connote and bring in others. Give out roles, eg, timekeeper, scribe, summarizer, reporter.
Students look for answers from tutor/too deferential	Stay silent. Throw questions back. Open questions to the whole group.
Discussion too abstract	Ask group to relate back to their own experience. Bring back to the 'here and now'. Use 'I' statements.

Discussion goes off point/ becomes irrelevant	Set clear theme at start, check group agree and then say, 'I'm wondering what the present discussion has to do with what we agreed.'
Distraction occurs	Give precedence to distraction.
Preparation not done	Share work out – teamwork Draw up contract. Use 'passport' scheme (see page 206).

References

Abercrombie, M L J (1969) *The Anatomy of Judgement*, Penguin, Harmondsworth

Abercrombie, M L J (1979) *Aims and Techniques of Group Teaching*, 4th edn, Society for Research into Higher Education, Guildford, Surrey

Allan, J (1994) Record of Achievement Project, University of Wolverhampton, Wolverhampton

Allport, F H (1924) *Social Psychology*, Houghton Mifflin, Boston, Massachusetts

Alverno College Faculty (undated) *Student Assessment-as-Learning at Alverno College*, Alverno Productions, Milwawkee, WI

Amaria P, Biran, L and Leith, G (1969) Individual versus cooperative learning 1: Influence of intelligence and sex, *Education Research*, **11** (2)

American Society for Engineering Education (ASEE) (1976) *Experiential Leaming in Engineering Education*, ASEE, Washington

Angelo, T and Cross, P (1993) *Classroom Assessment Techniques*, Jossey-Bass, San Francisco, CA

Argyris, C (1968) Some unintended consequences of rigorous research, *Psychology Bulletin*, **70**

Baker, F (1974) Personal Communication to M L J Abercromble (1979)

Bales, R (1970) *Personality and Interpersonal Behaviour*, Holt, Rinehart and Winston, New York

Banet, A G Jnr and Hayden, C (1977) A Tavistock primer, in *Annual Handbook for Group Facilitators*, eds W Pfeiffer and J Jones, University Associates Inc, San Diego

Barker, R (1968) *Ecological Psychology: Concepts and methods of studying the environment of human behaviour*, Stanford University Press

Barr, R and Tagg, J (1995) From teaching to learning – A new paradigm for undergraduate education, *Change*, November/December

Baume, D and Donne, C (1996) *Running Tutorials and Seminars*, Oxford Centre for Staff and Learning Development, Oxford Brookes University

Beard, R, Bligh, D and Harding, A (1978) *Research into Teaching Methods in Higher Education*, 4th edn, Society for Research into Higher Education, Guildford, Surrey

Beard, R and Harley, J (1989) *Teaching and Learning in Higher Education*, Harper and Row, London

Beaty, L and McGill, I (1992) *Action Learning: A practitioner's guide*, Kogan Page, London

Bennis, W, Benne, K and Chin, R (1985) *The Planning of Change*, Holt, Rinehart and Winston, New York

Berne, E (1968) *Games People Play: The psychology of human relationships*, Penguin, Middlesex

Biggs, J (1982) *Evaluating the Quality of Student Learning, The SOLO taxonomy*, Academic Press, London

Biggs, J (1999) *Teaching for Quality Learning in Higher Education*, Society for Research into Higher Education and Open University Press, Buckingham

Bion, W (1961) *Experience in Groups*, Tavistock Publications, London

Bligh, D (1998) *What's the Use of Lectures?*, Intellect Books

Bligh, D, *et al* (1981) *Teaching Students*, Exeter University Teaching Service

Bligh, D, Jaques, D and Piper D W (1981) *Seven Decisions When Teaching Students*, Exeter University Teaching Services

Bligh, D (1986) *Teach Thinking by Discussion*, Society for Research into Higher Education, NFER Nelson

Bligh, D (2000) *What's the Point of Discussion?*, Intellect Books, Exeter

Bloom, B S *et al* (1956) *Taxonomy of Educational Objectives Vol 1*, Longman, London

Bloom, B S *et al* (1964) *Taxonomy of Educational Objectives Vol 2*, Longman, London

de Board, R (1978) *The Psychoanalysis of Organisations: A psychoanalytic approach to behaviour in groups and organisations*, Tavistock Publications, London

Bonwell, C and Eison, J (1991) *Active Learning – Creating excitement in the classroom*, ASHE-ERIC Higher Education Report No. 1, Washington, DC

Boud, D (1981) *Developing Student Autonomy in Learning*, Kogan Page, London

Boud, D (ed) (1985) *Problem-Based Learning in Education for the Professions*, Higher Education Society for Research and Development of Australasia

Boud, D, Keogh, R and Walker, D (1985) *Reflection: Turning experience into learning*, Kogan Page, London

Boud, D (1991) *Implementing Student Self Assessment*, HERDSA Green Guide, 2nd edn, Staff and Educational Development Association, Birmingham

Boud, D (1995) *Enhancing Learning through Self-assessment*, Kogan Page, London

Boud, D and Feletti, G (eds) (1991) *The Challenge of Problem-based Learning*, Kogan Page, London

Bramley, W (1979) *Group Tutoring*, Kogan Page, London

Bronfenbrenner, U (1977) Toward an experimental ecology of human development, *American Psychologist*, July

Brookfield, S (1990) *The Skillful Teacher*, Jossey-Bass, San Francisco, CA

Brookfield, S and Preskill, S (1999) *Discussion as a Way of Teaching – Tools and techniques for university teachers*, Society for Research into Higher Education and Open University Press, Buckingham

Brown, G and Atkins, M (1988) *Effective Teaching in Higher Education*, Routledge, London

Brown, G, Bull, J and Pendlebury, M (1997) *Assessing Student Learning in Higher Education*, Routledge, London

Brown, S and Glasner, A (1999) *Assessment Matters in Higher Education – Choosing and using diverse approaches*, Society for Research into Higher Education and Open University Press, Buckingham

Brown, S, Armstrong, S and Thompson, G (1998) *Motivating Students*, Kogan Page, London

Carrier, M H (1981) *Take Five*, Harrap, London

Chesler, M and Fox, R (1966) *Role Playing Methods in the Classroom*, Science Research Associates Inc, Chicago

Chickering, A and Gamson, Z (1989) *7 Principles for Good Practice in Undergraduate Education*, Johnson Foundation, Racine, WI

Christopher, L and Smith, L (1991) *Negotiation Training Through Gaming*, Kogan Page, London

Collier, K G (1968) *New Dimensions in Higher Education*, Longman, London

Collier, K G (1969) Syndicate Methods: Further evidence and comment, *Universities Quarterly*, **23** (4)

Collier, K G (1983) *The Management of Peer Group Learning: Syndicate methods in higher education*, Society for Research into Higher Education, Guildford, Surrey

Cornwall, M C (1979) *Students as Teachers: Peer teaching in higher education*, COWO, University of Amsterdam

Cox (1978) in University Teaching Methods Unit (1978) *Improving Teaching in Higher Education*, Centre for Higher Education Studies, London

Creme, P (1995) Assessing 'seminar' work, in *Assessment for Learning in Higher Education*, ed P Knight, SEDA/Kogan Page, London

Cryer, P (ed) (1982) *Training Activities for Teachers in Higher Education*, Society for Research into Higher Education, Guildford, Surrey

Cuthbert, P (1994) Self development groups on a diploma in management studies course, in *Using Group-based Learning in Higher Education*, Kogan Page, London

Davey, A G (1969) Leadership in relation to group achievement, *Educational Research*, **11** (3)

Davison, A and Gordon, P (1978) *Games and Simulations in Action*, Woburn Books, London

Denzin, W (1969) Symbolic interaction and ethnomethodology – proposed synthesis, *American Sociological Review*, December

Deutsch, M (1949) Experimental study of effects of cooperation and competition on group process, *Human Relations*, **2** (3) (also in Cartwright and Zander (1968))

Dewey, J (1916 and 1944) *Democracy and Education*, Free Press, New York

Dolmans, H *et al* (1997) Seven principles of effective case design for a problem-based curriculum, *Medical Teacher*, **19,** (3)

Donaldson, A and Topping, K (1996) *Promoting Peer-assisted Learning amongst Students in Higher and Further Education*, Staff and Educational Development Association, Birmingham

Drummond, I *et al* (1999) *Managing Curriculum Change in Higher Education*, UCoSDA, Sheffield

Easton, G (1982) *Learning from Case Studies*, Prentice Hall, New York

Edwards, J (1980) The Engineering Syndicate Study, *Proceedings of Institution of Electrical Engineers*, **8**, November

Eitington, J (1996) *The Winning Trainer* (3rd edn) Gulf, Houston

Entwistle, N (1977) Strategies of learning and studying: Recent research findings, *British Journal of Educational Studies*, **XXV** (3), October

Entwistle, N (1981) *Styles of Teaching and Learning*, John Wiley, London

Entwistle, N (1992) *The Impact of Teaching on Learning Outcomes in Higher Education*, UCoSDA, Sheffield

Entwistle, N (1998) *Motivation and Approaches to Learning: Motivation and concepts of teaching*

Erikson, E (1971) *Identity: Youth and Crisis*, Faber & Faber, London

Festinger, L, Schachter, S and Back, K (1950) *Social Pressures in Informal Groups: A study of human factors in housing*, Harper and Row, New York

Forster, F, Hounsell, D and Thompson, S (1995) *Tutoring and Demonstrating – A handbook,* Centre for Teaching, Learning and Assesment, University of Edinburgh, and Universities and Colleges Staff Development Agency, Sheffield

Fransson, A (1976) Group Centred Instruction: Intentions and outcomes, in *Strategies for Research and Development in Higher Education*, ed N Entwistle, Swets and Zeitlinger, Amsterdam

Freud, S (1921) *Group Psychology and the Analysis of the Ego*, edited and translated by Strachey, J (1975), Norton, New York

Fry, H, Ketteridge, S and Marshall, S (1999) *A Handbook of Teaching and Learning in Higher Education – Enhancing academic practice*, Kogan Page, London

Gaff, J and Wilson, W (1971) Faculty cultures and interdisciplinary studies, *Journal of Higher Education*, **42** (3)

Gardner, H (1993) *Frames of Mind*, Fontana Press, London

Garland, D (1994) The upshot programme: Improving group-work skills for business and accounting students, in *Using Group-based Learning in Higher Education*, eds R Gregory and L Thorley, Kogan Page, London

Gibb, J (1961) Defensive communication, *Journal of Communication*, **11**, September

Gibbs, G (1981) *Teaching Students to Learn*, Open University Press, Buckingham

Gibbs, G (1984) Using role play in interpersonal skills training: A peer learning approach, in *Learning for the Future*, eds D Jaques and E Tipper, SAGSET, University of Loughborough

Gibbs, G (1990) *Improving Student Learning Project – Briefing Paper*, CNAA / Oxford Centre for Staff Development

Gibbs, G (1992a) *Improving the Quality of Student Learning*, Technical and Educational Services, Bristol

Gibbs, G (1992b) *Discussion with More Students*, Oxford Centre for Staff and Learning Development, Oxford Brookes University

Gibbs, G (1995*) Learning in Teams* (Tutor Guide, Student Guide and Student Manual), Oxford Centre for Staff and Learning Development, Oxford Brookes University

Gibbs, G, Habeshaw, S and Habeshaw, T (1989) *53 Interesting Things to do in Your Seminars and Tutorials*, TES Publications, Bristol

Gibbs, G, Habeshaw, S and Habeshaw, T (1989) *53 Interesting Ways to Appraise Your Teaching*, TES Publications, Bristol

Gibbs, G, Habeshaw, S and Habeshaw, T (1994) *53 Interesting Ways to Teach: 12 do-it-yourself staff development exercises*, TES Publications, Bristol

Gibbs, G, Habeshaw, S and Habeshaw, T (1995) *53 Interesting Ways to Assess your Students*, Technical and Educational Services, Bristol

Gibbs, G, Habeshaw, S and Habeshaw, T (1995) *53 Interesting Ways of Helping your Students to Study*, Technical and Educational Services, Bristol

Goldschmid, B and Goldschmid, M (1976) Peer teaching in higher education – A review, *Higher Education*, **5**

Goleman, D (1995) *Emotional Intelligence*, Bloomsbury, London

Goodlad, S (1978) Projects, *Improving Teaching in Higher Education*, Centre for Higher Education Studies, London

Gordon, W (1961) *Synectics*, Harper and Row, London

Grant, P (1996) Oral assessment in groups, *The New Academic*, **5** (2)

Guzkowska, M and Kent, I (1994) Facilitating teamwork in the curriculum, in *Using Group-based Learning in Higher Education*, eds R Gregory and L Thorley, Kogan Page, London

Harris, T A (1973) *I'm OK – You're OK*, Pan Books, London

Hartley, P (1997) *Group Communication*, Routledge, London

Heathfield, M (1999) Group-based assessment: An evaluation of the use of assessed tasks as a method of fostering higher-quality learning, in *Assessment Matters in Higher Education – Choosing and using diverse approaches*, eds S Brown and A Glasner, Society for Research into Higher Education and Open University Press, Buckingham

Hedley, R and Wood, C (1978) *Group Discussion for Seminar Leaders*, Mimeograph, University of Manitoba

Heron, J (1976) *Six-Category Intervention Analysis*, Human Potential Research Project, University of Surrey

Heron, J (1981) Assessment revisited, in *Developing Student Autonomy in Learning*, ed D Boud, Kogan Page, London

Heron, J (1989) *The Facilitator's Handbook*, Kogan Page, London

Her Majesty's Stationery Office (HMSO) (1964) *Report of the Committee on University Teaching Methods (Hale Report)*, HMSO, London

Her Majesty's Stationery Office (HMSO) (1997) *Report of the National Committee of Inquiry into Higher Education – 'Higher Education and the Learning Society' (The Dearing Report)*, HMSO, London

Hill, W F (1977) *Learning Thru Discussion*, Sage, London

Hudson, L (1966) *Contrary Imaginations*, Penguin, Harmondsworth

Jaques, D (1980) Students' and tutors' experience of project work, in *Higher Education at the Crossroads*, ed R Oxtoby, Society for Research into Higher Education, Guildford, Surrey

Jaques, D (1981) *Behind the Scenes*, Report to the Nuffield Foundation

Jaques, D (1987) *Supervising Projects*, Oxford Centre for Staff and Learning Development, Oxford Brookes University

Jaques, D (1988) *Supervising Projects*, Oxford Centre for Staff and Learning Development, Oxford Brookes University

Jaques, D (1989) *Independent Learning and Project Work*, Oxford Centre for Staff Development, Oxford Brookes University

Jenkins, A M (1992) Encouraging active learning in structured lectures, in *Improving the Quality of Student Learning*, ed G Gibbs, Technical and Education Services, Bristol

Johnson, D W and Johnson, F P (1987) *Joining Together: Group theory and group skills*, Prentice Hall, Englewood Cliffs, NJ

Johnson, D and Johnson, F (1990) *Learning Together and Alone: Cooperation, competition and individualisation*, Prentice Hall, New Jersey

Jones, K (1988) *Interactive Learning*, Kogan Page, London

Jones, K (1991) *Icebreakers*, Kogan Page, London

Jones, K (1995) *Simulations – A handbook for teachers and trainers*, 3rd edn, Kogan Page, London

Jones, R M (1972) *Fantasy and Feeling in Education*, Penguin, Harmondsworth

Kagan, N (1982) *Interpersonal Process Recall: Basic methods and recent research*, mimeograph, University of Michigan

Knight, P (ed) (1995) *Assessment for Learning in Higher Education*, SEDA/Kogan Page, London

Knowles, H C and Knowles, M (1972) *Introduction to Group Dynamics*, Association Press/Folletts, Chicago

Knowles, M (1975) *Self-Directed Learning: A guide for learners and teachers*, Association Press, Folletts, Chicago

Knowles, M (1979) *The Adult Learner: A neglected species?* Gulf, Houston

Knowles, M (1986) *Using Learning Contracts*, Jossey-Bass, San Francisco, CA

Kolb, D (1984) *Experiential Learning*, Prentice Hall, Harlow

Kolb, D, Rubin, I, and McIntyre, J (1984) *Organizational Psychology: An experiential approach*, 4th edn, Prentice Hall, New Jersey

Krupar, K (1973) *Communication Games*, Free Press, New York

Kuhn, T (1973) *The Structure of Scientific Revolutions*, University of Chicago Press, Chicago

Kuiper, R (1977) Group Project Work: A self-managed 'learn and work' process in *Project Orientation in Higher Education*, eds M Cornwall, F Schmithals and D Jaques, Brighton University Teaching Methods Unit, London

Lago, C and Shipton, G (1995) *Personal Tutoring in Action*, University of Sheffield Counselling Service

Lewis, V and Habeshaw, S (1990) *53 Interesting Ways to Promote Equal Opportunities in the Curriculum*, Technical and Educational Services, Bristol

Lewis, R and Mee, J (1981) *Using Role Play: An introductory guide*, National Extension College, Cambridge

Luft, J (1970) *Group Processes: An introduction to group dynamics*, Mayfield, Palo Alto, California

Luker, P (1987) *Some Cases of Small Group Teaching*, unpublished thesis, University of Nottingham

Marris, P (1965) *The Experience of Higher Education*, Routledge and Kegan Paul, London

Marshall, L and Rowland, F (1998) *A Guide to Learning Independently*, Open University Press, Buckingham

Marton, F, Hounsell, D and Enwistle, N (1997) *The Experience of Learning: Implications for teaching and studying in higher education*, Scottish Academic Press, Edinburgh

Marton, F and Säljo, R (1976) On qualitative differences in learning I and II, *British Journal of Educational Psychology*, **46** (1 and 2)

Massy, W, Wilger, A and Colbeck, C (1994) Overcoming 'hollowed' collegiality, *Change*, American Association for Higher Education, July/August

Mathews, B (1994) Peer evaluation in practice: Experience from a major group project, in *Using Group-based Learning in Higher Education*, eds R Gregory and L Thorley, Kogan Page, London

Matthews, R (1996) Collaborative learning: Creating knowledge with students, in *Teaching on Solid Ground – Using scholarship to improve practice*, eds R Menges and M Weimer, Jossey-Bass, San Francisco, CA

McGill, I and Beaty, L (1995) *Action Learning: A guide for professional, managerial and educational development*, Kogan Page, London

McHardy, P and Henderson, S (1994) Management Indecision: Using group-work in teaching creativity, in *Using Group-based Learning in Higher Education*, eds R Gregory and L Thorley, Kogan Page, London

McKenzie, J *et al* (1993) *Tutorials – teaching matters*, videos and booklets, University of Technology, Sydney

McLeish, J, Matheson, W and Park, J (1973) *The Psychology of the Learning Group*, Hutchinson, London

McNiff, J, Lomax, P and Whitehead, J (1996) *You and Your Action Research Project*, Routledge, London

Menges, R and Weimer, M (1996) *Teaching on Solid Ground – Using scholarship to improve practice*, Jossey-Bass, San Francisco, CA

Miles, M (1981) *Learning to Work in Groups: A program guide for educational leaders*, 2nd edn, Teachers College Press, Columbia, New York

Miller, C (1975) Evaluation of teaching and the institutional context, in *Evaluating Teaching in Higher Education*, ed R Cox, Centre for Higher Education Studies, London

Miller, C and Parlett, M (1974) *Up to the Mark – A study of the examination game*, Society for Research into Higher Education, Guildford, Surrey

Miller, N (1993) Perspectives on experiential group work, in *Using Experience for Learning*, eds D Bond, R Cohen and D Walker, SRHE and Oxford University Press

Millis, B (1994) Formats for group work, *The Teaching Professor*, May

Napier, R W and Gershenfeld, M K (1985) *Groups: Theory and experience*, 2nd edn, Houghton Mifflin, Boston

National Union of Students (NUS) (1969) *Report of Commission on Teaching in Higher Education*, NUS, London

Neath, M (1998) *The Development and Transfer of Undergraduate Group Work Skills*, unpublished thesis, Sheffield Hallam University

Neufeld, V R and Barrows, H S (1974) The McMaster Philosophy: An approach to medical education, *Journal of Medical Education*, **49**

Newcomb, T M (1967) Student peer group influences, in *The American* College, ed N Sanford, John Wiley, New York

Nicol, D (1997) *Research on Learning and Higher Education Teaching*, UCoSDA Briefing Paper 45, Universities and Colleges Staff Development Agency, Sheffield

Nisbet, S (1966) A method for advanced seminars, *Universities Quarterly*, **20**, Summer

Nuhfer, E (1994) Students as colleagues, *The Department Chair*, Anker Publishing, Winter

Osborn, A (1963) *Applied Imagination: Principles and procedures of creative problem solving*, Scribners, New York

Parker, J C and Rubin, L J (1966) *Process as Content: Curriculum design and the application of knowledge*, Rand McNally, Chicago

Parlett, M (1977) The department as a learning milieu, *Studies in Higher Education*, **2** (2)

Parlett, M and King, R (1971) *Concentrated Study – A pedagogic innovation observed*, Society for Research into Higher Education, Guildford, Surrey

Parry, S and Dunn, L (1999) Developing a community of leaders through online assessment practices in a distance education setting, paper presented at 1999 Northumbria Assesssment Conference

Perry, W (1970) *Forms of Intellectual and Ethical Development in the College Years*, Holt Reinhart, New York

Pfeiffer, W and Jones, J (1974) *Annual Handbook for Group Facilitators*, University Associates Inc, San Diego; and Mansfield, UK

Pfeiffer, W and Jones, J (annual 1973–90) *Structured Experiences in Human Relations Training*, University Associates Inc, San Diego; and Mansfield, UK

Pirsig, R M (1974) *Zen and the Art of Motorcycle Maintenance*, Corgi Books, London

Pressnell, M (1994) A case study of a group project in aerospace design engineering, in *Using Group-based Learning in Higher Education*, eds R Gregory and L Thorley, Kogan Page, London

Pretty, J *et al* (1995) *Participatory Learning and Action – A trainer's guide*, International Institute for Environment and Development, London

Prince, G M (1970) *The Practice of Creativity*, Harper and Row, New York

Prince, S and Dunne, E (1998) Group development: The integration of skills into law, *Law Teacher*, **32** (1)

Pring, R (1973) Objectives and Innovation: The irrelevance of theory, *London Educational Review*, **3**, Autumn

Pring, R (1978) Teacher as a researcher, in *Theory and Practice of the Curriculum*, ed D Lawton, Routledge and Kegan Paul, London

Prosser, M and Trigwell, K (1999) *Understanding Learning and Teaching – The experience of higher education*, Society for Research into Higher Education and Open University Press, Buckingham

Race, P and Brown, S (1993) *500 Tips for Tutors*, Kogan Page, London

Rainer, T (1980) *The New Diary: How to use a journal*, Angus and Robertson, London

Ramsden, P (1992) *Learning to Teach in Higher Education*, Routledge, London

Redl, F (1942) Group emotion and leadership, *Psychiatry*, **5**

Rice, A K (1971) *Learning for Leadership: Interpersonal and intergroup relations*, Tavistock Publications, London

Richardson, E (1967) *Group Study for Teachers*, Routledge and Kegan Paul, London

Rogers, C (1983) *Freedom to Learn in the 1980s*, Merrill, Columbus, OH

Rose, C and Nicholl, M (1997) *Accelerated Learning for the 20th Century*, Piatkus, London

Ross, M and Hendry, C (1957) *New Understandings of Leadership*, Association Press/Folletts, Chicago

Rowan, J and Reason, P (1981) *Human Inquiry: A sourcebook of new paradigm research*, John Wiley, London

Rowntree, D (1978) *Educational Technology in Curriculum Development*, Harper and Row, London

Rubin, L J (1967) *Facts and Feelings in the Classroom*, Ward Lock, London

Rudduck, J (1978) *Learning Through Small Group Discussion*, Society for Research into Higher Education, Guildford, Surrey

Säljö, R and Marton, F (1997) Approaches to learning, in *The Experience of Learning*, eds F Marton, D Housell and N Entwistle, Scottish Academic Press

Schroder, H and Harvey, O (1963) Conceptual organisation and group structure, in *Motivation and Social Interaction*, ed O Harvey, Ronald Press, New York

Shaffer, J and Galinsky, M (1974) *Models of Group Therapy and Activity Training*, Prentice Hall, Harlow

Shaw, M E (1977) *Group Dynamics: The psychology of small group behaviour*, Tata-McGraw-Hill, New Delhi

Shuell, T (1986) Cognitive conceptions of learning, *Review of Educational Research*, **56**, pp 411–36

Slavin, R (1990) *Cooperative Learning – Theory, research and practice*, Prentice Hall, Englewood Cliffs, NJ

Smith, A (1997) *Accelerated Learning in the Classroom*, Network Educational Press, Stafford

Smith, P (1973) *Groups within Organisations*, Harper and Row, London

Smith, P (1980) *Small Groups and Personal Change*, Methuen, London

Snyder, B (1971) *The Hidden Curriculum*, MIT Press, Cambridge, Massachusetts

SRHE (Society for Research into Higher Education) Working Party on Teaching Methods (1975) *Project Methods in Higher Education*, SRHE, Guildford

Stadsklev, R (1974) *Handbook of Simulation Gaming in Social Education*, University of Alabama

Stanford, C and Roark, A (1974) *Human Interaction in Education*, Allyn & Bacon, Massachusetts

Stefani, L and Nicol, D (1997) From teacher to facilitator of collaborative enquiry, in *Facing up to Radical Changes in Universities and Colleges*, eds S Armstrong, G Thompson and S Brown, Kogan Page, London

Stein, M (1975) *Stimulating Creativity, Vol 2: Group procedures*, Academic Press, New York

Stenhouse, L (1972) Teaching through small group discussion: Formality, rules and authority, *Cambridge Journal of Education*, **2**

Stenhouse, L (1975) *Introduction to Curriculum Development*, Heinemann, London

Stewart, I and Joines, V (1987) *TA Today – A new introduction to transactional analysis*, Lifespace Publishing, Nottingham

Talbot, M (1994) Learning journals for evaluation of group-based learning, in *Using Group-based Learning in Higher Education*, eds R Gregory and L Thorley, Kogan Page, London

Taba, H (1962) *Curriculum Development: Theory and practice*, Harcourt, Brace and World, New York

Taylor, W and Walford, R (1972) *Simulation in the Classroom*, Penguin Books, Harmondsworth

Thiagarajan, S (1978) Thiagi's Game – Game VI described as a fast-paced introduction to gaming, *Simulation/Gaming*, May/June

Thorley, L and Gregory, R (1995) *Using Group-based Learning in Higher Education*, Kogan Page, London

Tiberius, R (1999) *Small Group Teaching: A trouble-shooting guide*, Kogan Page, London

Toohey, S (1999) *Designing Courses for Higher Education*, Society for Research into Higher Education and Open University Press, Buckingham

Treadaway, J (1975) Do Seminars Work?, *Institute of Education Reporter*, University of London

University Teaching Methods Unit (UTMU) (1978) *Improving Teaching in Higher Education*, Centre for Higher Education Studies, London

van Ments, M (1983) *Effective Use of Role Play*, Kogan Page, London

Watzlawick, P, Bavelas, J and Jackson, D (1962) *Pragmatics of Human Communication*, Norton, New York

Wellington, P (1998) Multidisciplinary student teams motivated by industrial experience, in *Motivating Students*, eds S Brown, S Armstrong and G Thompson, Kogan Page, London

Wheeler, D K (1967) *Curriculum Process*, Unibooks, London

Wilson, A (1980) Structuring seminars: A technique to allow students to participate in the structuring of small group discussion, *Studies in Higher Education*, **5** (1), March

Yamane, D (1997) Group projects: Problems and possible solutions, *Teaching Professor*, February

Zinkin, L (1994) Exchange as a therapeutic factor in group analysis, in *The Psyche and the Social World: Developments in group analysis theory*, eds D Brown and L Zinkin, Routledge, London

Zuber-Skerritt, A (1992) *Action Research in Higher Education – examples and reflections*, Kogan Page, London

Index